SINISTER INFLUENCES

KENTUCKY'S FABULOUS FIVE AND THE POINT-SHAVING SCANDAL OF 1951

RON ELLIOTT

Acclaim Press
MORLEY, MISSOURI

P.O. Box 238
Morley, MO 63767
(573) 472-9800
www.acclaimpress.com

Book Design: Rodney Atchley
Cover Design: Emily Blattel

Library of Congress Control Number: 2014915041
ISBN-13: 978-1-938905-75-9
ISBN-10: 1-938905-75-X

First Printing 2015
Printed in the United States of America
10 9 8 7 6 5 4 3 2 1

This publication was produced using available information.
The publisher regrets it cannot assume responsibility for errors or omissions.

Contents

Preface 7
Chapter One – What Am I Gonna Do Now? 13
Chapter Two – Little Ralph 18
Chapter Three – The Baron of the Bluegrass 23
Chapter Four – 1945-46: NIT Championship 30
Chapter Five – The Beak 38
Chapter Six – 1946-47: Back to the NIT 43
Chapter Seven – 1947-48: The Fabulous Five 52
Chapter Eight – 1948-49: Back to Back Championships 68
Chapter Nine – On to the NBA 78
Chapter Ten – 1949-50: Third Time No Charm 89
Chapter Eleven – 1950-51: A Tale of Two Teams 94
Chapter Twelve – Scandal 133
Chapter Thirteen – See Anything? 140
Chapter Fourteen – Big Bill's Big Trouble 152
Chapter Fifteen – The Edict 160
Chapter Sixteen – Damned Yankees 170
Chapter Seventeen – Probation 177
Chapter Eighteen – Where There's Life, There's Hope 183
Chapter Nineteen – Adolph Rupp 191
Chapter Twenty – Alex Groza 195
Chapter Twenty-One – Bill Spivey 198
Chapter Twenty-Two – Ralph Beard 203
Chapter Twenty-Three – The Yardstick 207
Appendix A 214
Appendix B 215
Appendix C 216
Appendix D 217
Endnotes 218
About the Author 231
Index 232

Preface

Okay, let's get this out of the way right up front. Yes, I am a Kentucky basketball fan and have been since the Wildcats first came to my adolescent attention when they won the NCAA Championship in 1958. But, for purposes of this book, I must try not to be simply a fan, because I'm also a professional historical researcher and author. The latter attributes being much more important, I told the publisher to point it out if I wrote anything that sounded like I was trying to shade the truth in the Wildcats favor. My job as an author is simply to report the facts as I find them.

Everyone who follows basketball has at least heard of the UK's Fabulous Five and their involvement in the point shaving scandals, but nobody (initially including me) seems to know any of the details. It's as if there is an aura of mystery surrounding the activities which first brought disgrace to the UK basketball program (and several other schools) more than 60 years ago and tarnished the reputations of a few outstanding players. I quickly found out that, while there is no mystery, the aura exists because nobody who is in possession of any first-hand knowledge is willing to talk about it.

The one exception to that rule of silence is Ralph Beard. Mr. Beard left a collection of audio and video tapes in which he openly and honestly discussed his role in the drama. While he did not disclose any details of payoffs—he said he didn't know any—he did emphatically deny that he ever made any attempt to affect the point spread. "If taking the money makes me guilty, then I'm guilty," is his repeated theme. Mr. Beard also said that in the more than 50 years he had to bear his complicity, while he sometimes went as long as ten or fifteen minutes without thinking about it, he still could not find a way to explain why he took the money. With a shrug and a puzzled expression, he simply said, "I don't know, the money was nothing."

In the one instance I could find of Alex Groza discussing his role, he took the same tact, saying that he had no explanation for why he did it. Their teammate, Dale Barnstable, never made a single public pronouncement concerning his part. In these days of second and third and fourth chances for ball players who are caught using banned drugs and other wrongdoings, it's difficult to understand why Beard and Groza were made to pay such a terrible price for their transgressions.

On the other hand, Bill Spivey was far from silent. Mr. Spivey proclaimed, long and loud, that his only sin was failing to report the fact that he was approached by a "fixer." Try as he might—and he did put forth a mighty effort—the zealous New York Assistant District Attorney was unable to pin anything on Mr. Spivey. Nevertheless, he did manage to ruin Spivey's career.

So, most of the information had to come from contemporary newspaper accounts, a few books on the scandals, court records and magazine articles. There again, it would be pretty easy for me to ignore any statement which does not support the way I might be already leaning, but that will not do—I must report all the facts as they are found. On a separate but related topic, one of the more interesting aspects of this story is examining the on-the-spot newspaper accounts of the "fixed" games. With the perspective of knowing the history, it is easy for us to read players' motives into the accounts that the man who wrote the account back in 1949 probably did not intend to convey. I presented these accounts, verbatim, in Chapter 13 so you can draw your own conclusions.

Of the few books on the point shaving scandals, the most prominent and widely cited is *Scandals of '51: How the Gamblers Almost Killed College Basketball*, by Charles Rosen published by Holt, Rinehart and Winston in 1978. This book is written in historical novel style, relating "facts" via conversation among the participants. The problem is that Mr. Rosen included no source of his "facts," not a single footnote or even a bibliography. Hence, I have quoted no information from that source, although it was tempting to use some statement with which I agreed. Citing unsupported statements is how "facts" become facts.

For their help, I owe acknowledgements to the staff at the Louisville Free Public Library, most notably Joe Hardesty, Allen Ashman of the University of Louisville Library, the staff at the University of Kentucky Special Collections, especially Sarah Dorpinghaus, Herky Rupp who, despite ill health, tried to help, Professor Ron Bryant and especially John Snell and my wife Carol and the folks at Acclaim Press, in particular Doug Sikes and Monica Burnett. All these people treat me "better than I deserve."

So, here's everything I could learn about the Kentucky basketball players' involvement in the point shaving scandals. In my opinion, Ralph Beard, Alex Groza and Bill Spivey deserve a better legacy than history has so far afforded, and I sincerely hope this book helps add the weight of other opinions to mine.

KENTUCKY'S FABULOUS FIVE

AND THE POINT-SHAVING SCANDAL OF 1951

Chapter One

What Am I Gonna Do Now?

Although it was a seasonably cold late October night outside, there was plenty of heat inside Chicago Stadium. Not only was the furnace blasting, but the stands were packed for this early season basketball game. Hottest of all, however, was legendary coach Adolph Rupp. As the waning seconds of the 12th annual *Herald-American* All-Star game ticked off the clock, Rupp stalked the sidelines, shouting angrily at the referees and his players or anyone else who happened within earshot. At last, when the final horn sounded, the scoreboard indicated that the Rupp-coached college All-Star team, composed of the best players from across the nation, lost by a count of 76-70.[1]

Rupp headed the all-star team by virtue of the fact that his University of Kentucky (UK) Wildcats were reigning college champions, having defeated Kansas State for the 1951 title the previous March. All-Star game protocol dictated that the opposition be provided by the previous season's National Basketball Association (NBA) champion, in this instance, the Rochester Royals. At this moment, Rupp was not a happy man; he did not like to lose at any time, at any place, to anybody or under any circumstances. It made no difference that his cobbled together team, albeit talented, had had little practice time, did not understand his intricate offense or that the opponent was a cohesive and well-coached team of professional athletes.

Seated two rows behind Rupp's bench was a collection of his former UK players: Ralph Beard, Alex Groza, Wallace Jones, Joe Holland and Cliff Barker. Beard, Jones, Groza and Barker (along with Kenny Rollins) were starters on UK's "Fabulous Five," winners of 130 of 139 games, three national championships and one runner-up during their college careers.* The five men were in a jovial mood, comfortable in

*One NIT championship and runner-up, and two NCAA tournament championships. At the time, as the NIT was considered the more prestigious event, Kentucky opted for that tournament in '46 and '47.

their profession and looking forward to the upcoming professional season. On this occasion, they were also happy not to be a target of their former coach's wrath. Like many others before and after them at UK, they came to truly appreciate Coach Rupp only after their days of playing for him were over.

In addition to their UK success, these players comprised the nucleus of the basketball team that traveled to London, England in the summer of 1948 and brought the Olympic Gold medal home to America. When their college days were over, these men, plus Holland, who was a reserve player at UK, joined the professional ranks as a unit, becoming the core of the fledgling NBA's Indianapolis Olympians.

Scheduled to play an exhibition game against the Milwaukee Hawks in Moline, IL the next day, the Olympians left Indianapolis a day early to take in the All-Star game, pay their respects to and visit with their old coach and scout the Royals, who figured to provide their main competition in the NBA's Western Division for the upcoming season. After the game ended, the Olympians said a hasty goodbye to the still angry Rupp and wove their way through the crowd to the exit.

Refreshed by the cool air, the players' thoughts turned to the drive to Moline and the game against the Hawks as they crossed the parking lot. Reality crashed in on Cliff Barker when one of a pair of burly, well-dressed man grabbed his arm and announced, "Hold it, you're coming with us."[2]

Initially startled, Barker exclaimed, "What the hell's going on?" Cliff Barker, age 30 at this time, was a 6'2", 185 pound professional athlete. Also a World War II veteran and a survivor of 16 months in a German POW camp, he was a not man to fool with. Seeing the menacing glare in Barker's face, the man eased his grip and recoiled slightly, but did not release the player's arm.

"You're all under arrest," the man announced, identifying himself as New York City detective James Canavan. His partner was New York special investigator James White.[3] "We're taking all of you downtown for questioning."

Barker may have been surprised, but Alex Groza and Ralph Beard were not. Since the previous July, the newspapers had daily reported breaking news of a scandal in which some 30 players from seven colleges were accused of "point shaving," accepting monetary bribes from professional gamblers to "fix" the results of 86 college games in the 1948 and '49 seasons.[4] As the stars of UK's national championship teams, Groza and Beard were the ones gamblers had approached, knowing that those two could easily impact the outcome of a game. Unknown to them at this time, former UK teammate Dale Barnstable, now coach of Louisville's DuPont Manual High School, was being arrested at his home at the same time.

A "line" or "point spread" is a figure that gamblers assign to games establishing a betting standard. "Line setters," professionals at the task, generally located in Las Vegas or New York, try to predict that team "A," the favored team, will defeat team "B" by a given number of points. Local "bookies" all over the country then accept bets based on the line. If the line is, say ten points, one can bet that team "A" will win by more than ten or that team "B" will lose by more than ten. If "A" wins by one to ten points or loses, the bookie wins all bets. The game, then, can be "fixed" in two ways: by paying the favored team to go all out and go over the point spread or play at less than full capacity and hence go under. Events would prove that many games over the previous two years, some involving UK and Groza, Beard and Barnstable, had been fixed in both ways.

Groza, and especially Beard, were prime targets for the fixers. Both from impoverished backgrounds, the lure of easy money was a powerful motivator when they were college students. While Groza was older and perhaps more adapted to the ways of the world, having served a hitch in the Army during the war, Beard came to UK in the fall of 1945 as a seventeen-year-old freshman. Both were outstanding basketball players. They led Rupp's Wildcats through three years of unparalleled success from 1946-49, each being honored by being named to the All-America team three times ('47, '48 and '49) and each being chosen as the nation's most outstanding player one of those seasons. Groza led the 'Cats in scoring in those three seasons, posting 1579 points in 110 games over three seasons[5] to Beard's 1517 in 139 games through four seasons.[6] Both Beard and Groza were holders of many school and conference records. If one wanted to fix a UK game, these are the players one would want in his pocket.

Given the revelations of game fixing that pervaded the sports news all that summer of 1951, Groza and Beard had to know that their being apprehended was just a matter of time. In fact, when the players had gathered earlier in the day at Indianapolis' Butler Field house parking lot for the drive to Chicago, someone brought the *Chicago Tribune* containing an article stating that New York District Attorney Frank Hogan had "the goods" on several UK players in regard to point shaving. One (non former UK) member of the Olympians' team reported, "Alex just pushed the article aside and said, 'Well, there's nothing to that,' but Ralph read it rather intently."[7] Those who knew Beard were not surprised that he read intently—Ralph did everything that way—so the rest of the players forgot the incident as they loaded up for the trip.

Beard's involvement in point shaving would, however, come as a total shock to everyone who knew him. As disciplined, dedicated and straight-arrow as they come, Ralph's only vice was chewing too much gum—he played every game with five sticks in his mouth. No one who had any exposure to him would have suspected young Ralph of any illegal activity. "If the pressure of college athletics is such that a boy of Ralph's caliber can be reached by sinister influences," one of his high school teachers would declare, "there is something wrong with the system and no young man playing college athletics is safe."[8]

Although the authorities were to claim that the Wildcat trio were involved in fixing several games in various locales, they were in trouble for having accepted a total of $2,000 ($1,000 to Groza, $500 each to Beard and Barnstable) to shave points in a National Invitational Tournament (NIT) tilt against Loyola of Chicago played at New York City's Madison Square Garden on March 14, 1949. While point shaving would be considered bad ethics everywhere, in the State of New York, it was a crime. Back in 1919, the Chicago White Sox players had conspired with gamblers to intentionally lose baseball's World Series to the Cincinnati Reds. In the wake of that "Black Sox" game fixing escapade, the Empire State had enacted a statute making it illegal to offer or accept a bribe to impact the outcome of any professional game. In 1945, similar activity at Brooklyn College precipitated an amendment to expand the law to amateur sports. (Having overlooked the possibility that referees could also be bribed would later compel yet another amendment.) That law was what had brought the New Yorkers to the Windy City to arrest the former UK players. This was serious business; conviction on this charge would earn the offender a maximum of five years in a New York jail.[9]

The men were transported to the Cook County Courthouse where they were placed in separate rooms. Vowing that they could not control a game and thus had never been approached by gamblers, Jones, Barker and Holland were soon released, but Groza and Beard were grilled—without benefit of legal counsel—for the next seven hours. Both stubbornly denied the allegations at first, but eventually gave in and confessed when confronted with the over-whelming evidence that assistant New York D.A. Vincent O'Conner had gathered.[10]

In Louisville, Dale Barnstable, who was also expecting to be arrested, readily confessed to accepting the $500 bribe and begged the public to understand. "The thing about it is that you convince yourself that you are doing no harm at the beginning. You get $15 or $20 from the school for playing a good game and you figure it won't hurt to take some bigger money for winning with something to spare," he said.[11]

After his confession, an inconsolable and rumpled Ralph Beard was thrown into the drunk tank with "winos and psychos", where he remained for a very long night in the Chicago jail. Finally, at 3PM on October 20, 1951 after fifteen hours in custody, he was released on $1,000 bond posted by a local bondsman. He called his mother, Sue, to explain what had happened before boarding a plane for home. Picking up Ralph's wife, Marilyn, Sue met her son for a tearful reunion at the airport. Keenly aware that he had committed a life-altering error—one that he would rue every day for the rest of his life—Ralph turned to face the two women. "What am I gonna do now?" he sobbed."[12]

Chapter Two

Little Ralph

Legend has it that University of Kentucky basketball coach Adolph Rupp had a sign over the 6'7" door to his office reading, "If you don't have to duck, don't bother to come in."

If there is any truth to that, Rupp would have ripped the sign down when Ralph Beard walked into his office. When he came to UK as a seventeen year-old freshman in the fall of 1945, he stood 5'10" and his playing weight was 175 pounds. Beard would soon earn the title of "the biggest of the little men."

Ralph M. Beard Jr. was born December 2, 1927 in Hardinsburg, KY, first son of Ralph M. and Sue Anna (Moorman) Beard.[13] Like many another "Junior," (John Boy Walton being a notable exception) the boy was known in the family as "Little Ralph" to distinguish him from the father. That name would follow him outside the family home and, as he was usually the smallest member of his basketball team, stick with him throughout his athletic career.

Several generations of the Beard family were blessed with athletic talent. The grandfather, Marvin, excelled at track and baseball at Nashville's Vanderbilt University. Ralph Sr. was a professional baseball and basketball player. Both of these men had been standout athletes at Louisville's Male High School. Little Ralph made his athletic gifts manifest at an early age. "His first basket was his potty chair," said his mother, Sue. "As soon as he was big enough to stand, he'd throw a little rubber ball into it." The child loved hearing his parents applaud when he made a "basket." Thus encouraged, when he got older, he used the cutaway part of his high chair. "When that became too easy, we put up a miniature basket over his bed and then moved it into the kitchen. Finally, a barrel hoop was put up on the garage."[14]

Little Ralph spent so much of his spare time in the driveway throwing a ball through the hoop and perfecting his ball-handling skills that other neighborhood kids eventually joined in. Before long, Ralph Sr. started coaching the boys and organized a make-shift league for Ralph and the other local boys.

In 1933, shortly after another son, Moorman, was born, Ralph Sr. left the family, essentially putting an end to Little Ralph's association with his father. Senior moved to Dallas, Texas, where he became the golf pro at Cedar Crest Country Club and sired Little Ralph's half-brother, Frank, who became a successful professional golfer.[15]

Even though young Ralph delivered newspapers and did whatever else he could to help out, Sue Beard had great difficulty supporting herself and her sons in Hardinsburg. So when Ralph was 15, in the summer following his freshman year at Hardinsburg High School, she and Ralph moved to Louisville, leaving Moorman in the care of her parents.[16] The year was 1943. Sue quickly found employment on the swing shift in an aircraft assembly plant, and soon secured an additional position as supervisor of maids at a residential hotel where she cleaned six apartments and two sleeping rooms a day in exchange for an apartment for her and her son. Ralph pitched in by stoking the hotel's furnace before school, at lunch and in the evening.[17] Following the family convention, Ralph enrolled in Male High School which was, as the name implies, an all-boys' school. Introverted, and hence shy, Ralph stuttered whenever he was excited or required to speak in public. Only on a field of athletic competition was he truly comfortable. Ralph said that if you had talent, so much the better, but whether you had talent or not, his coaches at Male demanded 101% effort at all times[18] and that was fine by him—he did everything at full throttle anyway.

In that arena, even the tradition-rich state of Kentucky had never seen the like of Ralph Beard. He became the first four-sport letterman in Male's history, participating in basketball, baseball, track and football and starring in each sport. In football, he was the starting halfback, a dashing zigzag open field runner, one of the fastest players in the state. As a three-year starter, Ralph was one of the main cogs in Male's 1945 undefeated run to the State championship.[19] In track, he ran the half-mile, winning the state championship as a senior.[20] In baseball, he played all the infield positions, attracting major league attention at third base. Upon graduation, Ralph signed a professional contract with the Boston Braves organization.

As outstanding as he was in those sports, basketball was his game. "Some people are born good-looking, some are rich," said Ralph, "God gave me speed and quickness." Beard certainly put those assets to good use in basketball. It was often noted that when Ralph took off on the fast break, you could smell rubber burn in the gym. An interesting discussion could be had as to who was the fastest player to ever wear Kentucky's uniform. John Wall would certainly be on the list as would Dwight Anderson, whom broadcaster Cawood Ledford dubbed "the blur." Rajon Rondo was pretty speedy, too, but those who saw him play would insist that Beard would win the race.

As great as those physical gifts were, perhaps determination was Beard's most valuable inherent talent. As is said of many great competitors, whether playing for the national championship or mumbly-peg, Ralph would simply find some way to beat you. In Male's strict environment he added discipline to his game. Working hard on the facets of the game that can be learned, he developed into a tenacious defender, a good outside shooter and excellent ball handler. On defense, Ralph considered any score by the man he was defending as a personal insult. His outside two-hand set shot was effective enough to demand close defensive attention. If his defender made the error of getting too close, the cat-quick Beard would dart by his opponent and fly to the basket where he was equally proficient in making what was called a "crip shot"* in those days with either hand. Ralph was his team's leading scorer each of his three years at Male. He was named as an All-State performer as both a junior and as a senior, being elected captain by his teammates in his final year.

Among the Ralph Beard legends that abound at Male High School is the time Ralph grabbed the ball in a tight game against archrival DuPont Manual. As a surprise to Coach Paul Jenkins and his teammates, Ralph tucked the ball under his arm as he yelled, "Time out." As the referee blew his whistle to stop play, Ralph ran into the backcourt searching the floor intently. Soon, both referees and the players from both teams were searching as well, not knowing if they were looking for a sweatband, a contact lens or perhaps even a lost tooth. Suddenly, Ralph shouted, "Here it is!" He crammed his lost wad of chewing gum back into his mouth and tossed the ball to the ref to indicate he was ready to resume play.[21]

*The olden reference is to a shot under the basket "so easy a cripple could make it." Obviously, crip shots would be politically incorrect and so do not still exist, being "lay-ups" in today's game.

Beginning in 1940, at the end of the basketball season, All-Star high school players from across Kentucky assembled to play a game against their Indiana counterparts. Starting in 1956, one player from each state is honored by being named "Mr. Basketball," and recognized as the top high schooler in the state. The chosen player is honored by being assigned jersey number one in the All-Star game. The roll includes some illustrious names from each state including Kelly Coleman, Oscar Robertson, Jeff Mullins, Tom and Dick Van ArsDale, Wes Unseld, Rick Mount, Darrell Griffith, Kent Benson, Rex Chapman, Kyle Macy and Steve Alford, to list a few, names familiar to any basketball fan. Had that title existed in 1945, Ralph Beard's name might also grace that list.

However, that Ralph would have been named Kentucky's Mr. Basketball was not a lock: one of his All-Star teammates was a young man from Harlan, Kentucky named Wallace Jones. Like Beard, Jones had a family nickname, being dubbed "Wah Wah" when his baby sister couldn't manage "Wallace." At 6'4" and 205 pounds, Jones was a terrific athlete who, like Beard, competed in four sports. Wah led Harlan High to the State basketball championship in 1944 (they finished third in '45) and held a national record having once scored 100 points in a high school game.[22]

For a week in June, the All-Star team practiced at Western Kentucky State College (as it was known at the time, now Western Kentucky University) under the tutelage Western's renowned coach, Ed Diddle. All they had to do was play basketball, eat and swim in the pool. For the first time in his life, Ralph could eat all he wanted. "I swore I was in heaven," he said.[23]

In those days, the event was sponsored by the *Indianapolis Star* and played annually at Butler University Field House in Indianapolis. Up to that time, the Hoosier boys had dominated, winning all three games (due to the war, no game was played in 1943 or 1944.) Beard and Jones put a stop to that streak, leading the Kentucky boys to their first win in the series, besting the Hoosiers 45-40.[24]

Among the spectators that night was UK coach Adolph Rupp, who was favorably impressed with both Jones and Beard.** Coach Rupp used to say that when a baby boy is born in Kentucky, his mother hopes he'll grow up to be President of the United States while the father hopes

**Amid the troubles to come in 1951, Look Magazine alleged that Rupp, in violation of NCAA rules, visited with Beard and Jones in their Indianapolis hotel the night before the game.

he'll play basketball at the University of Kentucky. And so it was with Ralph Beard. Although he flirted a bit with Coach Peck Hickman at the University of Louisville and Western's Ed Diddle salivated, Beard knew about and liked UK and Coach Rupp, and so opted to attend college on the Lexington campus. In much the same way that John Calipari attracts talented players today, athletes of that era came from far and near to try for a scholarship offer from Rupp. Given his impoverished youth, Ralph's eyes must have lit up when he learned that the scholarship included room and board, tuition, laundry and $15 per month! As it happened, Coach Rupp was out of the country on a military assignment when Ralph was ready to sign a grant-in-aid in the summer, so he ended up entering UK in the fall of 1945 on a football scholarship.[25]

Chapter Three

The Baron of the Bluegrass

If one had a desire to learn any game from the ground up, to know all the subtle nuances and understand every step in the evolution of the sport, what could be better than learning from the person who invented the game? Not many of us would have such an opportunity, but Adolph Rupp did.

Born in Halstead, Kansas in 1901—a mere ten years after Dr. James Naismith invented the game of basketball—Adolph was the fourth of six children born to a German mother and an Austrian father. The Rupp's spoke only German at home, hence Adolph did not start speaking English until he began attending school. As a result, he was able to read in German throughout his life. While there was plenty of farm work to do, Rupp enjoyed the new game that he practiced by throwing a bag stuffed with rags through a hoop. A hard life got even harder when Rupp's father died in 1910.[26] Later, he found time to play on his high school team, which actually had a ball, and discovered that while his talent for playing the game was limited, he did have a flair for taking charge.[27]

After high school, Rupp, who would in time become a legend himself, attended Kansas University where he came under the supervision of another man who would also become a legend, Coach Forrest "Phog" Allen. Rupp was a guard and in his three years on the varsity did not score a point but he was a part of KU's championship basketball teams of 1922 and 1923.[28] More importantly to his future career, he became acquainted with Dr. Naismith, who was chairman of the physical education department at that time.[29] The two men, no doubt, had some interesting discussion on how the game should be played.

After graduating with a degree in economics in 1923, Rupp found that his idea of entering the banking business was not working out and so accepted a job coaching football and basketball at a Kansas high school. After a few intermediate stops, he ended up as basketball coach at the brand new high school in Freeport, Illinois. At Freeport, Rupp installed the style of play he'd learned from Allen and Naismith but gradually added his own ideas, most notably sometimes abandoning the zone defense preferred at Kansas for the man to man.[30] Incidentally, in his first year at this job (1926) Rupp coached a black player, William "Mose" Mosley. "He was a first teamer and a good athlete,"[31] the coach remembered. That fact is generally overlooked (or ignored) by those who—long after Rupp is not around to defend himself—would portray him as a racist.

During this time, the coach met Esther Schmidt who would become his wife in 1931 and attended graduate school in the summers, earning a master's degree in education from New York City's Columbia University in 1930. Here also one of the Rupp legends was born. Rupp says that with the big $300 annual salary increase he received to come to Freeport, he went out and bought a "nice blue suit" to supplement his only other game apparel, a brown suit. "We got shellacked," Rupp declares. "I decided that a blue suit just was not the thing to wear to a basketball game."[32] Thus, he earned the title, "The Man in the Brown Suit," by never wearing anything else to a game over the remaining 45 years of his coaching career.

Rupp's record at Freeport is variously reported at 66-21, 66-17 and 76-4. The man himself says it was 67-16, while they won 40 of their last 48 games[33] and his knowledge of his statistics, even though quoted late in his life, are usually accurate. Whatever the correct figure is, all agree that his career at the high school level was successful. Good enough, in fact, that following the 1930 season (when Freeport finished third in the state), University of Illinois basketball coach Craig Ruby mentioned to Rupp that University of Kentucky basketball coach John Mauer had resigned, creating an opening on the college level. Rupp thought that sounded good and asked Ruby if he would mind recommending him for the job.[34] Up to that time as many of UK sports administrators and coaches had come from Illinois, Ruby's recommendation would be tantamount. "First thing I knew, I got a telegram asking me to come to Lexington for an interview."[35]

Rupp was totally unimpressed with the University of Kentucky and Lexington, noting that Freeport High School had better basketball facilities than UK did.[36] Additionally, during the interview, they arrived at the cafeteria late for lunch to find that there was little left to eat. Offered only a small piece of fish, a stick of cornbread and a cup of coffee, Rupp concluded, "these people in Kentucky aren't eating very well." When the interview ended, Rupp was told that, as they had 55 other candidates, they'd let him know. Ten days later, he received a telegram advising that he'd been appointed basketball coach at UK and that he should wire his acceptance immediately. At that juncture, Rupp began to have second thoughts; he already had a good job, UK offered the same salary he was earning, so money was no incentive, he had a girlfriend in Freeport (he and Esther were seeing a lot of each other but had made no plans) and everybody in the school and town wanted him to stay. Finally, a local merchant advised, "take the Kentucky job. You might like it, but if not, you can go to a better job from there than you can from here." That did it: in early June 1930 Rupp wired his acceptance of the job as instructor in physical education, head basketball coach and assistant football coach at the University of Kentucky.[37] Thus began the Rupp era in the annals of the Kentucky Wildcats.

Informed that there was nothing for him to do in Lexington until football practice began in September, Rupp hung around Freeport through the summer, selling securities to earn a few extra dollars. Upon his arrival at UK in early fall, Rupp reported that the football coach, Harry Gamage, was happy to see him[38] —a situation that would last only until they quickly became rivals for the athletic budget. A couple of disappointing surprises awaited the new coach: the gym that wasn't as good as Freeport High School's was "the best in the (Southern) Conference"; many of his basketball players were on the football team and thus unable to work on their basketball skills; Rupp himself, due to his football duties, had no time to work with the few players who were available.

UK basketball lore indicates that things changed right away when the Rupp era began, but to think that is to ignore some facts. In the first place, John Mauer, an excellent coach who had gone 16-3 the previous season, left some good players with which for Rupp to work. Carey Spicer, Ellis Johnson and Forrest "Aggie" Sale, each of whom would be All-American players, were on that first Rupp-coached team. Secondly, the players were familiar and comfortable with Mauer's scheme of five or six basic plays executed at a deliberate pace. Years later, Carey Spicer, All-American under both coaches, revealed that before that first season began, "...Rupp called me into his office and picked my brain about the type of offense we had used the previous year. I told him that, as captain, I had John's playbook and he said, 'Would you mind if I look at it?'" At the end of the football season when Spicer reported for basketball practice he found that, "we were using the same plays and even the same numbers that we had under Mauer." Rupp was also familiar with the existing system as it was pretty much what Mauer had learned as a player at Illinois and was used by many Illinois high school teams as the coaches were also Fighting Illini products. Spicer also noted that Rupp added "variations" to the plays and encouraged the players to look for opportunities to utilize their natural abilities outside the system.[39] So, for the moment, the deliberate pace remained and only in subsequent years did Rupp's system evolve into the "race horse" style that would become his trademark at UK.

At one of the first team meetings, Rupp told his charges to "be aggressive and look for opportunities, not security." Most importantly, he said, that he "demanded perfect execution and perfect attention to detail." Most of those who played for Coach Rupp would state that those policies did not change much over his career. In fact, Ralph Beard remarked that as far as his teams were concerned, "perfection itself was not good enough to satisfy Coach Rupp."[40]

Also right away, Rupp established some rules of behavior for his "boys", including a dress code while they were on the road. This too persisted throughout his career. If you ever saw the Kentucky basketball team in an airport or hotel, they were wearing coats and ties and comported themselves as gentlemen.

That first season, 1930-31, Rupp's 'Cats won 15 games while losing 3. The final loss was to Maryland, 29-27, in the finals of the Southern Conference in Atlanta. Rupp expected that the fans would be disappointed and so, much to his surprise, the team was met by a "nice crowd" upon their arrival back in Lexington in bad weather. He was also pleasantly surprised by being awarded a new two-year contract.[41]

After the season, he drove back to Freeport and "snuck in and swiped" Esther from her parents' home. They were married August 29, 1931.[42]

The next winter, dissatisfied with the level of UK's regular competition, Rupp had a hand in the formation of the Southeastern Conference (SEC) late in 1932. The charter members, in addition to

Kentucky, were the Universities of Alabama, Florida, Georgia, Mississippi, Tennessee, Mississippi State, Vanderbilt, Auburn University, Louisiana State University, The University of the South (Sewanee), Georgia Tech and Tulane.[43] Over the years, the latter three schools dropped out while the conference has added South Carolina, Arkansas, Texas A&M and Missouri bringing the number of members to its current level of fourteen.

Over the next decade, Rupp recruited excellent players and refined his approach to the game. "It was 1934 or '35, I think, that something happened by accident in practice. I shouted, 'Hold it. Everybody go back and do that again.'" That accident resulted in basketball's "inside screen," which Rupp claimed as his contribution to the game of basketball. He also claimed that it kept them "undefeated in the conference for five or six years until the rest of the teams figured it out."[44] By the early 1940's, Rupp's teams had compiled an impressive record and "The Baron of the Bluegrass" was well on his way to becoming a legend.

Several factors conspired in creating the "living legend" status. First, of course, is Rupp's coaching ability and record. By 1946, his teams had compiled a record of 256-63, a remarkable 80.25% winning percentage. These factors were aided by the fact that fans turned out in droves packing Alumni Gym to see Kentucky's new "race horse" fast break. Other contributing factors were Adolph Rupp's brilliant mind, sharp wit, and ability to spout comments that made for excellent newspaper quotes. For example, asked the secret of Kentucky's success, Rupp instantly replied, "That's easy—good coaching." On another occasion, when a sportswriter asked how the game could be improved, Rupp replied, deadpan, "I'd bring back the center jump (after each basket,) take off the backboard just leaving the hoop and raise it five feet."

"Are you serious?" the newspaperman asked incredulously.

"Hell, no!" Rupp roared, "but it's a scoop for your column."[45]

Rupp was a man of many facets. One would think basketball was his entire life, but not so. He was interested in business, cattle, art, music and history and could speak knowledgably on all those topics. As Rupp matured and grew into the job at Kentucky, the number of adjectives required to describe him grew proportionally. Brilliant, maniacal, egotistical, witty, driven, single-minded, ambitious, astute, stubborn, motivated, sarcastic and clever are barely sufficient to cover most of it.

Long before the days that every move a college coach makes is scrutinized to ensure compliance with the myriad rules that the National Collegiate Athletic Association (NCAA,) the agency charged with policing college sports, imposes on them, Rupp held try-outs for his team. Sometimes as many as 50 players were invited to work out against each other vying for spots on Kentucky's roster. And it was serious business; Ralph Beard said that the first time he was ever in Alumni Gym, in the summer of 1945, was at such a try-out. Beard said that there were three All-American guards on the floor when he first walked out as a seventeen-year-old.

Another feature of UK lore maintains that one of the reasons that Coach Ed Diddle enjoyed such great success as Western Kentucky's basketball coach is that he hung around outside the gym during UK's try-outs and offered scholarships to Rupp's rejects as they were sent away.

Rupp's influence and Kentucky's success led to a couple of major rule changes in college basketball. In an effort to speed up the game to accommodate UK's fast break style, in 1933 the NCAA instituted the rule requiring the offensive team to advance the ball across mid-court in ten seconds. Three years later the three-second rule was introduced. This rule prohibits offensive players from remaining near their basket for longer than three seconds (the precise *restricted area* is also known as the *lane* or the *key*). A game central to this rule's introduction was an especially rough affair between UK and New York University on January 8, 1936. Because of this game and other similar contests, Kentucky's 6'5" All-American center, Leroy Edwards, is generally recognized as the player responsible for the three-second rule. According to Coach Rupp, Edwards was simply so big and strong that once he camped under the basket, the only way to dislodge him was by passing a new rule. Note that at the time, the lane was only six feet wide. In another effort to speed up the game, the center jump after each made basket was eliminated in 1937.[46]

Another development during these years was UK's long-standing rivalry with the University of Tennessee. Rick Pitino's "transgression" of accepting the coaching position at the University of Louisville is nothing compared to the fallout that stemmed from the Vols hiring Rupp's UK predecessor, John Mauer, in 1939. As previously noted, Mauer was an excellent coach and did well on the Knoxville campus, beating UK in regular season games in 1940, '41, '42 and '45 (all in Knoxville) and knocking the 'Cats out of the conference championship in 1941 and '43, those being the only interruptions in Kentucky's title runs from 1939 to 1945.

At the U.S. Army's request, Rupp traveled to New York in August 1945, enroute to Paris, France.[47] In the Big Apple, Rupp was commissioned as a Colonel and outfitted with the proper uniform and paperwork for the sports program he was ordered to establish for American troops in Europe. Rupp's habit of wearing starched khaki shirts and pants as he presided over UK's practice sessions may stem from this experience with the military.

The war years wreaked havoc on college athletics, as the military sucked away all available manpower. By 1945, the only players around who were eligible for college teams were those unfit for military service for some reason and those under the draft age of eighteen. Fortunately for Rupp and UK, two of those in the latter category were Ralph Beard and Wah Jones.

Chapter Four

1945-46: NIT Championship

When Ralph Beard walked into his first football meeting at UK in August 1945, he may have been surprised to learn that his friend Wah Jones was to be one of his teammates on the gridiron. Although they had been teammates on the Kentucky All-Star basketball team, they may not have discussed the fact that both planned to play football, and baseball in addition to basketball, in college. Both men were outstanding athletes, and Jones is the only person to become an All-American player under two legendary coaches: Paul (Bear) Bryant (who would come to Kentucky from the University of Maryland the next fall) and Adolph Rupp. Jones has his UK jerseys number 27 retired in both sports.

There was at least one other excellent football player in the room that hot August morning. George Blanda, who would become an SEC and National Football League (NFL) celebrity, was also a freshman in the fall of 1945. After his outstanding UK career, Blanda had the distinction of having played 26 seasons of professional football, the most in the sport's history, and had scored more points than anyone in history at the time of his retirement. Blanda retired from pro football in 1976 at the age of 48, having earned the nickname "The Fossil." He is one of only three NFL players to play in four different decades, and he holds the record for most extra points kicked and is a member of the NFL's Hall of Fame.[48] Also in the room that day was Nick Englisis, a sophomore lineman from Brooklyn, New York. "Nick the Greek" did not last long at UK after Coach Bryant showed up, but, as we shall see, he would figure large in Beard's future.

About the same time, although the athletes didn't know or care, things were changing on the administrative level. Under great pressure from alumni, state legislators and the fans, University President Herman Lee Donovan was struggling to find some way for the Wildcats to win more football games. Never very good, the team had compiled an 11 win, 16 loss and one tie record since Donovan became President in 1941. One of the problems, Donovan decided, was that as athletics were under the auspices of the College of Arts and Sciences, coaches fell under the Constitutional salary limit of $5,000 per year—not enough to hire a "big time" football coach. So, in September 1945, the University of Kentucky Athletics Association (UKAA) was established to operate, administratively and financially, the athletic programs as an independent entity. The establishment of the UKAA would bring on many changes in the athletic world, not the least of which was the environment that allowed the employment of Bear Bryant.

As another impact of WWII on college sports is that, given the shortage of manpower available for university teams, freshmen were declared entitled to play in the fall of 1945. So, unlike previous years when freshmen played on their own team, Beard, Blanda, Jones and the other newcomers were eligible for the varsity right away.

After a month of grueling practice under the watchful eyes of Coach Bernie Shively, UK's athletic director who was coaching on an interim basis, the 'Cats took on Ole Miss for their first game in Lexington on October 20. Beard saw only spot duty as the Rebels prevailed 21-7. After beating Cincinnati the next Saturday, the Wildcats traveled to East Lansing to battle Michigan State. UK's starting halfback was injured early in the game, so Beard got his first chance at extended playing time. On his first play, Ralph fumbled the exchange from Blanda, a miscue that provided one of the factors in the 7-6 loss. The Georgia Bulldogs came to Lexington for a game on November 10, a game that would prove a disaster for Ralph. Given the starting assignment, he played well enough early but injured his right shoulder near the end of the first quarter. Patched up by the trainer, Beard re-entered the contest in the second quarter only to go down with a separated left shoulder. Slumped on the sidelines, he realized his football career was over.[49]

Despondent and hurting and perhaps a little homesick, Beard sulked in his room for a while before, home for a weekend, consulting with University of Louisville basketball coach Peck Hickman. Hickman said he'd be happy to have Ralph on his team. As Athletic Director Shively had switched his scholarship to basketball, Beard had to wait until Coach Rupp, who was in Europe on his military assignment, returned to Kentucky. This is one of those Rupp stories that proves to be true. Beard walked into Rupp's office and informed the coach of his decision to transfer to Louisville. Rupp leaned back in his chair and fixed young Ralph with a glare. "Well, Beard," he intoned in his distinctive Kansas twang, "I don't know why you'd want to go to that normal school, but I can tell you that the University of Kentucky will not cancel its schedule." Ralph said that he learned early that no matter how good of a player one might be, "you're only a cog in the big machine."[50]

Ralph's shoulders were healed by the time basketball practice rolled around. Joining him on the team were guards Jack Tingle and Jack Parkinson both of whom had been all-SEC performers the previous season, Wilber Schu, a forward from nearby Versailles who, despite the two bad knees and a perforated eardrum which kept him out of the military, had made the SEC second team the previous spring and Joe Holland, a 6'4" forward from Benton in Western Kentucky, fresh out of the Navy. As the players settled into Rupp's practice routine, Parkinson and Beard worked into the starting guard spots and Tingle moved to forward opposite Schu. Wah Jones became outstanding at the center position, which was critical in Rupp's offensive scheme. Jones' nickname may have sounded childish but he was a big, strong guy who served as the teams "enforcer," meaning that to get physical with any of the UK players meant that you'd have to deal with the 6'4" 205 pound Jones also.

Those practices were brutal. As previously noted, Rupp demanded perfection and his theory was "practice makes perfect." Practice began at 3:30 in the afternoon and went full blast for three hours. One of Rupp's cardinal rules was for no one to speak "unless you could improve on the silence." According to Beard, Rupp was "hard, tough and, at times, mean" but Ralph and Rupp "got along fine." "His only interest was in winning games for the University of Kentucky," said Beard, "and that was my whole life at the time, too."[51] Famous New York sports writer Grantland Rice penned the legendary line: "When the last great scorer comes to write against your name, he marks not if you won or lost but how you played the game." One of Coach Rupp's favorite comments, taking a cue from that quote was, "If it matters not whether you win or lose, why do they keep score?" Beard and Rupp were a perfect match; both would do anything to win and Ralph personified the dedication and perfect execution his coach demanded. In later years, Rupp would say that Ralph Beard was "a nearly perfect basketball player."

Years later Ralph Beard would vividly remember those long days of practice. "Those scrimmages were twice as hard as games. I'm not exaggerating, they were bloodlettings.... That competition in practice is what made us so good."[52]

The only interruptions in the practice routine came when someone made a mistake. Rupp would blow his whistle—a signal for everyone to stop where he stood—and correct the offender, usually with biting sarcasm. One player remembered that when he fumbled a pass, Rupp told him to "get a handle on the ball and throw the ball to somebody who knows what the hell to do with it." On another occasion, Rupp told a player that he looked like "a Shetland pony in a stud horse parade." It could be said of Rupp just as a Green Bay Packer once observed that Coach Vince Lombardi "treats us all the same—like dogs." Ralph Beard commented that Rupp "asked for no quarter and gave none, making no allowance for whether a particular player would respond to his sarcasm."[53] If a player needed a par on the back, he was not going to get it from Rupp—he left that to his assistants. Over the years, many players who could not stand up to Rupp's system and sarcasm would transfer to seek their basketball fortunes in a perhaps less-demanding environment.

This edition of Rupp's Wildcats began the season with a warm-up against an "impressive" team of Army soldiers from Ft. Knox. Rupp's players easily outclassed the soldiers, much to the delight of a capacity crowd of 3,000 spectators crammed into Alumni Gym on UK's campus. Jack Tingle scored 17 points and Parkinson added 13 to pace the 'Cats while Beard, playing on the day before his eighteenth birthday, managed only two points on a single field goal and Jones chipped in three. Everybody on Rupp's bench saw action as they won going away, 59-36.[54]

A little over two weeks later, the Wildcats thoroughly stomped Arkansas, leading 39-9 at the half before winning 67-42. Jack Tingle led the way with 13 points and Wilber Schu, playing in the first game after gaining eligibility added 10. Still adjusting to the college game, Beard tallied only two and Jones added three.[55] When a time-out was called, Ralph was surprised when he noticed that the manager who handed him a towel was none other than Nick Englisis, the man he'd met earlier on the football team. Although no one seemed to take any particular notice, "Nick the Greek" took a seat at the far end of the UK bench, evidently having somehow wrangled himself an appointment as an assistant manager.[56]

Ralph Beard was not in the least happy with his slow start as a collegian. His first game in Louisville as a Wildcat was against Notre Dame. The Fighting Irish won 56-47, with Ralph held scoreless. Feeling humiliated in his home town, with his mother and all his high school friends in the stands, he was so despondent he stayed out all night rather than go home and face his mother.[57]

In March 1946, in need of an assistant, Rupp turned to an old friend, Harry Lancaster. Lancaster had been an assistant doing a lot of scouting back in '44 before he was tapped for a Navy assignment. Finished with his military obligation, he was happy to return to Kentucky. He and Rupp were an ideal pair in that Lancaster provided perfect counterpoint to Rupp's personality and abilities. This combination would last until Lancaster became UK's athletic director in 1968.

The 1945-46 Wildcats finished the regular season with a record of 20 wins balanced against the only losses inflicted by Temple and Notre Dame. It seems the Fighting Irish were always a thorn in Rupp's side. At the end of February, Rupp's 'Cats roared into Louisville prepared to rip through the SEC post-season tournament, where each of the games would be played at the Armory before capacity crowds in excess of 6,000 screaming patrons. In the opener against Auburn, the 'Cats "couldn't hit an elephant with a Greyhound bus in the first 14 minutes," but eventually routed the Tigers 69-24. Over the two next evenings, Kentucky blasted Florida and Alabama by counts of 69-32 and 59-30 to set up the championship match against LSU on March 2. That game was no contest due to the Tigers having suffered a bout of food poisoning prior to the game and UK's smothering defense. With the issue never in doubt, Kentucky led 31-15 at the half and never took their foot of the throttle, winning 59-36 to wrap up their eighth SEC tournament championship in 13 tries. As had become standard, Tingle, Schu and Parkinson carried most of the offense while Jones chipped in 11 and Beard 5. Worth a note in passing is that at that time no statistics were kept for rebounding, at which Jones excelled, or assists, which was one of Beard's strong points.[58]

Following an unusual regular season game following the post-season tournament, a 54-43 win over Temple, Kentucky prepped for a run at the national title. Although the NCAA began holding a post-season tournament in 1939, the National Invitational Tournament (NIT,) held annually at New York's Madison Square Garden, the "Mecca of Basketball" was a year older and much more prestigious at that time.[59] The NIT title was an honor that had eluded Coach Rupp so far and he very much wanted to win on the big stage, calling the rival NCAA tournament "a big YMCA" affair.

Rupp, who had spent four summers in New York while earning his advanced degree at Columbia, liked the big city. He enjoyed the atmosphere, the restaurants and the night clubs the Big Apple had to offer. He also took great delight in going in the hot bed of college basketball and showing that his Kentucky boys were as good as—and usually better than—what the Northeastern school had to offer.

And Rupp did like Kentucky boys as players. He knew all along what Rick Pitino learned in 1992 when he had to depend on the likes of Richie Farmer, Deron Feldhaus and John Pelphrey—when you put that blue and white jersey on a native of the Bluegrass State, he will play hard. With reference to the terrain of Eastern Kentucky, Coach Rupp liked to note, "I lift up mine eyes to the hills from whence commeth my help."

Perhaps it was this trip to the Garden that the most famous of all Adolph Rupp stories occurred. During a practice in the Garden, Rupp became very upset with Jack Tingle's performance. "Tingle," Rupp roared, "I want you to go over there in the corner, pull your pants down and take a crap." As the players waited, Rupp delivered the punch line. "Then, when the folks back in Lexington say that Tingle didn't do shit in Madison Square Garden, you can say, 'Oh, yes, I did, too.'"[60]

When Ralph Beard went along with the team to New York for the first time, he imbibed the sights, sounds and smells in awe of the metropolis. "Man, I'm a long way from Hardinsburg," he thought.[61] In fact, the naïve eighteen-year old was much farther than he knew. While the boys back in Breckinridge County might venture so bold as to wager a nickel in the pool room, New York City in general and Madison Square Garden in particular were havens for bookies and gamblers. Outside, ticket "scalpers" sometimes got $50 for a five dollar seat and inside, bookies teemed in the concourses. Sometimes bettors formed a line waiting to get their money down, considering the point spread, of course.

Kentucky fans were not yet The Big Blue Nation, but they were in abundance, even in New York City. In the days before television, Ralph

Beard was amazed to find that people on the sidewalk recognized him. "They loved Kentucky basketball in the Garden," he said. "They even knew the players' names, home towns and point averages."[62]

The 'Cats roared through the opening round, beating Arizona 77-53 on March 16. The next game, against a determined West Virginia squad, was much tougher, but UK prevailed over the Mountaineers 59-51 setting up the final game with Rhode Island on March 20.

A crowd of 18,000, many of them cheering for the underdog Rams, showed up on a chilly evening in New York. With Kentucky heavily favored, the battle turned out to be much closer than expected with Rhode Island's stars Ernie Calverly and Dick Hale matching Beard, Jones and Tingle basket for basket. Beard had the defensive assignment on Calverly, an All-American guard and a great scorer, averaging 26.7 points per game. "I want him stopped," Rupp told Beard in the locker room before the game.

Beard, who had already established himself as a "stopper," able to play outstanding defense on the opponents' best scorer, calmly crammed the fifth stick of gum in his mouth. "Don't worry about it, Coach," he answered.[63]

After a first-half run by each team, the Rams led 27-26 the half and both teams expected a tense struggle after intermission. Expectations were met; Jones and Beard each scored to begin the second period staking the Wildcats to a 30-27 lead, but it was nip and tuck after that. When Wah Jones fouled out, to join Tingle on the bench with four minutes remaining and the Rams leading 42-40, the situation looked bleak for the Kentuckians. Despite the two UK starters disqualified on the bench, still, the game stayed close. With the scored knotted for the twelfth time at 45 and only seconds left on the clock, Beard took the ball to the left of the circle, paused momentarily before darting past his defender. As Ralph sped for the basket, the Rams' off-guard, Calverly, moved in to block his path. Deftly, Beard veered to his left past the defender. Calverly reached, but Ralph was already by him and all the Rhode Islander could do was try to disrupt the sure "crip" shot with a hard foul. The whistle sent Calverly to the bench with his fifth foul while Beard picked himself up and stepped to the free throw stripe for the single free throw allowed for a non-shooting foul.

His jaws chomping his mouthful of gum like a piston was the only sign that the eighteen-year-old competitor felt any pressure despite the national title opportunity resting on his shoulders. "I was scared to death," Beard would say 50 years later, "that was my way of calming myself."[64] Ignoring a trickle of blood from the knee injured by the foul, "Calmly the little Louisville athlete stepped to the stripe—the screams of 18,000 persons were hushed momentarily—and dropped in the free throw that won the ball game for Coach Adolph Rupp and his brilliant Kentuckians." The Rams were unable to score as the remaining 40 seconds clicked off. The free throw gave Ralph 13 points in Kentucky's first NIT Championship. Jones and Schu tallied ten each. Beard also won defensive honors and kept his word by holding the high-scoring Calverly to two field goals and four free throws.[65]

If he had not been previously, that free throw elevated Ralph Beard to bona fide hero status across Kentucky. The term "rock star" had not been invented yet, but with his winning smile, gracious manners, unassuming personality and fiery on-court demeanor, Ralph would qualify. A Lexington drug store proudly announced that it would supply him with all the gum he could chew. For those readers too young to remember, throughout the 1930's and 40's millions of American boys thrilled to the daily exploits of fictional character "Jack Armstrong, the All-American boy" in a popular radio program. In every Kentucky boy's heart, Ralph Beard gave ol' Jack a run for his money. Little Ralph may have not been the tallest guy, but he was certainly a big man on campus and UK's media guide touted him as "the perfect Wheaties ad."[66] If the rule, now in effect, requiring players to spend one year in college before turning pro (the "one and done" rule) had been in force then and if professional basketball had had any popularity, Ralph Beard may have been one of the first "one and done's." As it was, he would return to Kentucky.

The Wildcats ended that glorious season with an over-all record of 28 victories in 30 tries, which was a lot of games for the time. Jack Parkinson led the team in scoring, averaging 11.3 points per games. Ralph Beard scored 279 points in those 30 games for an average of 9.3, and Wah Jones' 290 put his average at 9.67. Parkinson (who was also named to several All-America teams), Tingle, Beard and Jones were named to the All-SEC first team and Wilber Schu, the fifth starter, was named to the second squad.[67]

Kentucky basketball seemed at a zenith, but as the saying goes, "You ain't seen nothin' yet." Nobody suspected that true—dare I say, fabulous—greatness waited just around the corner.

Chapter Five

The Beak

In the spring of 1944, while the Allies prepared for the invasion of France, back in Ohio, Martin's Ferry High School basketball coach Floyd Baker thought he had a pretty good player on his state runner-up team. Baker's problem was that he could find no college coach to agree with him despite the fact that the young man in question had been named to the Ohio All-State team each of the two previous years and scored a state record 628 points as a senior. Also, despite the fact that the young man's brother had been on a football scholarship at Ohio State, for reasons no one has been able to fathom, the Buckeyes showed no interest. In desperation, Baker invited UK's famous coach to speak at Martin's Ferry's athletic banquet.[68] Thus was Adolph Rupp introduced to Alex Groza, a player destined for college and professional basketball stardom.

Alexander John Groza was born in Martin's Ferry October 7, 1926, the youngest of four brothers in a family of Hungarian emigrants. All the Groza boys were active in sports, so it was only natural that ever since baby Alex was big enough to get out of the house, his brothers, Frank, Lou and John, looked out for him and guided his athletic career. Lou, who would become a famous football player, steered Alex away from football, advising "you might get hurt." Lou "The Toe" Groza played one year (1942) at the Buckeye school in Columbus before he went into the Army. Returning from the service in 1946, Lou, a tackle and place kicker, went straight to the NFL's Cleveland Browns, where he lasted 21 years, helping the Browns to eight professional championships. When Lou finally retired in 1967, he held NFL records for the longest and most field goals. Lou Groza was elected to the NFL's Hall of Fame in 1974.[69]

The Grozas were a hard-working family and all the boys chipped into the family fortunes. Alex started work at age twelve, plucking chickens at a poultry house. From there, as he progressed through school, he moved on to more responsible jobs at a box factory and finally, a can factory.[70]

Although all the brothers played basketball (in addition to other sports,) it was Frank who guided Alex into basketball and helped him develop his skills. Alex was always tall for his age, but skinny and awkward for much of his youth. His big feet didn't help any either, as he was always tripping over them. Additionally, his big nose would earn him the nickname "The Beak."

All the Groza boys played the center position in basketball, but, in 1941, when Alex's turn came to take over, Martin's Ferry won the Ohio freshman's championship. With Alex on the varsity at 6"4" the next season, Martin's Ferry won their district and sectional titles but lost out in the regionals. By the time he was a senior, he had grown to 6'5" but only weighed a beanpole-ish 167 pounds. Alex was named Captain of Ohio's All-State team and voted its most valuable player.

Groza was a good student, graduating with an "A" average. He ranked sixteenth in a class of 177 and was a four-year member of the National Honor Society.[71]

After meeting Groza at the banquet, Rupp invited Alex to his annual workout session, held in Lexington. When Alex arrived in Big Blue Country, he may have been surprised to learn that he was one of 30 hopefuls who would display their skills for Rupp that year. These players scrimmaged against each other, with the line-ups changing for each match, all weekend. In the end, Groza was offered a scholarship to Kentucky. "To my knowledge, I was the only guy he invited back," Groza says.[72] As difficult as it is to understand, Groza said that UK's was the only scholarship offer he received.

When practice began in the fall of 1944, Kentucky's prospects for the season looked pretty good. Bob Brannum, All-American center the previous season, was gone to the Army, but Rupp figured Groza would provide an adequate replacement. Alex was underweight, and at a mere 6'5", pretty short for a major college center, but he was cat-quick and had excellent moves under the basket. Armed with a lethal hook shot that made up for his lack of height, Groza knew how to score. Additionally, the 'Cats had proven performers Jack Tingle and Wilber Schu at forward, Jack Parkinson and Tom Moseley at guard. These players, teamed with Groza's skills, should be able to produce as Rupp hoped.

However, two events that would impact the season occurred before the first game. Moseley, who had previously committed the cardinal sin of talking back to Rupp, missed an extra practice session and was summarily dismissed from the team. The other, more disastrous event: Alex Groza received his "greetings" from Uncle Sam. He was ordered to report for induction into the armed forces in three weeks.

Nevertheless, the season began on December 1 with the usual tune-up against an Army team from Ft. Knox. Groza looked good, scoring 19 in Kentucky's easy 56-23 victory. Alex played well in the next two games against a Navy squad stationed at Berea, Kentucky (featuring Joe Holland, a blonde 6'4" Kentuckian, who caught Rupp's eye), and Indiana, both easy wins. Late in December, Alex Groza's eyes lit up, not in anticipation of Christmas, but the prospect of playing undefeated Ohio State in Lexington on December 23. Groza was out to prove that the Buckeyes had made a mistake in failing to offer him a scholarship.

Ohio State's attack revolved around Arnie Risen, a standout 6'9" native of Williamsburg, Kentucky, who had transferred to the Columbus campus from Eastern Kentucky State College. Risen, who would battle Groza many times in the professional ranks, was bigger, stronger and more experienced than Groza, but Alex had something to prove. Snow swirled outside, but the stands were packed, as usual, inside Alumni Gym. When the dust settled, Groza had outscored Risen 16 to 14 as Kentucky won 53-48 in an overtime thriller. Rupp had designed his offense to feature Groza distributing the ball to cutting teammates if no shot was available for him. So, the big guy handled the ball a lot. Unfortunately, at this time, no statistics were kept for rebounding or assists. It would be interesting to know how Groza stacked up against Risen in those areas.

After the game, OSU coach Harold Olsen approached a sweating and jubilant Groza. "Alex," he asked, "why didn't you come to our school?"

Groza had dreamed of this moment and had his answer ready. "Nobody asked me,"[73] Alex said as he turned to walk away, smiling in sweet revenge.

After Christmas, the 'Cats went on a road trip for games against Wyoming in Buffalo, NY, Temple in Philadelphia and number one rated Long Island University in New York City. Groza scored fourteen in the runaway 50-16 victory over Wyoming's Cowboys. Then, on December 30, he tallied 27, including the game-winner, in a 45-44 squeaker at Temple. On New Year's Day against highly regarded LIU at Madison Square Garden, Kentucky fell far behind in the second half before Rupp turned to a little used reserve, Buddy Parker. Parker provided the spark the Coach had hoped for as the Wildcats rallied to tie the game at 52 as regulation time ended. Rupp's charges outscored LIU 10-0 in the extra period for a huge win. Groza led all scorers with 27.[74]

Rupp allowed Groza to miss the next game, a laugher against Arkansas Teachers College in Lexington on January 8, but told his big man to be back in time for a much tougher contest against Michigan State five days later. In that Arkansas Teachers (now University of Central Arkansas) game an incident occurred which will stand forever as one of the crown jewels in Wildcat/Rupp lore. As the story goes, Rupp stormed into the locker room at halftime, apparently madder than a wet hen. No matter that his Wildcats were leading by a score of something like 40-4, his concern was that one Bear player had scored all four points. "Who the hell is guarding that number 12?" Rupp demanded.

Slumped on a stool in front of his locker, Jack Parkinson timidly raised his hand. "That's my man, Coach," he sheepishly admitted.

"Well get *on* him," Rupp roared, "he's runnin' wild!" The players looked at each other, everybody afraid to laugh.

That is a true story. Well, almost anyway. The incident did occur and the actual halftime score was 41-4. Of course, the 'Cats went on to win. The fact is, however, that one Arkansas Teachers player, named Wells, had three of the four points. So, the story, as usually related, is only a very slight embellishment of the facts.[75] I once heard Coach Rupp, quizzed by a sportscaster, admit that the story was true, "But I was kidding," he said. "What are you going to say to your team with a score like that?" After a slight pause, Rupp added "They knew I was joking," a bit wistfully, I thought. Coach Rupp then got back at the sportscaster. "What was the final score of that game?" Rupp queried. The TV man just shook his head. "It was 75-6," Rupp announced with a chuckle. "They took my lecture to heart and held the other team to a single field goal in the second half." The Coach then conjectured that was probably the only time a team had been held to only two points for an entire half.*

*www.wikianswers.com says: "On November 3rd, 1978 Duke lost to instate rival Davidson 49-33. Amazingly, Davidson came back from a 31-4 halftime deficit. This is the fewest number of points ever scored in a half of NCAA men's basketball."

Groza had used the time away from the team to visit his parents as his date to report to the Army was rapidly approaching. The game with Michigan State on January 13 was billed as "Farewell to Groza Night." As was often said in those days, the only thing dependable about wartime travel was that it was undependable. Sure enough, Groza's train was late and the game had already started by the time he arrived in Lexington. He rushed from the depot to Alumni Gym in time to dress and score one basket as the Spartans led 24-20 when the horn sounded ending the first period. During halftime, the president of the student pep organization presented Alex with a gold key to the University and other farewell gifts in an elaborate and emotional ceremony.[76] Groza scored twelve in the second half as the 'Cats prevailed 66-35. Until that time, Alex Groza had been a Buckeye, but "I became a Kentuckian right then and there," he vowed.[77]

As Coach Rupp scratched his head wondering how to replace his star center, Groza reported to basic training. During the ten games in which he participated during the season, Groza had scored 165 and UK was undefeated in eleven contests. The back-up center, Kenton Campbell was a good player and with Groza gone he helped the Wildcats to a 22-4 record and another SEC Championship in the 1944-45 season. At season's end, Groza's average of 16.5 points per game was a team high.

In the Army, Groza completed infantry combat training before being sent to Texas to await an overseas assignment at Fort Hood. One day an officer approached Alex to ask if he'd rather remain at Fort Hood and play with a basketball team being organized there. Groza, of course, did not hesitate to accept the offer. Subsequently, he was assigned to the medical corps and worked in a hospital until his discharge. The officer who recruited Groza for the military team was former UK great and future Groza teammate Bob Brannum.[78]

As I have been preaching for some time, we cannot pay enough homage to those men and women who sacrificed so much during WWII to preserve our way of life. While that is a debt that can never be fully paid, we can take every opportunity to honor them. So, before we move on, it is worth noting here that former UK basketball players Melvin Brewer, Kenny England, Jim Goforth, Walter Johnson and Jim King were among the thousands of Americans who did not return.[79]

Chapter Six

1946-47: Back to the NIT

By the fall of 1946, the war was over and most of the men being discharged from the military were returning to America looking for their old jobs back. Many others were eager to resume a college education interrupted by their military service. Congress had provided the GI Bill, which allowed many to do just that. Several such men would work to UK's basketball advantage. These men would give a whole new meaning to the term "veteran team."

As Coaches Rupp and Lancaster donned their starched khaki outfits to begin practice for the 1946-47 season, they had every reason to smile about the upcoming Wildcats' prospects. Waiting on the floor were sixteen players who would form a team that the coaches were sure could go a long way into the post-season tournaments, perhaps even secure another national championship.

Lost to graduation was Wilber Schu, who had been an integral part of the previous season's team, and All-American Jack Parkinson had been inducted into the military service. Returning, however, from the 28-2 squad were Ralph Beard (sophomore,) Joe Holland (sophomore,) Jack Tingle (senior), Kenton Campbell (junior)and little used reserves Mulford "Muff" Davis, Buddy Parker, and Malcolm McMullen. Bob Brannum (sophomore,) an All-American in '44, was back from the military as was Kenny Rollins, a 6'0' junior guard who had lettered in the 1942-43 season before his stint in the Navy.

Not on the floor that October day was Wah Jones, as he was still involved with Coach Bryant's football team whose season was not finished yet. They were scheduled to wrap up the year in Knoxville on November 23 with the annual grudge match against the Volunteers. UK's 13-6 loss in that game would bring the record to 7-3, matching Bryant's first year record at Kentucky. These were the first steps in the legend that would come to surround Bear Bryant. Given the low football expectations in Lexington, winning seven games in two consecutive seasons was great by UK standards. Jones, now a sophomore, would be along to basketball practice when the pigskin season ended and his bruises healed.

Newcomers who were expected to contribute included Jim Line, a 6'2' freshman forward from Akron, OH, Jim Jordan, a 6'3' forward who transferred as a junior from North Carolina's final four team of the previous campaign and Dale Barnstable, a good-looking blonde freshman from Antioch, IL. Rupp had recruited these players during his time in the military.[80]

Another returning player was Cliff Barker, an Army Air Force veteran. Cliff had participated in one of Coach Rupp's famous try-outs in 1939 and had been so totally unimpressive that Rupp simply dismissed him. Barker's Yorktown, IN coach, Ken Sigler, pleaded with Rupp to reconsider, vowing that Barker was a much better player than he had shown in the try-out. Rupp agreed to reconsider, and Barker did come to UK in the fall. Barker worked out with the team for a while before he "went home, fell in love, got married and went into the Army Air Force"[81] before he got much of a chance to show Coach Rupp what he could do.

The B-17 bomber on which Barker was serving as the flight engineer was shot down over Brunswick, Germany on January 30, 1944.[82] Cliff was one of five of the ten crewmembers to survive.

Parachuting safely to earth, Barker and his fellow crewmembers were captured and sent to a POW camp. Over the next fifteen months, the prisoners had to find their own ways to fill the long empty days. One of the available activities was playing basketball, although they had no ball. Just as Adolph Rupp had done back in Kansas, they threw a bag stuffed with rags at a hoop. "You didn't dribble that thing much," said Barker.[83] So Cliff became a deft ball handler. Eventually a Red Cross package containing a basketball showed up and Barker spent many of his long hours rolling and spinning the ball on his fingers and practicing other ball-handling tricks. At age 25, Barker would be a 6'2" 185 pound sophomore this season. His nifty passes would be a big part of this Wildcat team's success. Cawood Ledford, long-time radio broadcaster of Kentucky's games (who was a Centre College student at the time,) said that Barker was the first player he ever saw deliver a no-look pass.[84]

The best news of all, however, was that Alex Groza was back for his sophomore year. When he was discharged from the Army, Alex made his way to Lexington, where he was surprised to see Coach Rupp waiting at the train depot. Groza approached, expecting a warm welcoming smile. Instead, Rupp continued to peer past Groza down the line, looking for something or someone. "Coach?" Groza said, hesitantly.

Rupp glanced up, a bewildered look on his face. Suddenly, his confusion changed to joy as he recognized his star player. Rupp's difficulty in recognizing him was due to the fact that Groza had grown two inches and gained 70 pounds while in the Army, now a robust 6'7" and weighing in at 238.[85]

The Coaches' dream of so much talent was a nightmare for the players. The competition in practice was hot for starting assignments. The only lock was Beard at shooting guard. After the previous season's NIT heroics, Ralph, being Ralph, had asked Rupp what he should work on over the summer. Rupp told him that he needed to become a better free throw shooter, make better use of his left hand and improve his running one-hand shot from near the free throw line. The latter was the 1940's version of today's jump shot. In addition to playing baseball, his second love, in his time away from school, Beard had indeed worked diligently on the suggested areas and had indeed improved in each, much to the Baron's delight.[86] Steady and mature Kenny Rollins claimed the point guard spot. An adequate scorer when need be, Rollins was a good ball-handler and an excellent floor general, a veritable "coach on the floor."

There were a number of contenders for the forward positions. Barnstable, Line and Jordan all caught the coaches' notice, but in the end, proven performers Tingle and Holland won the starting assignments.

Hottest of all the competitions was the battle for the center position. Wah Jones, who had had an outstanding campaign at the pivot the previous season, was not yet on hand, leaving All-American Brannum, Campbell, an All-SEC performer, and Groza to fight it out. Bigger and stronger than before his Army stint but just as quick, agile and crafty, "Big Al" emerged with the prize, much to Brannum's dismay.

Those five players took the floor as Rupp unveiled what figured to be his strongest UK team so far. The first game was against cupcake Indiana Central in Lexington on November 28. Since arriving at UK, Rupp's general philosophy had been to pick five starters and let them play the whole game unless somebody was injured or in foul trouble. In fact, Buddy Parker, one of the reserves once reported that Ralph Beard, after diving for a ball ended up at the feet of the bench players, writhing in pain. Rupp yelled, "Parker!" who thought he'd be substituted. Instead, Rupp demanded, "Help Beard up!"

However, the overabundance of talent with this group forced the coach to depart from form when the score was well in hand; running up the score on an overmatched opponent was considered bad manners. The starters didn't play long and everybody on the bench would see action in this season-opening game. On the first possession, Ralph Beard flashed by his man to the basket but missed the first field goal attempt of the season. No matter; the fat lady sang the National Anthem on this one as the 'Cats were soon up 20-0. Beard led all scorers with 15 and Groza added nine. Eleven other Kentuckians dented the scoring column as UK rolled to an easy 78-36 victory for the season's first win.[87]

Reserve Buddy Parker, who would become a long-time Lexington real estate agent and auctioneer, noted that in some of the early season games this year, Rupp would have only half his players dress before the game. That group would play the first half. At halftime, the other half of the squad would dress while the first group showered and donned their street clothes so they could sit in the stands with their girlfriends through the rest of the game.[88]

Wah Jones joined the team following UK's 24-14 football victory over Villanova in the one and only occurrences of the Great Lakes Bowl played on December 6 in Cleveland, Ohio. Jones immediately began a daily battle with Tingle for his starting position. Eventually, Jones' strength and rebounding ability won out. At that point, UK's starting line-up became Beard and Rollins at guard, Holland and Jones at forward and Groza at center.

These 'Cats did pretty well, sailing along through December outclassing all opponents by big margins including a twenty point win over DePaul on December 12 in Louisville and a big win by the same count over highly regarded St. John's in Madison Square Garden. In that game, played on December 22, Alex Groza, the big center, dominated the rebounding despite six-foot-nine-inch Harry Boykoff of St. John's, and scored well. Ralph Beard, Joe Holland and Ken Rollins played fine floor games and also scored heavily. An impressed New

York scribe noted that "Kentucky, a fast-break team, never tired of running, maintained a strong defense and showed a strong reserve power in totally outclassing St. John's."[89]

A story Ralph Beard liked to tell involved a Jack Tingle performance, perhaps in this game. It seems that Jack, who was a bit of a rounder, showed up at the Garden that night somewhat the worse for wear following an afternoon spent lounging in some of the local watering holes. Nonetheless, Tingle poured in an amazing seven field goals. Beard, who would not so much as drink a Coke during training, asked Tingle how he could play so well under those circumstances. "Hell, Ralph," Jack replied, "when you look up there and see four baskets, you're naturally bound to hit one of 'em."

Back home two nights later, Rupp again played everybody while ringing up an 83-18 pummeling of Texas A&M. Those 83 points was a Kentucky record for the most points scored in a single game, but, as the saying goes, records are made to be broken. Five days later, the 'Cats posted 96 on hapless Wabash while winning by 72.[90]

Since 1936, Louisiana's Sugar Bowl had offered a basketball game in conjunction with the celebrated football game. A record crowd of 9,000 showed up to see the Wildcats take on Hank Iba's Oklahoma A&M team in the 1947 Sugar Bowl Classic in New Orleans on December 30. Kentucky had an eleven game win streak going but was not prepared for Iba's slowdown tactics. With no shot clock or 5-second dribbling rule, the Aggies held the ball for most of the game and came away with a 37-31 win. In response to a sportswriter's query, the usually loquacious Rupp snapped, "You can't score if you don't have the damned ball!"[91]

Athletic Director Bernie Shively observed that, "We were just over confident.... They fought hard but it wasn't enough."[92] *Courier-Journal* writer Earl Ruby swore that A&M had more players on the court than Kentucky. "On every rebound, there were three or four Aggies and never more than one Wildcat. It was so noticeable than on more than one occasion, I forsook my scorebook to count noses." Ruby said he got five for each team at every count, but still wasn't convinced.[93] Rupp added, "It's a pity we had to pick a spot like this to play the worst game of our lives. The boys didn't follow a single instruction."[94] That comment is vintage Rupp. It was common knowledge around the campus that in his career, Rupp won 876 games while the players lost 190. This would prove to be just one of several Sugar Bowl games in which the 'Cats were to be disappointed.

In the wake of that bitter loss, Rupp—for once—sought his players' advice. Informed that there was a leadership problem on the floor, Rupp decided to allow the players to choose a captain—a practice that had been suspended for the last few seasons because his players were so young. They promptly elected dependable Kenny Rollins.[95]

UK then reeled off ten more wins with no victory margin less than ten points. One of those games was against Notre Dame in Louisville's Armory on February 1. Returning to the scene of his total embarrassment the previous year, Ralph Beard redeemed himself by scoring 17 while limiting the Fighting Irish's All-American player he guarded to just two points.[96]

This brought up a much anticipated return engagement with DePaul. The 'Cats shooting that evening was every bit as cold as the Chicago weather. They hit a frigid 21 percent on 16 of 75 shots, which won't win many games. Actually, DePaul didn't shoot much better; connecting on only 18 of 61, but it was good enough to allow the Blue Demons to pull off a 53-47 win. The sportswriters thought—again—that Kentucky appeared over-confident as they took the floor, but any cockiness soon evaporated as the Blue Demons led 19-16 after ten minutes of play and 33-28 at the half. Behind the inspired play of Groza, the 'Cats battled back in the second half, eventually closing to two at 46-44, but that was as close as they came. The papers called it a "stunning setback" for Kentucky. Groza led the way with 21, Wah Jones added eight while Beard was held to four free throws.[97]

The 'Cats sailed through their remaining conference games ending up the regular season with 27 wins against two losses. That brought up the SEC tournament in Louisville late in February. According to conference rules, each team was allowed only ten players, so clearly Rupp had to leave somebody at home. As one of his choices, he said that Bob Brannum was simply "not good enough" to make the traveling squad. Rupp told Brannum that he was not going to the tournament and then brazenly asked him to continue to practice with the team. It is probably a good thing that Brannum's response to that request is not recorded. Brannum, having been a consensus All-American in the 1943-44 season, had played in each of this season's 29 games but his time was sparse behind Groza and Jones. In his limited action, he'd scored a mere 125 points. He'd been steaming for some time and being left off the traveling squad was the last straw—he told Coach Rupp that he'd be transferring. Asked about Brannum's being left at home, Rupp added insult to the player's injury by giving out Brannum's Lexington phone number, "if any of you coaches are interested."[98] At least one coach was interested; we shall hear from "Tank" Brannum again.

The early rounds of the tournament were easy as UK defeated Vanderbilt, Auburn and Georgia Tech, besting the old single game tournament scoring record of 74 in each game. That set up the final against surprising Tulane who had knocked off Tennessee and second-seeded LSU for the right to take on the 'Cats. "The lead swapped hands numerous times leading up to halftime, with Kentucky clinging to a slim 25-20 lead." Then Kenny Rollins, "previously most greatly lauded for his leadership, floor work and brains came through with three straight field goals to give Kentucky a 31-23 lead." They would not relinquish the advantage, winning 75-53, going away. Rollins paced the UK attack with 17 points and Joe Holland added 15.[99]

A gasp and then a roar went through the capacity crowd of 7,500—then as now mostly Kentucky fans—when the newspaper men and coaches' picks for the All-Tournament team were announced. Named to the select squad were Beard, Jones, Tingle, Holland and Rollins. Not only were they five UK players, they were all native Kentuckians! "Where's Groza?" you ask as well you should. Kentucky had won by such run-away margins that Alex had not played enough minutes in the tournament to be considered for the first team. He was named to the second team.[100] Worth a note in passing is that the fact that freshmen were eligible during the war allowed Tingle to be the first player ever to be named to the select quintet four times.

After the now usual postseason game with Temple, which UK won 68-29, Rupp and his players packed their bags to head back to the National Invitational Tournament, once again opting out of the rival "YMCA" tournament. The NIT was to be played at Madison Square Garden where the 'Cats had won what they considered to be the National Championship the year before on Ralph Beard's heroics. The games began on March 17 and the 'Cats had a little trouble in the opening rounds, squeaking by LIU 66-60 and then whipping North Carolina State 60-42. That brought up the title match against the tournament's "Cinderella," Utah who had surprised everyone by defeating

Duquesne and then West Virginia to gain the finals. The Utes played a slow-down game, much like Coach Iba's Aggies, and the anti-thesis of Kentucky's fast break pattern. The gamblers set the line at Kentucky by 12 over the lightly regarded and sixth seeded Utes.

"Cautious to the point of being monotonous, Utah slowed the game down to a snail's pace. But when the Utes moved, they moved with deadly accuracy."[101] Jim Line, Groza and Jones struggled against the Utes, but the Kentuckians could never close the gap. In the end, Utah won 49-45.

Much was made in the New York papers that a Utah-born Japanese player named Wat Misaka had "held" Ralph Beard to one point. It is a fact that Beard scored only a single point, but in a 2002 interview, Ralph recalled that game as a nightmare and he was still angry about it. "What they didn't say was that I had spent the previous week in the infirmary before we went to New York," declared Beard. Ralph went on to say that Joe Lapchick, who would later coach the NBA's New York Knicks drafted Misaka because he was "a better player than me." Beard reminded that while he never played against Misaka in college again, the first time they met in the pros, Ralph scored 32 on him. Forty-six years later, you can still see the competitive fire in Ralph Beard's eyes as he says he told Lapchick, "you might have thought Misaka was better than me, but this is what you're gonna see from now on, except that, next time, I'm going to double the effort."[102] There would be no next time, the 5'7" Misaka lasted a total of three games as a professional basketballer.[103]

Rupp, of course, was extremely disappointed. Still, his team went home with a record of 34-3, SEC Champions for the ninth time in the fourteen years of the conference existence and national runner-up. In other post-season honors, Groza and Beard were named censuses All-Americans. The little Hardinsburg boy was named Player of the Year by True Magazine and the New York writers voted him the best player to appear in the Garden all season.

This was the beginning of the end of Rupp's love affair with New York. With Kentucky ranked number one in all the post-season polls, Rupp was incensed when the Metropolitan Basketball Writers named Navy Coach Ben Carnevale as Coach of the Year instead of him.[104] This was a grudge "The Baron" would nurse for a long time.

Ralph Beard, despite his accolades, again asked his coach what he could do to improve his game. Rupp told him to work on his long two-hand set-shots. Over the summer, Beard was in the gym at least three days a week, putting up 500 or more outside shots per session. When the next season rolled around, Beard would show himself to be one of the best long-range shooters in the game. That outside accuracy added to his driving skills and quickness made Beard, just a sophomore, an excellent player in every phase of the game.

Ralph Beard and Alex Groza finished out the year with nearly identical scoring averages, 10.9 and 10.6, respectively. Rollins, Holland and Jones followed up with nice scoring averages, as well. Unlike what we witness today, the fans and coaches licked their chops in a situation John Calipari can only dream about; all these players, plus Jim Line, Cliff Barker, Jim Jordan and Dale Barnstable, would be returning for the next season. In most SEC locales, basketball is considered to be nothing more than something to fill in the time between the end of football season and spring practice, but Kentuckians ached to get football out of the way so the next edition of Rupp's 'Cats could take the floor.

Chapter Seven

1947-48: The Fabulous Five

By the time the yellow ginkgo leaves around the Lexington campus shuffled under the students' feet as they hurried to classes in the fall of 1947, Coaches Rupp and Lancaster were gearing up for the basketball season in which they fully well expected to go undefeated. Sound familiar?

That expectation was actually not too unrealistic; their 'Cats were, indeed, loaded for bear and the only games which figured to be tough were a December 20 match-up with Temple in Philadelphia and a February date with their old nemesis in South Bend. Additionally, early season foes St. John's and DePaul were usually troublesome.

For personnel, Kentucky had 19 players, including four All-Americans: Beard, Groza, and Jones, juniors now, and Jack Parkinson who was returning for his senior campaign. Additionally, two of the previous season's All-SEC performers, Cliff Barker and Kenny Rollins were back. There were also plenty of other veterans including Jim Line, Joe Holland, Dale Barnstable and Jim Jordan. So talent-laden, in fact, was this squad, that neither Jack Parkinson, who had made All-American in 1946 nor Jim Jordan, a two-time All-American while stationed at North Carolina in '45 and '46, could ever crack the starting line-up!

Once again, as we can imagine, the competition in practice was hot. Ralph Beard would comment that the competition in practice was what made them so good and Alex Groza observed that practice was much harder than a game because the opponent was tougher and, these sessions held long before the NCAA decreed that teams can only practice 20 hours per week, sometimes lasted three exhausting hours.[105] As the November 29 opener against weak-sister Indiana Central approached, the starters emerged as Rollins and Beard at guard, Groza at the pivot and Barker and Holland at the forward spots. Once again, Wah Jones would report to practice only when the football season ended.

As expected, Indiana Central's (now University of Indianapolis) Greyhounds posed no problem and Rupp cleared his bench in the 80-41 victory. Two nights later, the 'Cats defeated a Ft. Knox Army team by the same score. In a scheduling anomaly, the Wildcats played hapless Tulsa on consecutive nights, steamrolling in both games, 72-18 and 71-22.

Those were all home games and the word spread quickly that this basketball team was worth watching. If you think it's tough to get into Rupp Arena to see a game, consider this: Alumni Gym, the home of these Wildcats, had a seating capacity of 2,800. For any game, more than half of the spaces were allotted to students. All the rest went to University faculty and staff and the press. The only public sale of tickets occurred while the students were on Christmas and semester break, just six of the seventeen home games.[106] So, usually everybody in attendance had some connection with the University. Well, in theory, anyway. Wah Jones once commented about the comedy of seeing a Lexington bank president sitting in the stands wearing a Kentucky letter sweater.[107]

The games were so popular that the administration was forced to divide the student body into two groups who were admitted to games on an alternating basis. But, people found ways to get in so that the crowds cheering their blue and white clad heroes were sometimes as large as 5,000 patrons. "There were many games where nobody had room enough to sit from the time they came into the building until the game was over," one player commented.[108] Although it was considered a huge facility when it opened in 1924, as small as that building is by today's domed stadium or Rupp Arena or even Memorial Coliseum standards, conditions must have been pretty cozy in old Alumni Gym on a cold 1947 winter evening.

Kentucky looked invincible in defeating DePaul at Louisville 74-50, Cincinnati in the Queen City 67-31 and Xavier at home 79-37. This brought up the much anticipated match against powerful Temple on their floor in Philadelphia on December 20.

Right from the tip-off, the Temple Owls demonstrated that they were unimpressed by Kentucky's newspaper clippings. Before 8,623 screaming fans, the Owls scored the game's first three points. The 'Cats fought back to tie the game at ten after a brisk four minutes of play. The remainder of the game was nip and tuck, with neither team able to gain a lead larger than five while the lead changed hands eleven times. Near the end of the game, "Big Al" stole the ball, drove the length of the floor in four loping strides for a "crip" to put his team up 58-57. A Temple basket put them up one before an added free throw made the margin two. Then a Temple player fouled Kentucky's free-throw ace, Kenny Rollins. The crowd roared as Rollins calmly stepped to the line and deposited his first toss into the net. "Then bedlam became almost silence as he made ready for his second try. Kenny's second shot hit the rim, rolled around and out. And with his failure went Kentucky's chances to tie the game."[109] And also with it went the myth of invincibility and Rupp's dream of an undefeated season. Each team had 20 field goals; Rollins' missed free throw was the difference as the Owls won 60-59. Worth noting is that Ralph Beard's playing time and effectiveness were limited by an injured hip and Wah Jones, not yet in basketball shape, did not even get in the game.[110]

Despite a relatively easy win over St. John's in Madison Square Garden before heading south, Rupp was still fuming when the team arrived back in Lexington. He knew this team had the stuff of greatness and he intended to get it out of them. "Coach was a terror, a tiger in practice the following week," Joe Holland remembered. "We'd had plenty of rough practices before, but we'd never seen him like that."[111]

Ralph Beard received a brief respite when he attended a ceremony in honor of his being named *Sport Magazine's* "Top Performer in Basketball for 1947." Unfortunately, *Sport* had pictured teammate Jim Line, not Beard, on the cover of the issue honoring Beard. For copies sold in Lexington, *Sport's* staff pasted a likeness of Beard over Line's. Ralph laughed off the gaffe, but his smile faded just a bit when he observed that the presentation watch he was awarded was engraved to Maurice Richard, Sport's top hockey performer, not him. The players later exchanged for the proper watches.[112] Relief from Rupp's wrath did not come for anybody else until the team travelled to Louisville to take on Creighton on January 2.

An event that was to have historic consequences occurred that evening in Louisville's Armory. Despite the lopsided score, Coach Rupp was still in a foul mood occasioned at the moment by sloppy play. When somebody threw an errant pass that sailed out of bounds untouched, "The Baron" could tolerate no more. He called time-out and ran out on the floor to meet the offending player before he got to the sidelines. Rupp's face was beet red as he administered a proper chewing-out. When play resumed, Joe Holland, seated next to Rupp on the bench, remarked, "Coach, if you'd get off our cases, maybe we could play."

Momentarily ignoring the game, Rupp whirled to face Holland. "You mean the referees?" the Coach demanded.

Apparently fed up with Rupp's dictatorial attitude, Holland replied, "No, dammit, I mean you."

Returning his attention to the game, Rupp muttered, "I'll see you after the game."[113]

Holland slumped, no doubt thinking "me and my big mouth." He knew that Rupp did not tolerate criticism from anybody and most certainly not from his players. Sitting at the far end of the bench for the rest of the season would be his fate. That is if Rupp was charitable enough not to dismiss him from the team outright. Joe was good player—All SEC, in fact—though, so when the other players interceded on his behalf, Rupp consented to let Holland remain on the team. But he would never regain his starting position and hence not be one of the "Fabulous Five."

Consequently, for the next game against Western Ontario the following night, Rupp started Wah Jones, finally in basketball shape and who had had a great game against Creighton, in Holland's forward spot. So, in Alumni Gym on Euclid Avenue on the campus of the University of Kentucky, on January 3, 1948, as Jones, Beard, Groza, Barker and Rollins walked out for the tip-off to begin the game, The Fabulous Five was born. UK, incidentally, won that game 98-41.

This line-up was truly a coach's dream as they had everything a basketball team could hope for: speed, quickness, strength, enough height, stamina, experience and toughness. As individuals, Beard and Jones were young and enthusiastic; Groza and Barker were seasoned as was Rollins, who was as steady as a boulder.

As these individuals bonded together, an incredible team emerged as each player had his role and matched it perfectly. Beard may be the fastest man ever to play for UK, quick to the basket and a deadly outside shooter. If the game had had a three-point line in Ralph's day, his career point total would have been increased by perhaps 20%. Rollins was an excellent ball-handler and floor leader. Although the high-scoring Beard played excellent defense, to protect him from foul trouble, Rollins always defended the opponent's best guard and usually shut him down.

In the pivot, Groza was amazing. A bit short by major college standards at 6'7", he was as quick as a cat, very agile and clever. While not a great leaper, he was an above average rebounder and more than adequate on defense. His deadly hook shot was indefensible and was only one factor in his usually leading the team in points. Unfortunately, at the time, no statistics were kept for rebounding or assists. Groza would have ranked high in both categories.

Jones and Barker were both big, strong tenacious rebounders. Neither of them was anybody you'd want to fool around with, either—whoever guarded Wah Jones usually finished the game with more than a few bruises. Jones could shoot if need be. Although content to rebound and defend, he'd scored enough to claim All-Conference honors and, eventually, All- American. And while everybody on the team was quite capable of defending himself, to get at any of Kentucky's players, you'd have to go through Jones or Barker. Barker's ball handling skills were the stuff of legend. He was able to put enough "english" on the ball to get it, through traffic, to Groza on a 45-degree angle to the direction from which it was thrown. Such a pass invariably caused a defender to do a double take, wondering if he actually saw what he thought he did. Barker's outlet passes on the fast break were amazing.

Perhaps this line-up greatest feature was its "killer instinct." "When we got twenty up on somebody, that was just the beginning," said Kenny Rollins. "No mercy! None whatsoever. We never had any compassion for anyone."[114]

And finally, with three war veterans on the floor, this team simply did not rattle. They'd take whatever an opponent and a hostile crowd threw at them, eat it up and spit it out. It was also in this era that the phrase "they went to war," used by the broadcasters and newspaper men to describe a great rally, was born.

These players patented Rupp's fast break. A typical play went like this: The opponent shoots and misses. The ball comes off on the left to Jones, who whirls and hits Barker on the run to the right near midcourt. Barker deftly whips the ball to Rollins streaking down the middle of the floor, Beard ahead to his right and Groza even with him on his left. Rollins barely touches the ball as he funnels it to Beard flying under the basket for a lay-up. The ball moved smoothly and rapidly from one end of the court to the other, in three or four passes, without touching the floor! This type of action happened routinely and was executed with every bit as much precision and rhythm as a Glenn Miller jive tune.

Bob Brannum had transferred to Michigan State following his tiff with Coach Rupp, and was ready and waiting when UK's team arrived in East Lansing on January 10. Brannum knew, of course, all of Kentucky's offensive patterns and so was a terror on defense. Extra motivation was provided by the fact that he was out to prove that he was "good enough." In fact, as good as anybody Rupp could send out. "Tank" Brannum did, indeed, out score Alex Groza, gathering 23 points to Groza's ten. Nevertheless, the 'Cats squeaked by 47-45.[115]

The Wildcats sailed along, defeating Ohio, Tennessee, Georgia Tech, Georgia and Cincinnati by an average margin of better than 22 points before linking up with DePaul in Chicago on the last day of January 1948. Rupp noted that DePaul was always a tough opponent and that "we never look good in Chicago. I wish we get it going tonight." He got his wish, as "…an amazed crowd of 16,500 sat spellbound throughout the second half…when the "'Cats practically burned the netting off the goals."[116] Each member of UK's "Fabulous Five" was quick to point out that their success was not limited to five players, but involved other teammates. So it was this night with Dale Barnstable leading the scoring with 17. Wah Jones, in addition to "an aggressive, sparkling defensive game" added 15 and Beard tossed in 11.[117]

With the season's record at 19 wins versus a lone one-point loss, the 'Cats' train steamed through a snowstorm to South Bend, Indiana for a contest with Notre Dame on February 2. The newspaper reported that the fact that the groundhog saw his shadow was not to be the worst news of the day for the Wildcat faithful as the Fighting Irish knocked off the number one rated 'Cats 64-55. The "kid as Irish as Paddy's pig, Kevin O'Shay," whom Ralph Beard had embarrassed the year before in Louisville, was out for revenge, but to his chagrin, he drew Rollins and Barnstable, not Beard as his defensive assignment. However, that eventuality did not deter O'Shay from his purpose as he proceeded to drop 25 points on the Kentuckians.[118] Perhaps wounded pride was a factor, but the Wildcats would not lose again for a while.

A notable event occurred in Alumni Gym on February 14, 1948 when Ralph Beard threw in a two-hand set shot from 52.5'. "Happy"

Chandler, Kentucky's former Governor who considered himself UK's biggest fan, raced out onto the court to mark the spot. A nail, driven in the floor later, denotes the longest shot in Wildcat History. After that Tennessee game, they cruised through the remainder of the regular season, defeating Alabama, Georgia Tech, Temple and Xavier to close out the campaign with a sterling 27 wins and two losses. That brought up the SEC tournament, once again held at Louisville's Armory. The 'Cats breezed by Florida, LSU and Tennessee in the opening rounds to set up a meeting with a surprising Georgia Tech squad in the final.

The game was tight for the first 35 minutes, with nine ties while the lead changed hands eleven times. Then Kenny Rollins came to the rescue. "Aside from the points he scored (14), he was alert and aggressive on the floor. And Groza (who scored 13), coming to life in the second half, teamed with Rollins to make the tournament finale a happy one for UK fans."[119] Ralph Beard had to go out with severe leg cramps with about 6 minutes left, but Kentucky held on for a 54-43 win to wrap up their fifth straight SEC title. Rollins and Jones joined Beard on the All-Tournament team while Groza and Barker made the second team.

Heaven moves in mysterious ways and that's about the only explanation for Coach Rupp's deciding to take his team to "that other" post-season tournament, the NCAA, to be held in what was fast becoming what used to be Rupp's used-to-be favorite venue, Madison Square Garden. It was a single elimination affair, featuring eight teams, four in each of two regions, with the games beginning on March 19. It is interesting to note that in those days, a third place game was held in each region as well as a national third place game between the semi-final losers.

In the lower bracket, Baylor defeated Washington and then Kansas State to reach the final. In the upper, Kentucky easily beat Columbia and then had to face defending NCAA Champion Holy Cross who featured a terrific guard named Bob Cousy. The Crusaders had won 19 consecutive games including a first round drubbing of Michigan. In that game, Cousy had poured in 23 points and dazzled the crowd, as well as the Wolverines, with his shooting, dribbling and deft ball-handling. When the 'Cats entered the arena, they saw the banners notifying all that "Cousy is the GREATEST" and "The BEST PLAYER IN THE WORLD." Without comment, Rupp turned to Rollins. "Kenny," he said quietly, "that's your man."[120] Rollins, accustomed to such assignments, simply nodded.

"Barney (Barnstable) and I talked about what we'd try to do with him in the locker room before the game," Rollins said later. "We decided to try to deny him the ball because he was such a wizard once he got it. We also decided to try to force him to the middle of the floor as he seemed to prefer the sides."[121] Rupp would later gloat that "Rollins covered Cousy like a new fallen snow." Cousy scored only three free throws as the Wildcats won 60-52 behind Alex Groza's 23. Cousy, of course, would go on to basketball immortality as a member of the Boston Celtics. After the game, someone presented one of the Cousy banners to the Kentucky captain. It would become a prized possession. The win over Holy Cross set up the title match with Baylor.

A packed house in excess of 16,000 showed up for the Championship Game on March 23. And they got their money's worth as the Wildcats played a nearly perfect game while tying one tournament record and setting another. They joined Utah as the only teams to have garnered both NIT and NCAA Championships. In winning the latter, they had scored a record 194 points in three games besting the 179 posted by Oklahoma A&M in 1945.

Everybody played well, but Groza had scored 54 of those points (14 on Baylor) and gathered enough rebounds to be named the tournament's Most Valuable Player by the "small army of writers" covering the event.[122] After Alex's 14, Jones had 9, Barker 5, Line 7, Holland (who had finally gotten out of the dog house long enough to play a few minutes) added 5. Beard scored 12 and Rollins chipped in 6. Barnstable did not score but turned in some fine defense in a true team victory by a count of 58-42.

With his first NCAA Championship trophy in hand, their coach was a proud man. "You boys have done everything you've been asked to do," he said behind the locked dressing room door following the game. "You won the SEC tournament and now you've won the NCAA Championship. You've kept training and made many sacrifices and I thank you from the bottom of my heart." With tears in his eyes, Rupp turned to "Big Al," and said, "You undoubtedly played the greatest game of any center who ever played in the Garden." Rupp would later say that this was "the greatest team ever assembled in college sports."[123]

As miserly as the Coach normally was with compliments, his players must have been honored.

The Lexington furniture stores may have had to order additional merchandise to replace the couches burned at Chevy Chase in celebration of Kentucky's first NCAA Tournament Championship, but the team had little time for festivity. The International Olympics Games, which had been suspended during the war, were to be resumed in 1948. This would be the first international Games since Jessie Owens embarrassed Adolf Hitler in Berlin in 1936, and so the eyes of the world would be on Wembley Stadium in London, England where the games were to be held. On the same day the 'Cats defeated Baylor, the American Olympic Basketball Committee met in New York to decide how the United States' team would be selected. After much, and probably heated, discussion a kind of playoff system involving college champions of various divisions as well as Amateur Athletics Union (AAU) championship teams was chosen. These games were also to be held in Madison Square Garden beginning the following Friday, so the UK team remained in the Big Apple.

In the post-war period, all across America and especially in New York, college basketball was king in the world of sports. The professional league teams were mostly small market entities and the college game garnered more widespread attention than any other sport. After college, many of the stars opted to go to an AAU team sponsored by a business concern rather than the professional leagues, of which there were two. These AAU players were essentially professionals, in that they held "jobs," but were, in fact, paid to play basketball. One such aggregation was sponsored by the Phillips Petroleum Company. The 66'ers, also sometimes called the Oilers, had a terrific team headed by 7'0" former Oklahoma A&M star Bob Kurland. Kurland was simply a great player, having been the main cog in the Aggies NCAA Championships of 1945 and '46 and named the tournament's Most Outstanding Player both years.[124] The road to the Olympic playoff win would definitely go through the Oilers.

Kentucky's first playoff game was scheduled for March 27 against the University of Louisville Cardinals, who were chosen by virtue of being the current National Association of Intercollegiate Basketball (NAIB) Tournament Champions. Despite Coach Peck Hickman's team's best efforts, UK won easily, dispatching the Cardinals 91-57. Two days later, the 'Cats were still hitting on all cylinders as they defeated Baylor again, this time by a count of 77-59. That brought up the mighty 66'ers on March 31 in the Garden.

The Committee's decision that the Olympic team would consist of the starting fives from these two finals teams diminished this game's importance a bit, but still, more than 18,000 fans showed up to witness the contest and both teams and coaches, of course, wanted the win as a matter of pride. The main prize at stake was that the winning coach would be the Olympians head coach while the loser would serve as his assistant.

The game was a slugging match—almost literally—between two heavyweights. Kentucky was up 16-10 when Cliff Barker went out with a broken nose after eight and a half minutes of play. Despite the absence of Barker and Wah Jones, who went to the bench with three fouls, throughout the first half, the score was knotted five times and the lead see-sawed seven times before the horn sounded with the score deadlocked at 26.

The 'Cats, with Jones and Barker still missing, got off to a slow start in the second half and fell behind 37-27 before Rupp reinserted Jones for defense and rebounding. At the same time, Ralph Beard went to work. "During the next five minutes, with Beard throwing in every other Wildcat goal and Jones holding the Oilers defensively, the wily Wildcats chopped the Oiler lead down to 39-36."[125] Jones fouled out just before Rollins banked in a long shot to cut the Oiler lead to 41-39. Two consecutive long shots and a free throw by Beard put the 'Cats up 47-45. Then Kurland took over. Two hook shots sandwiched around a Jesse Renick basket and free throw put the 66'ers up 51-47. With no shot clock to force the action, the 66'ers held the ball for the last four minutes to sew up the victory, 53-49. A New York scribe reported that this game was "perhaps the greatest basketball game ever staged in the history of the sport."[126] Does that sound familiar? Groza, although he and Holland rebounded well, did not have a good offensive game against Kurland, scoring only four points to the big guy's 20. Ralph Beard, who was spectacular for the 'Cats, matched the 66'ers basket for basket until the last of the game, finished as high point man with 23.[127] Had the game featured a three-point shot, Ralph Beard's long two-hand set shots may have altered the outcome.

The winning, and hence Olympic head coach, Omar (Bud) Browning complimented the Kentuckians, "That Beard is the best basketball player I have ever seen."[128] Adolph Rupp was a bit less magnanimous.

Remembering that he had come to a major college head coaching job straight from a high school, he told his team, "I want to thank you sons of bitches' for making me an assistant coach for the first time in my career."[129] That sounds more typical of Rupp than his praise following the national championship game.

The tired but happy 'Cats arrived back in Lexington after their extended stay in New York at 7:50 AM on April 2, 1948. A crowd estimated at 15,000 accompanied by four or five marching bands waited at the Southern Railway Depot to welcome their heroes. After appropriate ceremonies, the team was carried to the campus in a grand parade, which followed a round-about route, passing through the downtown area.[130] Banners along the way praised this as "the greatest college basketball champion of all time." Rupp's old coach and mentor, Phog Allen, spoke at a celebratory luncheon. Allen praised his former pupil and UK's team for an outstanding season. Near the end of his talk, in a more somber note, Allen noted that gamblers in this country were trying to control the outcome of basketball and football games. Allen warned that colleges would have to find ways to protect their athletes from this unsavory element.[131] Kentuckians paid little attention; after all, these boys were above reproach and, as Rupp noted, they had done everything asked of them.

Adding All-Americans Vincent Boryla (Notre Dame,) Don Barksdale (UCLA,) Raymond Lumpp (New York University) and Jack Robinson (Baylor) to Kentucky's Jones, Groza, Beard, Rollins and Barker, plus the 66'ers starters Lewis Beck, Gordon Carpenter, Bob Kurland, R.C. Pitts and Jesse Renick rounded out the American Olympic roster.

To raise money for the trip to England for the games, the teams agreed to play three exhibitions, first at Tulsa, Oklahoma, near the Oiler's home base of Bartlesville, on June 30. Don Barksdale and Jack Robinson joined the 66'ers for this game while Boryla and Lumpp supplemented the Wildcats. Barksdale led his team to a hard-fought 60-52 victory before 6,000 screaming fans. Kurland had 10 and Barksdale added 9 for the winners while Groza and Boryla each had 11 for Kentucky. Ralph Beard, who played sparingly with an injured leg, scored only a single goal.[132] With the count at Oiler's two wins to Kentucky's zero, the next game was scheduled for Kansas City on July 2.

This game was a nip-and-tuck affair right from the beginning. Kentucky, playing without the injured Beard, matched baskets with the

66'ers throughout regulation and then an overtime period and then another overtime period. Mid-way through the first overtime, a firecracker went off in the stands. Thinking it was the gun, all the players stopped. "We had the game won before that stopped play," Rupp commented.[133] Then, with nine seconds remaining in the second overtime and the 66'ers leading 69-68, a spectator seated nearer the floor lit another firecracker. Again, the players apparently thought the loud sound was the gun ending the period and started for the bench. UK's Joe Holland, who had the ball, noticing that the clock still showed a few seconds, dribbled down the court to lay the ball in the basket as the gun—the real one—sounded. Hence, Kentucky won the game 70-69 in double overtime.[134]

The final game, in what had evolved from a string of fund-raising exhibitions into a heated rivalry, was a dream come true for Adolph Rupp. For years, the Kentucky coach had advocated that basketball would draw huge crowds if played outdoors in the summertime. For this game, a basketball floor, rented from the Louisville Armory, was assembled on UK's football venue, Stoll Field, for the rubber match in the exhibition series. Rupp was vindicated; ticket sales exceeded 14,000 for the game to be played on July 9. Once again, Beard, still hurting, would play only sparingly, but the match-up everyone wanted to see was Groza against Kurland. "Thus far, Mr. Groza has given Mr. Kurland the hard way to go, twice out-scoring him and not allowing him to explode with the devastating scoring wrath that has made him a hardwood great," said the newspaper.[135]

In the days before every game was televised and with the limited availability of seats in Alumni Gym, this was the first opportunity for many Kentucky fans to see their heroes play in person. Here was a chance to see images previously provided only by static-filled radio broadcasts come to life. Win or lose, the UK fans were proud of their team and would turn out in droves to witness this contest. Clearly it was the largest crowd to ever witness a basketball game in The Commonwealth of Kentucky.

All those who showed up on the sweltering Kentucky summer night received their money's worth as these were two truly great teams. As "fabulous" as Kentucky was, the AAU team was tougher competition than any college squad in the country could provide. Despite the heat, the collegians decided to utilize their advantage, which was speed.

Running at a break-neck pace, although the score was knotted five times in the first half, the 'Cats shot out to a 31-26 half-time lead. The writers, baking in the glass-enclosed Stoll Field press box, doubted that the game could continue at such a torrid tempo.[136]

But it did. For seven minutes into the second period, anyway. At that point, with UK up 46-36, Oilers' coach Browning inserted Barksdale into this line-up. "Rebuffed with a single point in the first half, he came through with twelve in the second. And most of those came in the crushing five minutes when the Oiler's erased the ten point UK lead and drove on to victory."[137]

"And Barksdale, incidentally, was the first Negro to play opposite a Kentucky athletic team in Lexington. He received a big ovation when he was introduced before the game and another when the tilt ended," noted the *Courier-Journal.*[138]

When the dust settled, the AAU team had won 56-50, inflicting the first loss on a Wildcat team in Lexington since 1942! For the losers, Groza was high with 15 with Boryla right behind at 14. Beard, in limited action scored 5 while Rollins and Holland played brilliant defense. Kurland led all scorers with 19, Lew Beck added 11 and Barksdale's contribution was 13.[139] And so, the rivalry ended a great financial success. Ticket sales had netted $25,000. That, plus donated money, provided enough to include Barnstable, Holland and Line on the trip. Now, the competitors would merge to become the United States Olympic Basketball Team and sail for London, England to participate in the "Games of the XIV Olympiad."

On July 13, the U.S. Olympian athletes, who included decathlon specialist Bob Mathias, assembled in New York to organize for the trip. The checking of passports, immunizations and the issuance of uniforms and identity cards had a flavor familiar to the many military veterans among the athletes—hurry up and wait. Everybody was on board the SS American, though, when it eased out of New York harbor the next day beginning the eight-day trip across the Atlantic.[140]

After three game balls were lost overboard, the coaches refused to allow the players to scrimmage and only allowed them to exercise by running on deck. No conditioning was lost, however, and the guys were ready to play by the time the ship arrived at Southampton on July 22, eight days before the official opening of the Games. That timing allowed an opportunity for the team to tour a bit, playing exhibitions aimed at popularizing the American sport in Europe. They traveled to Paris, where Ralph Beard said he saw things an old Hardinsburg boy had never even dreamed of and to St. Andrews, Scotland, where Beard saw his first golf course, before settling into the Olympic Village, a refurbished Royal Air Force base at Uxbridge.[141]

London was a bombed out shambles and Harringay Arena, where the basketball games were played, was in very poor condition. Beard reported that two windows at the top of the building were broken out, making for a drafty interior. Additionally, the lighting was poor, the baskets were not level and the floor was uneven and teeming with soft spots. Additionally, the British cared little for basketball, so the U.S. team played in much less-than-ideal conditions before sparse crowds.[142] That made little difference to the players as they were competing for the pride of the good ole U.S. of A.

During this trip, the two sets of players got to know each other and formed some relationships, although Beard reported that they were not close. The whole experience was an education for the twenty-year-old in that he saw some different cultures, had exposure to, and opportunity to learn from, the older "pro" players and became acquainted with Don Barksdale, his first black teammate. Beard describes Barksdale as "very easy-going, a great guy and a tremendous basketball player." The two men became good friends.[143]

Head coach Bud Browning and his assistant-in-name only, Adolph Rupp, figured to have little trouble in the Games. Basketball was, after all, an American game and war-torn Europe had had slight time for such frivolity since the bombing stopped. As each man firmly believed that he had the best squad, they compromised by agreeing to play each team as a unit, exchanging all five 66'ers for all five Kentuckians at intervals. As Olympic rules allowed only ten players for each squad, some of the American's 14 players had to sit out each contest and nobody played in all eight games.

That strategy worked well as the Americans breezed through the opening rounds, defeating Switzerland 86-21 and Czechoslovakia 53-28. On August 3, somebody—presumably Browning—made the decision to let Kurland, Beard, Renick and Barker sit out the third game and the Americans mixed up the line-ups, placing some Oilers and some Wildcats on the floor at the same time, due, in part, to foul trouble.[144] The starters, Jones, Groza, Rollins, Lumpp and Boryla were up

14-9 when the second group came in and lost the lead to put Argentina up 33-26 at the half. The lead see-sawed back and forth throughout the second half, with ties at 37, 39, 42, 53 and 55 until Rollins, Jack Robinson and Carpenter took charge and built a 59-55 margin with seconds left. A wild heave by an Argentine player went through the hoop as the buzzer sounded. The Americans thought the shot was too late, but the officials (Swiss and Chinese) decided to allow the basket. Thus the U.S. team squeaked by 59-57.[145]

As Coach Rupp sat on the Olympic bench watching Bob Kurland, who was a great player, the visions dancing in his head were not of sugar plums, but of his own seven-footer. The young man's name was Bill Spivey and Rupp had recruited him out of Warner-Robbins, Georgia. Unfortunately, Spivey was as raw as he was tall and weighed a mere 165 pounds. When Rupp departed for England, he left Assistant Coach Harry Lancaster in charge with orders to "put some meat on Spivey's bones." Lancaster worked with Spivey in the gym, teaching him a hook shot and footwork in the lane. Lancaster also had the young man eating four helpings of mashed potatoes a day along with several quarts of milk in addition to his regular meals. As Rupp was keenly interested in Spivey's progress, Lancaster wired the player's weight to Rupp daily. Finally, when Lancaster's telegram reported that it had reached 185 pounds, Rupp wired back, "All right, he's proved he can eat. Now let's find out if he can play basketball."[146] Actually, Rupp and Lancaster knew he could play basketball; Spivey racked up more than 1,800 points in his three-year high school career.[147]

As the Argentines were the best team the Americans were to face, the remaining games were anti-climatic. Egypt proved no match for the U.S. in a lopsided 66-28 U.S. win the next day. Then, with Wah Jones leading the way with 12 points, the U.S. crushed Peru 61-33 on August 6. Kurland scored 19 points as the Americans handed South American champion Uruguay a 63-28 setback on August 9. Alex Groza scored 19 in the defeat of Mexico, which moved the Americans to within one victory of Olympic gold.

Facing France in the finals, Browning decided to start his five 66'ers. Only leading 9-4, the unit system was abandoned and Browning began substituting one player at a time. At the half the U.S. was in command 28-9, and the Americans went on to record an easy 65-21 victory over

France. The U.S.'s scoring was led by Groza and Raymond Lumpp, who tallied 11 points each.[148] *

So the Americans came home with Olympic Gold medals. Everybody involved, most especially Adolph Rupp and Ralph Beard, would say that standing at the top tier of the medal platform while the Star Spangled Banner played was the high point of his life.

What a season Kentucky had! They finished the regular season with 27 wins against two loses, went 4-0 in winning the SEC tournament, 3-0 in capturing the NCAA championship, 2-1 in the Olympic trials, for an overall record of 36-3. As for individual honors, Alex Groza and Ralph Beard were named consensus All-Americans, Groza was the NCAA Tournament's Most Valuable Player, Wah Jones was named to some All-America teams and those three, in addition to Cliff Barker, were named to the All-SEC first team. Then they went 1-2 in exhibition against Phillips and 8-0 in winning the Olympic gold. On the way home, Coach Rupp gloried in what John Calipari can only joke about: they're all coming back!

---

*See Appendix A for Olympic Games details

Chapter Eight

1948-49: Back to Back Championships

When the fall of 1948 rolled around, America had finally put the war behind. The "hot" war, anyway. The Berlin Airlift and rumors of communists in the U.S. government filled the headlines along with the scandalous arrest of Hollywood movie actor Robert Mitchum on possession of marijuana charges.

As classes took up in Lexington, the campus was awhirl with visions of a repeat national championship for Kentucky's team. And the chances looked pretty good, too. Gone were Joe Holland, who was selling cars in West Virginia and Kenny Rollins, who was drafted by the Chicago Stags of the professional Basketball Association of America (BAA.) Returning, however, were the "Fabulous Four," Alex Groza, Ralph Beard, Cliff Barker and Wallace Jones. Additionally, plenty of experienced back-ups were available in Dale Barnstable, who would take over for Rollins, Jim Line, Walt Hirsh, Roger Day, John Stough and a kid from Cynthiana, Kentucky named Joe B. Hall.

Once again, competition was rough in practice. The NCAA had reverted to ruling freshmen ineligible for the varsity. So, the freshman team played its own schedule and battled the varsity in practice. Among this year's freshmen were the aforementioned Bill Spivey, "Skippy" Whitaker, Guy Strong and Shelby Linville, all of whom would become familiar names to the Wildcat faithful. Also, Charles Martin Newton, a 6'2" Floridian, figured to get some playing time against the other SEC school's freshmen teams.

Had John Calipari been around at the time, he probably would not feel so often compelled to remind fans that if the jersey says "Kentucky" on the front, it always has a target on its back as that has been the case for a long time. Just as most non-New York baseball fans hate the Yankees, many basketball fans dislike Kentucky. Rupp had alienated the New York media and everybody in the SEC was tired of UK's domination in basketball. Had the 'Cats played more games in the West, there would probably had been animosity there, too.

The only expected tough games were in the non-conference schedule, an early season match with DePaul in Louisville, Holy Cross in Boston on December 6, and St. John's as part of a double-header scheduled for Madison Square Garden two days later. Once again, the 'Cats would play in the Sugar Bowl Classic. Who they would be up against in New Orleans was unknown as the season began, but it seemed that whoever they matched up with in this venue always presented problems for the Wildcats.

The season began in Lexington on November 29 with the usual victim, Indiana Central. Also as usual, Wah Jones was still involved in football, so smooth lefty Jim Line joined Beard, Groza, Barker and Barnstable in the starting line-up for this game. The defending National Champs looked every bit the part as they raced out to a 10-1 early lead, flashing a stifling defense that would hold the Greyhounds to a paltry 19.3 field goal percentage for the night. Offensively, Groza and Beard sparkled while Barker elicited ooh's and ah's with his passing wizardry. The starters played every minute until Rupp began to substitute at the mid-way point of the second half. Eleven players would see action before the final horn. Beard led the scoring with 20, Groza added 14 while Barker and Barnstable each had 10.[149]

Next up was a usually strong DePaul quintet. The Blue Demons rolled into the Louisville Armory winners of their first two games, but they, too, proved impotent against Kentucky's sparkling defense as the 'Cats dominated in winning 67-36. Beard and Barnstable each had 15 and Groza added 12, much to the delight of the 7,500 fans in attendance.[150]

After dispatching Tulsa and Arkansas (Jones made his first start of the season in the latter game) by huge margins, Kentucky arrived in Boston for the anticipated match with Holy Cross. The Crusader's star guard, Bob Cousy, was out for revenge for last year's embarrassment at the hands of the departed Kenny Rollins. Holy Cross, not caring to run with UK, took a cue from Oklahoma A&M's style and held the ball, refusing anything less than a wide open shot in the first half, much to the annoyance not only of Rupp, but most of the nearly 14,000 fans on hand as well. That scheme worked for ten minutes, giving the Crusaders a 15-13 lead at that point. The 'Cats put on a flurry and led 27-20 at half. The second period was a battle, although Kentucky led most of the time. When the game ended, the 'Cats won 51-48, handing Holy Cross its first defeat in Boston Gardens in more than two years. Bob Cousy, probably glad that he did not have to contend with Rollins, managed 11 points, but it was too little as Jones matched his total and Groza added 17. Near the end of the game, as Wah Jones, who had fouled out, sat on the bench, a spectator, who clearly didn't know who he was fooling with, hit him on the back of his head with what appeared to be a rolled-up paper bag. Jones did not appreciate the gesture much and turned to face the man who began throwing punches. Coach Rupp stepped in and caught a glancing blow. Ushers and the police put a stop to the affray, but not before Wah Jones decked the unruly fan.[151] As Holy Cross was also slated for the Sugar Bowl Classic later in the month, these two teams might meet again in New Orleans.

In Madison Square Garden on December 18, Long Island University beat Kansas State before Kentucky took the floor to face St. John's in the double-header's nightcap. The Redmen (political correctness hadn't been invented yet) proved no match for Kentucky's stellar defense as the 'Cats rolled to a 57-30 victory.[152] UK then played a tight one, beating Tulane 51-47 in Louisville for their seventh consecutive victory.

A quirk of scheduling slated Tulane again as the first opponent in the Sugar Bowl Classic on December 29. Rupp evidently read his boys the riot act concerning that narrow victory margin in the previous game, as UK trounced the Green Wave by 31 this time. In a surprise, St. Louis University bested Holy Cross 61-52 in the other semi-final, so the UK-Holy Cross rematch was not to be.

The actual match-up was more interesting. The St. Louis Billikins, winner of the previous season's NIT, were led by the 6'8" "Easy" Ed Macauley, who figured to give Alex Groza a battle. Macauley was a hometown product who would go on to greatness with the St. Louis Hawks and Boston Celtics in the NBA. The two big guys essentially cancelled each other out, so it was a little man who made the big difference.

The battle was tight most of the way with Kentucky looking great. The 'Cats led 27-18 at the half but shot very poorly to begin the second period. Still, they cling to a 36-30 advantage with five minutes left. Then little Lou Lehman, who had not started a game in the Billikins

NIT run, went to work. St. Louis outscored UK 12 to 4 in the final minutes, with Lehman having seven of those points. For the last minute, St. Louis froze the ball to secure the win, 42-40.[153] Macauley and Lehman each had 14 points while Groza scored 13 for the 'Cats. This win gave the undefeated Billlikins a legitimate claim to the nation's top ranking and would, once again, lead to later scrutiny.

Perhaps the 'Cats still had a hangover from that defeat when they rolled into Cleveland to play Bowling Green ten days later. The Falcons seven-foot center gave Groza plenty of problems and UK appeared to be in trouble when "Big Al" fouled out with 12 minutes left in the game. Ralph Beard, who had played a brilliant floor game, stepped up his scoring at that point and led his team to a hard-fought 63-61 victory by pouring in 20 points.[154]

Rupp went to work and righted the ship as the Wildcats rolled through the rest of their schedule including wins over non-conference foes DePaul, Bradley and Notre Dame.

The game with DePaul, played in Chicago on January 22, was interesting in that Kentucky had already routed the Blue Demons by 31 points back in early December. This time, they "found the Demons vastly improved."[155] Groza scored 18 and Beard chalked up 16 in the 56-45 win, but, "the aggressive Kentuckians committed 26 fouls and had to slow up their whirlwind attack somewhat in the second half when Wallace Jones, Cliff Barker and Jim Line all went out with five personal fouls."[156]

In the middle of the conference season, Tennessee came to Lexington on February 8. With little to complain about as the 'Cats were up big at the half, Rupp decided to pick on Cliff Barker. "Cliff," he began, "why do you always run in the middle of the floor when you know you're much more effective on the wing?

"Well, Coach," Barker replied, "if I run on the bench side of the floor, you give me hell as I run by. My wife sits in the front row on the other side, and she gives me hell if I go over there. So, I stay in the middle away from both of you."[157] For once, the quick-witted Rupp had no comeback. As snow piled up outside Alumni Gym that evening, Alex Groza kept things hot inside, racking up 34 points to set a new SEC single game scoring record as the 'Cats won 71-56.[158] That single game point record would not last very long.

In early March, the Wildcats entered the SEC tournament in Louisville with 25 wins against the lone, Sugar Bowl loss. They breezed by

Florida and Auburn in the opening rounds, defeating each by more than 30 points. That brought on third-seeded Tennessee in a 10 AM Saturday morning contest. The Volunteers, remembering Groza's earlier performance, proved to be no problem as they chose to concentrate their defense on Big Al, thereby freeing Jones and Beard to do all the damage they could. And they did plenty. With the championship game scheduled for 8 PM, Rupp was able to give his starters plenty of rest as the Wildcats romped to an 83-44 victory behind Jones' 17 points and Beard's 15.[159]

All had gone according to form, so the nightcap featured second seeded Tulane against the top rated 'Cats. If the Green Wave, having lost to UK twice already, hoped the third time would prove to be a charm, they were to be disappointed. Alex Groza made his last SEC game a memorable one as his 37 points (which eclipsed his three week-old mark) set the tournament record for the most points in a single game as part of his also record 94 points for the tournament. The 68-52 win annexed Kentucky's eleventh straight SEC Championship and extended the streak of SEC wins to 63. When Kentucky's Groza, Jones and Beard and two Tulane players were named to the All-SEC team, Beard and Jones joined former teammate Jack Tingle as the only four-time All-SEC performers. With the freshman eligible rule gone away and in these days of "one and done" that trio's record may be forever safe.

Adolph Rupp's intended follow up to last year's NCAA title was not to simply win that tournament again. No, a much better encore would be to win both the NIT and NCAA tournaments and he saw to it that they had invitations to both. Accordingly, the Wildcats travelled to Madison Square Garden where they, as the top seed, were slated to take on sixteenth- seeded Loyola of Chicago in the opening round of the NIT on March 14. According to the sports writers, while the Wildcats were much the better club, "the Ramblers are a deceptive, hot-and-cold team and there's danger in their blowing hot while UK blows cold."[160] The fact that Western Kentucky was to play Bradley earlier in the day had fans of both schools looking forward to a UK verses Western Kentucky match up in the second round.

A dreary New York day became even darker when Bradley beat fourth-seeded Western Kentucky in the afternoon's first game. When Kentucky and Loyola of Chicago took the floor after the break, the

Kentucky fans were not concerned when the Ramblers jumped out to a 4-0 lead—the 'Cats would fight back. And so they did, taking the lead at 8-5. Then Loyola rallied to tie the game at 9. From that point on, the teams battled on even terms with Loyola ahead 32-31 at the half. Now Big Blue Nation found room for concern as UK had connected on only seven of fifteen free throws while the Ramblers had scored 14 of 16. Additionally, Kentucky's big men, Jones, Groza and Walt Hirsh were all in foul trouble as was Loyola's outstanding center, Jack Kerris.

Wah Jones was having a brilliant game on the boards when he fouled out with his team ahead 47-46 and 10:20 showing on the clock. Kerris had four fouls, so the coaches screamed for the 'Cats to get the ball to Groza, although Big Al had the same number of whistles blown against him. The team did not respond and, on the other end, Groza played tentatively against Kerris' hook shots. "The result was disaster for Kentucky. Kerris kept shooting; Groza, who played one of the poorest games of his career"[161] fouled out five minutes after Jones went to the bench, also disqualified. Groza sat with the same 12 points he'd had at the half, having gone scoreless in the second stanza. When Walt Hirsch fouled out a few seconds later, the Wildcats had no chance of rebounding with all three "bigs" on the bench. Despite an inspired effort by Ralph Beard, who led Kentucky's scoring with 15, the number one rated Wildcats were stunningly defeated 67-56, the eleven point margin in made free throws accounting for the exact difference.[162] Curiously, in addition to the upsets of the two Kentucky teams in the afternoon, in the evening session, San Francisco knocked out third-seeded Utah and Bowling Green upset defending champion and second-seeded St. Louis, providing upsets in all four first round games!

Even the New York press was shocked. "Lightning struck twice inside the Garden during the matinee and the shock was felt way down in Kentucky. It is doubtful if any bolt from the blue ever wrought so much havoc in the Bluegrass State as the setbacks suffered by both its representatives.

"If ever a team was confident of victory, Kentucky was. Its 29 and 1 record for the season, including a 21 game winning streak; its magnificent personnel—Alex Groza, Ralph Beard, Wallace Jones and Cliff Barker—and its awesome success pointed to success against the Ramblers from Chicago."[163]

A swarm of reporters awaited Kentucky Coach Adolph Rupp outside the locker room following the game. Interestingly, their questions did not focus on how Loyola accomplished the win, but rather how Kentucky managed to lose. With the rims of his eyes reddened, Rupp said, "We were flat, awfully flat." Then with a deep sigh, he added, "That's all there was to it." Pressed by the scribes, he elaborated as best he could. "We didn't hit, not even the free throws. When you can't do that, you are gonna get beat. And Loyola played well, they deserved to win."[164]

"Why didn't your team feed the ball to Groza when Kerris had four fouls?" a reporter asked.

"That's another question I'd like answered," Rupp replied.[165]

The future would bring many other major questions concerning this game.

With their tails tucked between their legs, the Wildcats headed home, dreading the grueling practice sessions sure to follow this shocking defeat. There was little time to lick their wounds, though—a few hours after the loss, the pairings for the NCAA tournament, slated to take place in the same venue six days hence, were announced. Kentucky would play Villanova in the opening round.

It was an angry pack of Kentuckians that showed up in the Garden on March 21. The Pennsylvania based Wildcats featured a hometown boy named Paul Arizin who, although a bit shorter than Groza, figured to give Big Al quite a game. Arizin, who would go on to NBA fame, matched Groza point for point as they both finished with 30. Jim Line and Cliff Barker aided Kentucky's cause with 21 and 18, while Ralph Beard claimed only three free throws as the 'Cats won, going away, 85-72. Three NCAA records were set: Kentucky's 85 was the highest score for one team in a single game; the two teams' combined 157 points set a new standard and UK's 23 made free throws was also a new norm.[166]

Next up was Illinois, who had defeated Yale in the other quarter-final the previous evening. This was no contest: "Exploding all over Madison Square Garden with a dynamic attack that never faltered, Adolph Rupp's Wildcats from Kentucky romped to a 76-47 victory over Illinois in the NCAA Eastern Regional final last night."[167] The *Times* reporter observed that if famous boxing referee Ruby Goldstein, who was among the 15,126 spectators, had been in charge, he would have, "intervened to save the loser further unnecessary punishment." Interestingly, he also noted that, "The Wildcats of last night—Alex

Groza, Ralph Beard, Cliff Barker, Wallace Jones and Jim Line (who had replaced Barnstable as a starter following the NIT loss)—were unrecognizable alongside the squad that floundered so dismally in the recent National Invitational Tournament."[168] Obviously, questions concerning the Loyola loss lingered in not only the fans' minds, but many others as well.

Rupp loaded his charges on a train bound for Seattle and a finals match up with Oklahoma A&M, the Aggies having emerged from the Western bracket by handily defeating Wyoming and Oregon State. The game was tight for only a moment. The Aggies scored first before the 'Cats knotted the score at 5. Then Groza took an intercepted pass the length of the floor to put UK up 7-5. Kentucky would retain the lead for the remaining 35 minutes of the game. Groza, who got every vote for the Tournament's Most Valuable Player, was magnificent, adding seven free throws to his nine field goals before fouling out late in the game. Kentucky captured its second consecutive NCAA title, dispatching Henry Iba's Aggies 46-36.[169] Ironically, these two teams were the only ones(at that time) to ever have won back-to-back NCAA titles, Oklahoma A&M having done so in 1945 and '46 behind their great seven-footer, Bob Kurland.

While the bulk of Kentucky's team headed home, the 'Fabulous Four"—Groza, Beard, Jones and Barker—along with Coach Rupp flew to New York for the annual *Herald-Tribune's* East-West All-Star game scheduled for the Garden on April 2. The East squad clearly had an advantage as the Kentucky players were accustomed to playing together, a rarity in All-Star competition. Groza, again matched up again with St. Louis's Ed Macauley, chalked up 12 (to "Easy Ed's" 9) and was named—yawn—the game's Most Valuable Player. The West squad, which also featured Texas' Slater Martin and Vern Mikkelsen, both bound for NBA stardom, did put up a fight, but in the crunch, the Kentuckians carried the East as they eked out a 65-64 victory.

A crowd estimated at 20,000 welcomed the Wildcats back to Lexington on April 4. Convertibles, interspersed with high school marching bands and floats, carried the "Fabulous Four" and their Coach in the parade from downtown to the campus. At the ensuing banquet, UK President H.L. Donovan, Lexington Mayor Tom Mooney and other speakers declared this Wildcat aggregation to be "the greatest team in the history of basketball" and the jerseys of Jones, Groza, Beard and

Barker—winners of two NCAA Championships and 130 of 139 games were retired. The jersey worn by the departed Kenny Rollins was also retired.[170] As a climax to the evening, Coach Rupp admitted that while flying with his players from Seattle to the All-Star game, he had considered retiring as he felt he'd never be able to build another team like this one.[171] Then he flatly denied the rumors that he'd be accepting a job in the professional leagues. "This is where I made my reputation and this is where I'm going to remain. This will be the last coaching assignment of my life."[172] Sound familiar?

The Helms Foundation once again declared Kentucky as the National Champion. Individual accolades came, too, as Helms named Alex Groza as its Player of the Year. Groza and Beard were voted consensus All-Americans and Wah Jones joined them on several honor squads. To this day (2014), Alex Groza remains tenth on the all-time UK career scoring list with 1744 points in 120 games for an average of 14.4 points per game. Ralph Beard is not far behind, ranking fifteenth with 1517 point in his 139 games for a 10.8 average.

Their careers as Wildcats were over, but they were far from through playing basketball together. Almost coincident with the welcome home, rumors to the effect that the seniors would go on a barnstorming tour began circulating. As a measure to capitalize on their popularity plus earn some money, the boys planned to rent a gym in communities where they thought people would turn out to see them play against a team of "independents," local amateur players. UK President Herman Donovan said that the University would be "embarrassed" should they follow through with that plan.[173]

Embarrassment notwithstanding, on April 8, the four seniors announced that had employed former *Lexington Herald* sports editor J.R. "Babe" Kimbrough as their business manager. Kimbrough, in his newspaper capacity, had travelled with the team and hence he and the players knew each other well. Further, the "Fabulous Four" announced that they, plus former teammates Kenny Rollins (whose professional season was over) and Joe Holland and ex-Kentucky Wesleyan star, Fairce Woods, had scheduled four exhibition games: April 8 in Charleston, WV, April 9 in Huntington, April 12 in Pikeville, KY and April 14 in Ashland.[174]

Those initial games were wildly successful, drawing packed houses at each stop, and these patrons were all paying customers, too. With no student tickets and no faculty and staff occupying seats, many fans had their first opportunity to see these heroes in person, and they flocked to the rented arenas and plunked down the price of admission. So, more games were scheduled, including a "dream game" with Western Kentucky's seniors, who had a pretty good year as well, in Louisville on April 18. The ex-Hilltoppers put up a good tussle, but the barnstorming ex-Wildcats came out on top 80-65.[175]

On April 22, the ex-Wildcats, who were calling themselves the Olympians now, took on a group of former Lincoln Memorial University players on their floor in Harrogate, TN. They dazzled the fans. "... Alex Groza exhibited some great shooting, but it remained for the old magician, Cliff Barker and Fairce Woods to provide the real treat.... It is impossible to describe the basketball delights provided by these Kentucky boys."[176] Groza lit up the scoreboard with 27, and Beard added 14 as the Olympians cruised to a 72-24 rout.[177]

When all was said and done, they had won each of the nineteen exhibition games they played. They had appeared all around the Commonwealth and surrounding areas and performed before packed houses at each stop.[178] They'd pocketed a nice piece of change in the process, too.

As spring deepened, the players pondered whether they would now go their separate ways, each having been drafted by two different professional teams (one in each league) or if, by some miracle, they could find a way to not break up such a marvelous team and continue to play as a unit. Kentucky Coach Adolph Rupp had things to wonder about, too: How could he replace such a team and would he ever reach such a zenith again?

Chapter Nine

On to the NBA

Sometimes, as the laws of probability dictate, the bread will land on the kitchen floor jelly side up. And sometimes, yes, miracles do occur. But, even then such happenings take a great conspiracy of time, people, place and circumstance. And still, one has to be aware enough to take advantage when opportunity knocks. For the Kentucky Olympians to remain together, as each was sought after by at least two professional teams, would require a bona-fide miracle and the cognizance to take advantage.

As the first piece of the puzzle, Kentucky's Olympians had a stroke of luck or, perhaps, showed great foresight when they engaged J.R. "Babe" Kimbrough to manage their barnstorming tour of basketball games all across Kentucky with stops in West Virginia and Tennessee. Kimbrough, as sports editor of The *Lexington Herald*, had followed the boys' careers for every minute since they enrolled at UK and was therefore well acquainted with each player. Additionally, he had previously served as city editor and political editor for several papers and as managing editor of a paper in Shelbyville, Kentucky. Kimbrough had managed his college fraternity house as well. Hence he was uniquely qualified to handle such diverse fine points as scheduling, transportation, meals and hotel accommodations.[179] He skillfully managed these, and myriad other details, that the players left in his capable hands.

Secondly, in the spring of 1949 as the Olympians barnstormed roughshod over all competition, there was trouble in the world of professional basketball. At that time, there existed two professional leagues; the senior being the National Basketball League (NBL), founded in 1937. The NBL featured franchises in such metropolises as Anderson, Indiana, Oshkosh and Sheboygan, Wisconsin and Moline and Rock Island in Illinois and nearby Davenport, Iowa, which comprised the

Tri-Cities Blackhawks. The league also offered four more stable teams based in Indianapolis and Ft. Wayne in Indiana, Rochester, New York and Minneapolis, Minnesota, but their main claim to greatness as the summer of 1949 approached was that their teams boasted better players than the rival league. These included the Rochester Royals' Bob Davies, the man after whom Ralph Beard patterned his game and former DePaul great, George Mikan, who, some would argue (with apologies to Michael Jordan, Wilt Chamberlain, LeBron James and many others who deserve mention), is the greatest basketball player of all time.

The younger league, The Basketball Association of America (BAA), which had struggled for existence since its 1946 inception, could not match the NBL's players, but presented more attractive venues, having teams located in Baltimore, New York, Boston, Chicago and St. Louis, among others cities. In the two years of the BAA's existence, the two circuits had constantly bickered, each trying to pirate away the other's most valuable assets.

On May 10, 1948, the BAA pulled off a coup, enticing the Indianapolis, Ft. Wayne, Rochester and Minneapolis teams to defect from the NBL. The new teams, especially Ft. Wayne and Minneapolis, would certainly boost the BAA's overall attendance figures, but still, there were a few problems.[180] The Indianapolis club, suffering financial problems during the previous season, sold their star player, Arnie Risen, simply to get cash, much to the dismay of the local writers and the fans. "The (Indianapolis) management which has broken faith with its players many times now breaks faith with the fans," said the newspaper.[181] The resulting turmoil led to a change of ownership, and the team became the Jets for the 1948-49 season. The Indianapolis team posted the second worst record of all league teams, losing 42 games against just 18 wins. So, the Jets proved a financial flop and were in deep trouble.[182]

During the Olympians barnstorming tour, Leo Ferris, owner of the NBL's Tri-Cities franchise, and vice president of the league, visited the boys after a game in Louisville, hoping to recruit Cliff Barker for his Blackhawks team. Informed that the players would like to continue as a unit, Ferris saw an idea that would serve as the perfect solution to both the Olympians and the NBL's problems. Accordingly, he made an appointment to meet with their manager, Babe Kimbrough. By the time Ferris arrived in Lexington in late April, he was sure that getting the Kentucky boys as a unit would be a huge coup for the NBL, so he arrived ready to make a definite proposal. He offered to organize the Olympians into a corporation in which the players would own all the common stock. Further, the league would loan the new corporation sufficient funds to establish the organization and grant them an NBL franchise in a location to be decided later.[183] There's your miracle!

But would the players' take advantage? Their decision was not as easy as it might appear. Each of them had been drafted by BAA team: Wah Jones by the Washington Capitols, Groza and Barker by the faltering Indianapolis Jets and Beard was the selection of the Chicago Stags.[184] Incidentally, had Beard opted to go with the Stags, he'd be reunited with his old running mate, Kenny Rollins. Rollins, by the way, was unsuccessful in an attempt to obtain a release from the Chicago team so he could join his former mates.

Owning their own brand new franchise was a risky venture, while playing for an established club would bring a more secure paycheck. However, the barnstorming tour had proven their popularity and been a financial success, so wouldn't the same be true in a professional setting? Their talent was beyond question, but did they possess the ability to compete with the professional teams day in and day out? In the end, the boys, along with Joe Holland, decided to stick together and accepted Ferris' offer. So, they became members of a team whose name and home had yet to be determined. The corporation was chartered with Kimbrough as President, Beard, Barker and Groza were named Vice Presidents, Jones was appointed secretary and Holland became treasurer.[185] Those assignations should create some interesting radio play-by-play if the announcer had any imagination. There was some discussion about attempting to hire Adolph Rupp as coach and he was offered the position, but he wanted to remain at UK. So, Cliff Barker, who had coaching aspirations, accepted the post as player-coach. The NBL officials wanted a team in Indianapolis, but the players were also considering locating their team in Louisville or Cincinnati. Using the tri-cities concept—playing "home" games in all three cities—wasn't out of the question, either.

Alas, there was a fly in the ointment. BAA President Maurice Podoloff (known throughout the league as "Poodles") convinced that Alex Groza would be the savior of the Indianapolis Jets, continued to apply his substantial charm to woo Big Al. In addition, he waved $16,000 under Groza's considerable beak—a $6,000 signing bonus and $10,000 for his first year's salary. That was significantly more than the new corporation would be able to pay for Groza's services. In late May, Groza finally gave in and accepted Podoloff's check for $6,000 even though he had already signed, along with his teammates, with Ferris and the NBL. Almost immediately, Groza realized that he'd made an enormous error and returned the contract and money to Podoloff.[186]

"Poodles" was not a happy man. He said that Groza had made the initial contact and that, "He (Groza) indicated that he had been practically forced into signing some kind of cooperative agreement by the high pressure tactics of Mr. Leo Ferris..." Podoloff told the press. He also expressed his determination to hold Groza to his BAA agreement.[187]

The next day (May 27) Ferris and Groza held a press conference. Groza denied that he had initiated the contact with Podoloff and also denied that he had been pressured into signing with the NBL as that was his actual desire. Emotionally, he admitted that he'd been swayed by the money but quickly realized that accepting the BAA's offer was a mistake. "I want to stick with the boys and I now realize that the original agreement we made (with the NBL) should stand" he declared. Ferris added that if Podoloff wanted to go to court, "we're certain he has no case."[188]

Alex Groza heaved a huge sigh of relief two months later, in July 1949, when the rival leagues finally decided to stop the war for players and cities by merging their strongest franchises. All the details were not worked out at the August 3 organizational meeting, but the new entity was to be called the National Basketball Association (NBA) and would consist of the BAA's Minneapolis Lakers (where that name made some sense,) the St. Louis Bombers, Ft. Wayne Pistons, Chicago Stags, Washington Capitols, Baltimore Bullets, New York Knickerbockers and Boston Celtics. Survivors from the NBL were the Syracuse Nationals, Anderson Packers, Sheboygan Redskins, Tri-Cities Blackhawks, Milwaukee Hawks and the Denver Nuggets.[189] BAA commissioner Maurice Podoloff was elected president of the new organization. This left Indianapolis, considered to be one of the stronger venues—when they fielded a decent product—with maybe one team, maybe two and maybe none.

While all this action was going on in New York and Indianapolis, Ralph Beard, having signed a contract to play professional baseball in the Boston Braves organization, was playing in the Appalachian League in Bluefield, West Virginia. Somehow, he found the time to marry Marilyn Bauer, a young lady from Morgantown, WV whom he'd met while at UK. Thus Beard joined Barker, Jones and Holland as married men; Groza remained the sole bachelor among the Olympians.

The merger of the professional leagues not only let Groza off the hook, but solved a couple of other problems as well. The viability of the Jets was no longer an issue, clearing the way for the Olympians, which the team officially was now, to establish their base in Indianapolis, a hotbed of basketball. Additionally, the Jets had played their home games in Butler University's Hinkle Field House, so their demise made that excellent facility available to the Olympians. With its huge 15,000 seat capacity and rock-solid dedicated basketball floor, the Butler Field House was considered by one and all to be the finest basketball arena in the country.

An NBA check for $30,000 was handed to the Olympians, allowing them begin operations. The players voted to make Babe Kimbrough a full partner, dividing the common stock into six full shares. Thirty shares of preferred stock were offered at $1,000 per share to repay the NBA loan. The citizens of Indianapolis, delighted to have a new team, snatched up the stock and the Indianapolis Olympians were ready to begin play as the first, and only, all-rookie team ever to compete in professional sports. This team was also unique in that the Olympians are the only team ever in professional sports to be owned by the players.

There was, however, one more college chore before their professional careers began—the annual college All-Star game played in Chicago on October 26 against the NBA Champion Minneapolis Lakers. Beard, Groza, Jones and Barker were joined by former Olympic teammate Vince Boryla, and some other standout players including Loyola's Jack Kerris (you do remember Jack from the previous NIT, don't you?) and St. Louis' "Easy" Ed Macauley. This would provide a much anticipated first match-up of Groza and the great Lakers' star, George Mikan, as well as provide an opportunity for the Olympians to play one last time under the direction of Coach Rupp. The All-Stars were, beyond doubt, talented, but proved no match for the Lakers. The professionals jumped out to an early lead and did not look back. Wah Jones led a late rally, but it was too little as the Lakers won 94-86 behind Mikan's 31 points.

Jones totaled 22 for the collegians, Groza scored 18 against the Lakers' big man, Beard added 13 and Boryla chipped in 17.[190] If the Olympians needed any reassurance that they could play at the professional level, it was surely provided by holding their own against the NBA champions.

Organization of the fledgling NBA presented many problems that had to be ironed out rather quickly. The first decision allocated the seventeen teams into three unequal divisions. New York, Boston, Baltimore, Philadelphia and Syracuse composed the Eastern Division, while Minneapolis, Ft. Wayne, Chicago, Rochester and St. Louis former the Central Division. Joining Indianapolis in the Western Division—which turned out to be the weakest of the three—were Waterloo, Anderson, Denver, Tri-Cities and Sheboygan. Another decision, which did the Indianapolis club no favor, was that the former BAA teams would play at the former NBL cities just once during the regular season. Likewise, former NBL teams would visit BAA courts a single time, while NBL teams would play their former mates four times! This gave the Olympians a tough and packed schedule and denied them frequent access to the more desirable (read "profitable") venues.

As summer turned to fall, all the administrative details may have been hammered out, but plenty of questions remained for the Indianapolis Olympians. In the first place, could these college boys stand up to the professional pace? College games are played in twenty-minute halves, while the NBA would play twelve-minute quarters. As the professional season is at least twice as long as the typical college campaign, could these boys tolerate the longer—and more physical—pro game for a grueling 64 game season?

Everybody knew that the Olympians would run Coach Rupp's Kentucky offense. Would that work in the pros as well as it did in college?

Would Cliff Barker, past his prime as a player nearing age 30 and who had never coached so much as a grade school team, be effective in his role as player/coach? Would his teammates/friends obey his dictates?

Then there was a question of back-up players. Five men, no matter how talented, simply cannot play all the minutes and win at the professional level. Before the season began, the Olympians signed Carl Schaeffer, formerly the leading scorer for the University of Alabama, Malcolm McMullen, who had been at Kentucky for a short stint before he transferred to lead Cincinnati's Xavier University in scoring, came next. Then two former NBL players, Marshall Hawkins (formerly of Tennessee) and Floyd Volker both Oshkosh veterans signed on. Bob Evans, a recent graduate of Butler University, passed a tryout and completed the roster. Before the season was over, Hawkins and Volker would be gone, replaced by Bruce Hale, who had played in both the NBL and BAA and Paul Walther, the former Tennessee Volunteer who had given the Fabulous Five plenty of trouble in the SEC wars.

All things considered, the most important question was whether the public would turn out and pay money to see these men play? One writer, considering the failure of previous teams in the Hoosier city, expressed his opinion with, "If these kids can revive interest in professional basketball in Indianapolis, I'll say they're able to perform miracles."[191] They'd already accomplished one miracle, so maybe there would be another. All these issues could be answered only on the court.

The National Basketball Association began its inaugural season in October with a series of exhibition games in which the professional teams faced each other. The Olympians, charging prices ranging from 65 cents for a child to $2 for prime seats, won five of their eight exhibition games and garnered enough profit to purchase their snazzy red, white and blue uniforms and all other necessary equipment.[192]

November 1 was opening day. The Olympians took on the Denver Nuggets at the Butler Field House and jumped out to a 20-6 early lead. With a big lead the starters watched most of the second half from the bench, and when it was over, they'd won their inaugural game 71-64 behind 19 points by Groza and Jones' 9. Beard scored 8 in his first contest and Barker added 4. A good crowd watched the first regular season game in the Butler Field House.[193]

A week later, the veteran New York Knicks paid their only visit of the season to Indy. When the smoke cleared, the Olympians suffered their first defeat, losing 79-64 to even their record at 1-1. This time, Groza and Beard led the way, scoring 18 and 14 respectively.[194]

Life on a professional road trip then became a reality. The boys embarked on a fourteen-day trip in which they would play eleven games in cities ranging from Indianapolis to New York to Sheboygan to Minneapolis. The highlight of the trip was a return engagement with the Knicks. The Olympians revenged the earlier defeat by winning 83-79 behind Groza's record 41 points before the largest crowd (18,135) ever to witness a professional game in Madison Square Garden.[195] One by one, the nagging preseason questions were being answered.

November 20 brought the much anticipated first professional match-up between the Minneapolis Lakers' George Mikan and the rookie sensation, Alex Groza. The 6'10" Mikan was the undisputed king of professional basketball scoring, at least until Groza came along. The two had gone head to head twice before, first in the college All Star game and then in a preseason exhibition, but this would be the first meeting with money on the table. Groza gave the big man a good game, but Mikan and the Lakers prevailed 121-95. The 121-point total was a new NBA record for a single game score. Mikan outscored Groza 29 to 21 and Ralph Beard, who was proving to be the best guard in the league, chipped in 24 for the losers.[196]

The December 1 rematch between the two teams had a little extra spice in that Groza and Mikan were neck-and-neck for the league scoring lead. So far in the season, Groza had scored 355 points to Mikan's 312, but Mikan had the better per game average at 26.0 to Groza's 23.7. Big Al and Coach Barker lined out a new technique for defending Mikan and were ready when the Lakers arrived in Indianapolis. In the previous meetings, Groza had held the ball high, which played into the taller Mikan's strength. Barker advised Alex to keep the ball low—dribble it near the floor—and then move quickly when Mikan bent over.[197] It worked. Groza outscored big George 38 to 33 as the Olympians recorded their first win over the Lakers 86-68. The more than 11,000 fans also saw Beard score 18 while Wah Jones added 17 to the satisfying victory.[198]

More questions now had answers. Barker was proving his mettle as a coach and took himself out of the game often enough to, acting as coach, observe the play and define offensive and defensive strategy. Additionally, fans packed the arenas everywhere the Olympians played, especially at home in the Butler Field House and in Madison Square Garden where the ticket-buying public was familiar with the ex-Kentucky players. In fact, gate receipts were so good that before the season was over, all expenses had been paid with enough extra revenue to allow each player (and Kimbrough) a $5,000 bonus to accompany their $5,000 salary.[199] Pretty good money considering that the average worker's annual income at the time was around $3,000.

A late December evening brought the Chicago Stags and former teammate Kenny Rollins to town. Ralph Beard held his friend to two points while Groza rang up 41 to keep the pressure on Mikan as the ex-Kentuckians posted a 104-92 win.[200]

When the regular season ended in mid-March, the Olympians were atop the NBA's Western Division standings with a quite respectable 39-25 record. The season was a success in many ways, not the least of which was at the ticket office. In addition to players' compensation, they paid the city back the $30,000 start-up money and still had more than $28,000 in the bank.[201] The Olympians drew more fans than any other team in the league. This was due, in part, to the large seating capacity of their home venue, but also because the fans loved their style of play and their proficiency at it. For the first time, somebody had challenged George Mikan for the NBA scoring title. Groza finished the season with 1496 points in 64 games for an average of 23.4, while Mikan compiled 1865 in 68 games (the Lakers won the championship) averaging 27.4. Big Al set a new standard for field goal accuracy, hitting 47.8 percent of his shots. Ralph Beard came in twelfth in scoring, averaging nearly 15 points per game and was seventh in assists. Ralph was proud of the fact that he ranked first in the fewest number of fouls, averaging less than two whistles per game.[202]

As Division winners, they would face the fourth place Sheboygan Red Skins (not politically incorrect at the time) in a best of three series in the first round of the post-season playoffs. Every member of the packed house who showed up for the first game in the Butler Field House on March 21 witnessed a tight game in which all five former Wildcats scored in double figures as the Olympians squeaked by 86-85.[203]

Two nights later, the teams met again on the Red Skins home court. Despite a 20 point effort by Jones, 26 for Groza and 15 by Beard, the Wisconsin team won by a count of 95-85 to set up the rubber match in Indianapolis on March 25.[204]

Once again, the game was played before 15,000 screaming Olympians' fans. Balanced scoring was the rule in this game as the Indy team prevailed 91-84 to advance to the next round where they would face the Anderson Packers, who had eliminated Tri-Cities in their first round playoff.

The intrastate rivals had raced neck-and-neck through the regular season. Anderson's players, having finished a mere two games behind the Olympians, were eager to prove that they were the superior team when they met for the opening game in Indianapolis on March 28. The physical play in the early going revealed that these teams did not like each other very much. The battle under the boards between Wah Jones and the Packer's Ed Stanczak was particularly rough. "He (Jones) kept holding me and grabbing my shorts until he finally grabbed me where the shorts were the shortest, if you know what I mean," said Stanczak. "I told him he was getting too personal." When the Anderson's Coach Ike Duffy told Stanczak to "do something about it,' he did. In the final minutes as the Olympians surged from behind, Stanczak found an opportunity to smash an elbow into Jones' face just below his right eye. Writhing in pain, Wah went to the locker room where, once the bleeding was stopped, eight stitches were required to close the gash[205] Stanczak was ejected from the game, but the fans did not see it as an even trade. Back on the court, Jones' teammates won 77-74 to take the series lead.[206]

Stanczak may have been a villain in Indianapolis, but he was a hero in Anderson when the teams took the floor there on March 30. The fans, hanging from the rafters, were at a fever pitch, cheering every move by the home team and booing every action of the Olympians. Even Wah Jones, sitting on the bench with his face heavily bandaged, was not spared the abuse. The Jones-less Olympians, also playing without Beard, who was suffering from a severe stomach virus, lost 84-67 to even the series at a game each.[207]

So the stage was set for the deciding game at the Butler Field House on April 1. Beard was out of the hospital and Jones declared he'd play regardless of his condition. All the seats were sold by 5 PM and an hour later, a long line, including a contingent who had driven up from Lexington, extended away from the ticket window clamoring for admission. Enough fans were allowed in to occupy all available standing room and sat around the edges of the floor four deep. Still, an estimated 10,000 ticket seekers were turned away. Despite a raucous effort from the crowd and heroic exertions from Groza and the sub-par Jones and Beard, the Packers ended the Olympians' phenomenal initial season with a 67-65 victory.[208]

With the season over, the boys went their separate ways for the summer. Groza went home to Martins Ferry, Jones and Barker remained in Indiana while Holland went to tend to his car dealership in West Virginia. Ralph Beard, on top of the world, set off for his second year of minor league baseball, playing for the Evansville Braves in the Indiana-Illinois-Iowa (Triple I) League.[209] He simply could not imagine anything better than doing what he loved—playing ball—and getting paid, quite handsomely, to do it.

Chapter Ten

1949-50: Third Time No Charm

Try to imagine an emotional farewell between Coach Rupp and the Fabulous Four as they shook hands in parting on the night of October 26, 1949 after the All-Star game in Chicago. Now try to imagine Rupp wringing his hands over UK's prospects with these players, who won 130 of 139 games over the past four seasons, now gone to the professional ranks.

If you know very much about Adolph Rupp, you'll find it impossible to envision either of those scenarios. The moment those players left UK for their barnstorming tour was the instant Coach Rupp began thinking about winning the conference championship the next season. While it is certainly true that when Jones, Groza, Beard and Barker departed, UK lost four great players, but it is not true that Kentucky's cupboard was left totally bare. As Rupp pointed out to Ralph Beard four years before, even with them gone, the University did not plan to cancel its 1949-50 season schedule.

Holdovers that had seen significant playing time the previous year were seniors Jim Line and Dale Barnstable and junior Walt Hirsh. Rupp was counting on the guys from Coach Lancaster's undefeated freshman team, most notably, seven-footer Bill Spivey who had, indeed, demonstrated that he could play basketball as well as he could eat. Spivey simply dominated the SEC freshmen games the previous season. Also moving up to the varsity were Bobby Watson, a 5'10' sparkplug from Owensboro, KY. Shelby Linville a 6'5" forward from Middletown, Ohio, Lucian "Skippy" Whitaker, a guard from Louisville, Guy Strong another guard from Irvine, KY and the aforementioned C.M. Newton. Clearly, this edition of the Wildcats would be a sophomore dominated squad, but still the coaches had high hopes.

Spivey was the chief reason for those hopes. Now packing a robust 230 pounds on his lanky frame, Spivey had improved his game by working out with and against the Phillips 66'ers while they were in town for the Olympic fund-raiser. The great Bob Kurland took the time to help Spivey improve his shooting and footwork. Additionally, having gone against Alex Groza in practice every day the previous season taught him a lot about playing the pivot. He was not only tall, he could run the court, too and had mastered an unstoppable hook shot. Spivey was clearly in control of the Wildcats center position.

Veterans Line and Hirsh would man the forward spots and Dale Barnstable would move back to guard, leaving his running mate as the only vacancy in the starting line-up. Rupp took long looks at Strong and Whitaker, but Watson's fiery play won him the assignment.

Against the opening sacrificial lamb on December 3, Jim Line led the way with 37 points while Spivey added 16 in his debut as the 'Cats rolled past Indiana Central 84-61. Against Western Ontario a week later, the proverbial fat lady again sang the National Anthem as they piled on an embarrassing 90-18 win. Next, they faced St. John's in the nightcap of a double header at Madison Square Garden. When asked about the persistently growing rumors that games at that venue were "fixed," Rupp dismissed that as "poppycock." As the players were constantly under his protective wing, he said, there was nothing to worry about.[210]

Despite the fact that the Redmen came into the game with a spotless 7-0 record and rated as a three point favorite by the odds-makers, they surprised the Kentuckians. "They are better than we thought," Rupp admitted in the wake of the 58-69 defeat. As one of the keys to victory, St. John's double teamed Spivey, thereby negating his rebounding. One of the men who dogged the big guy's every step was Dick McGuire, not to be confused with Al McGuire. Al, who was destined to become the legendary coach at Marquette and then a celebrated television analyst, was on the team, but Dick was the star. Late in the game, Kentucky rallied behind the sharp-shooting of Guy Strong and Bobby Watson to close the gap to 56-61, but that was as close as they came as the Redmen froze out the time.[211]

Following wins over DePaul and Purdue, the 'Cats made the pilgrimage to New Orleans for the Sugar Bowl Classic, which usually presented problems. In the opener with Villanova, the Wildcats came from behind to tie the game in regulation. In overtime, they hung on to win 57-56, handing the Philadelphia-based Wildcats their first defeat in eight games.[212] That set up the title match against a tough and highly-rated

Bradley team led by All-American Gene Melchiorre, "a small (5'10") but flashy forward." Jim Line had a lack-luster game until late when he made a basket to tie the score at 47. Line then proceeded to pour in five consecutive baskets to break the game open. Spivey topped Line's 19 points with 22 while Melchiorre led Bradley's scoring parade with 20.[213] Rupp told his young team that he was proud of them for winning the Sugar Bowl, "something the Fabulous Five never did."[214]

The year 1950 began with a tight win over Arkansas followed by a blow-out of Ole Miss at Owensboro. Then the North Carolina Tar Heels traveled to Lexington to take on the 'Cats. The Heels were outclassed 83-44 behind Walt Hirsh's 19 and Spivey's 16. At this point in the season, Kentucky held the number two rating in the national polls and Bill Spivey was third in SEC scoring.[215]

Then came the January rough patch, a trend that would become a Wildcat tradition. UK lost at Tennessee on the 14th, bested Georgia Tech two days later in Atlanta then lost to Georgia in Athens the next evening. That brought the record to 10-3 and their rating had slipped to fifth. Following a rousing victory over DePaul, Rupp took his charges to South Bend to take on Notre Dame on January 23rd. Spivey, now being mentioned as an All-American candidate, posted 27 points, sinking 12 of 20 attempts from the field but it was not enough as the Fighting Irish upset the 'Cats 64-51. The national press roasted Kentucky and Rupp, noting that this was the third defeat in the last five games and the four losses so far was one more than they had suffered during the entire previous two seasons.[216]

The Big Blue Nation was encouraged, however, as the Wildcats reeled off eleven consecutive wins leading into the SEC tournament which was to be held, once again, at the Louisville Armory. The last of those regular season games was a 70-66 victory over Vanderbilt in the final game the 'Cats would play in Alumni Gym. For a time, it appeared that the 'Cats might close out the old floor with a loss, but they rallied in the second half to come from behind for the win, which was the 84th consecutive win on that floor.[217] For the 1950-51 season, Kentucky would move to the new Memorial Coliseum then under construction down the block on Euclid Avenue. Interesting, enough, the last game in that facility, 25 years later, followed a similar script as Kentucky squeaked by Mississippi State 94-93 in overtime. UK's record on the old floor was a sparkling 262 wins against a mere 25 losses.[218]

In the SEC Tournament, Kentucky dispatched Mississippi State by ten in the opener and then took their revenge on Georgia to set up the championship game with Tennessee. The newspapers hailed Coach Rupp's rebuilding effort in the wake of the 95-58 blowout of the Volunteers behind Spivey's 37 points. That total tied the record, set by Groza, just the year before for the most points in a tournament game. The 95 points rung up by the 'Cats represented the most points by a team in tournament history, and the 37 point victory margin was also a new record as UK celebrated their seventh straight conference crown.[219]

Now Rupp and his players turned their attention to the post-season. In those days, the NCAA tournament field consisted of eight at-large teams selected by a committee. Coach Rupp claimed that the fact that his team was not invited was the only thing that prevented him from winning his third consecutive National Championship.[220] Maybe so, but the rest of the story, however, is a bit more complex. The committee asked Kentucky for a play-in game against North Carolina State. Rupp pointed out that not only did his team have the better record, at 25-4 as opposed the Wolfpack's 24-5, but were rated higher in the final regular season polls. Not to even mention that his team was the back-to-back defending National Champion. Based on those facts, and the Wildcat's victory over Villanova, who had defeated N.C. State, Rupp demanded that Kentucky be given the bid. The Wolfpack's venerable Everett Case readily agreed to the play-in but Rupp was adamant. The berth went to the Carolina school.[221] So, except for Rupp's stubbornness, there might be another national championship banner hanging in the Joe Craft center.

Instead, Kentucky accepted a bid to the NIT, where a first-round bye produced a match with the City College of New York (CCNY) on March 14. The NIT was to be played, as usual, in Madison Square Garden. The second-seeded Wildcats were a four-point favorite over the Beavers, but were hit by the flu as soon as they stepped off the train.[222] Seeding notwithstanding, CCNY was the better team, according to Coach Rupp. "If we played them again tomorrow night, we couldn't beat 'em," The Baron lamented. "(The Beavers) could do no wrong,"[223] said the newspaper. They raced out to a 13-1 lead and were still ahead 45-20 at the break. The 'Cats closed to within 16 in the second half, but wilted as the crowd—who usually cheered the Kentuckians—chanted, "pour it on, City, pour it on."[224] When the dust settled, CCNY had handed Rupp the worst defeat of his career, winning 89-50. The rumblings of "fixed" games coming out of New York City got a little louder following this game.

Rupp was a little less eloquent with his team than with the press. "I want to thank you boys. You get me voted Coach of the Year and then come up here and embarrass the hell out of me."[225] Spivey, too sick to start, still managed to score 15 while Jim Line and Walt Hirsh had off nights, scoring five and two, respectively as the 'Cats were amazingly bounced out of the NIT in the first round for the second year in a row. City's stars Ed Warner and Ed Roman combined for 43 points against Kentucky's defense. CCNY went on to win the NIT and then also captured the NCAA title for 1950 thus becoming the only school ever to win both. Given that participation in the two tournaments is now mutually exclusive, CCNY's feat of winning both championships is likely to stand as a singular accomplishment. Top rated Bradley, incidentally, was the runner-up to CCNY in both tournaments.

As a result of the controversy surrounding Kentucky's failure to receive an NCAA bid, the tournament rules were revised for the following year. The field was doubled to sixteen so that each region would be allowed two selections.[226] This, hopefully, would prevent any deserving team from being snubbed ever again. Sound familiar?

Thus Rupp closed out his twentieth campaign at the helm of Kentucky basketball and went home disappointed. But the cry "wait 'til next year" is the most common theme in sports. These green sophomores would be seasoned juniors when autumn rolled around.

Chapter Eleven

1950-51: A Tale of Two Teams

As the shortening days portended the approaching fall season in 1950, in Korea the "police action," as the politicians styled it, seemed more like a war to the troops on the ground that were doing the bleeding and dying.

In Indianapolis, the Olympians re-assembled determined to make a better run at winning the NBA Championship as sophomores than they had in their inaugural season the year before. Groza, Beard, Jones, Barker and Holland were as good as ever but felt that their bench had let them down. Consequently, they acquired the services of former Notre Dame (and Chicago Stag) great Leo Barnhorst, hoping to improve the supporting cast this season. They began the season slowly and by the first of the year their record stood at 14 wins against 15 losses. Groza and Beard were bright spots, averaging 21.7 and 16.8 points per game, respectively, while emerging as stars of the professional league.

In Lexington, the Wildcats were gearing up for a fresh run at the national championship. In addition to proven performers Bill Spivey, Shelby Linville, Bobby Watson and Skippy Whitaker, Rupp had a couple of sophomores, (and future All-Americans) Frank Ramsey and Cliff Hagan, who looked like they might be able to contribute. On December 9, Kentucky defeated Purdue 70-52 in the official dedication of the University's new Memorial Coliseum. The innovative facility was built to honor all Kentuckians who died in World War II, but it would become more famous over its productive life span, as "The House that Rupp Built." Incidentally, with its 12,500 seating capacity, many dubbed the new building a "white elephant" and predicted that the games would never attract enough patrons to fill all the seats.

Sparked by Bill Spivey, who had rounded into All-American form, by mid-December, Rupp's 'Cats were the nation's number one team with a spotless 6-0 record. The post-Christmas season brought yet another loss in the Sugar Bowl Classic, this one a one point setback in overtime at the hands of the St. Louis Billikins. Late in the game, the 'Cats were leading by two when Hirsh threw the ball away. A Billikins' score at the buzzer forced overtime. In the extra period, Spivey hit his lone free throw and Hirsh missed two to set the final margin at 42-43.[227] UK's loss erased the top rating, but they soon regained the pinnacle of the polls as they welcomed 1951 by reeling off 21 consecutive wins. Coach Bryant's 'Cats, incidentally, had better luck in the gridiron portion of the Sugar Bowl, defeating number one rated Oklahoma 13-7, snapping the Sooners' 31 game win streak.

The Olympians were involved in a historic game at Rochester on January 6. When regulation play ended with the score knotted at 65, both teams came up with the same scheme; hold the ball for one shot. Each team scored one basket in overtime and then went scoreless in the second extra period. Two more overtimes produced the same result while the fifth was a high-scoring affair with each team racking up four points. Most of the fans had already walked out in disgust before the Olympians made a decision. As the hour grew late and they had a game scheduled in Moline the next afternoon, they sent the half the team out to catch the train for Chicago, opting to finish the game with the five players on the floor and an empty bench. In the sixth extra period, a new NBA record, the Royals got the tip and held the ball for a final shot, which missed with four seconds remaining. Paul Walther snagged the rebound. Whirling, he saw Ralph Beard streaking for the basket at the other end. The high-arcing pass hit Beard in stride as his lay-up at the buzzer gave the Olympians the win 75-73. Angry fans' reaction to this game created such uproar that this and a similar game prompted the adoption of a shot clock, that limits the time a team can hold the ball in professional basketball.[228]

In both Lexington and Indianapolis, little notice was taken of a story that broke in the newspapers on January 18, 1951. Junius Kellogg, a star player at Manhattan College, reported to his coach and the local police that two former Manhattan players, Henry Poppe and John Byrnes, had offered him $1,000 to "throw" a game against DePaul played at Madison Square Garden earlier in the week.[229] Manhattan, a ten point underdog, won the game 62-59.

Subsequent police investigations led to the arrest not only of Poppe and Byrnes, but also three men "described by the authorities as gamblers with long police records." All five men were charged with "conspiring to commit a crime of bribery in violation of section 382 of the (New York) penal code, which makes it illegal to 'attempt to bribe a participant in any sport.'" The charges were a result of these men "fixing" several Manhattan College games in the 1949-50 season. Poppe had already confessed that he and Byrnes had each accepted money for "shaving points" in five games at the rate of $1,000 per game.[230] Manhattan was upset in two of the games in question and beat the point spread in the other three.

Manhattan Coach Ken Norton sounded a somber warning. "...if the fixers are putting money before my players faces, men on other teams must have been similarly tempted," he remarked before observing, "This racket is not purely local."[231]

Well, nobody in Lexington or Indianapolis was too surprised to learn that there was crime and corruption in New York City but, adopted a "after all, what does all that foolishness have to do with us?" mentality. Adolph Rupp's old Coach Phog Allen summed up the prevailing attitude: "College basketball isn't in any nationwide danger. All that is needed is to scramble the rotten eggs."[232]

As the winter of 1951 deepened, while it was true that most residents of Kentucky and Indiana paid little attention to the also deepening scandal, New York District Attorney Frank Hogan certainly was hot on the case. The 'Cats were well into their win streak when the next bomb exploded on February 19. DA Hogan announced that his on-going investigation had revealed that three CCNY players, Ed Roman, Ed Warner (you'll remember them from UK's loss in the previous NIT) and Al Roth admitted accepting up to $1,500 each per game to fix three games: CCNY versus Missouri, Arizona and Boston College, all three losses for CCNY. Also arrested were a former NYU player and a former Long Island University player and a gambler described as the "money man."[233]

The next day Hogan announced that three LIU players, Adolph Bigos, Leroy Smith and the most renowned of the trio, Sherman White, who was the nation's leading scorer, had been arrested and subsequently admitted accepting a total of $3,000 to shave points in LIU's game with Kansas State, played the previous December in—wait for it—Madison Square Garden. LIU blew a big lead before holding on to beat K State 60-59. Added to another CCNY player, this brought the

The Fabulous Five: Beard, Rupp and Rollins sit, Jones, Groza and Barker stand. This group lost just 9 of 139 games and, according to Ralph Beard, "shouldn't have lost any." Courtesy of University of Kentucky basketball and football negatives, University of Kentucky Archives.

Wallace "Wah Wah" Jones. Earned All-America honors playing under two legends: Adolph Rupp and Paul "Bear" Bryant. Courtesy of University of Kentucky basketball and football negatives, University of Kentucky Archives.

Alex Groza. "Big Al" was a consensus All-American three times. Courtesy of University of Kentucky basketball and football negatives, University of Kentucky Archives.

Ralph Beard, like Groza, was named All-American three times. He was named Player of the Year for the 1947-48 season. Courtesy of University of Kentucky basketball and football negatives, University of Kentucky Archives.

Kenny Rollins was a steady performer who always drew the toughest defensive assignment to protect the high-scoring Beard. Courtesy of University of Kentucky basketball and football negatives, University of Kentucky Archives.

Cliff Barker shows off his ball handling skills. Courtesy of University of Kentucky basketball and football negatives, University of Kentucky Archives.

Rupp in his practice outfit. All that's missing are the sergeant stripes. Courtesy of University of Kentucky basketball and football negatives, University of Kentucky Archives.

Long time UK assistant coach Harry Lancaster also served as Rupp's straight man. Courtesy of University of Kentucky basketball and football negatives, University of Kentucky Archives.

Dale Barnstable coached in high school following his UK days. Courtesy of University of Kentucky basketball and football negatives, University of Kentucky Archives.

Jack Parkinson was one of two former All-Americans who could not crack the starting line up once the Fabulous Five showed up. Courtesy of University of Kentucky basketball and football negatives, University of Kentucky Archives.

Jim Line became implicated in the scandals after the Fabulous Five moved on. Courtesy of University of Kentucky basketball and football negatives, University of Kentucky Archives.

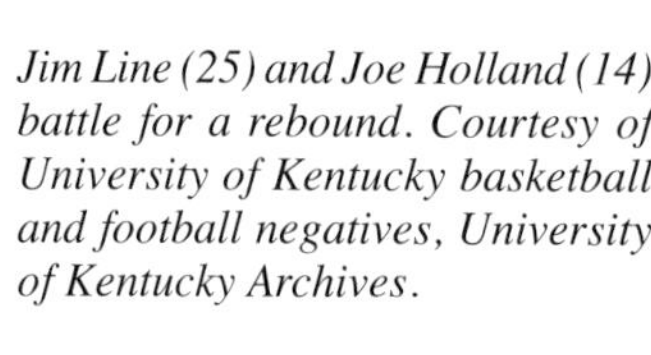
Jim Line (25) and Joe Holland (14) battle for a rebound. Courtesy of University of Kentucky basketball and football negatives, University of Kentucky Archives.

Coaches Lancaster and Rupp reaction to the action on the floor. Courtesy of University of Kentucky basketball and football negatives, University of Kentucky Archives.

Rupp and a player in the early days. Courtesy of University of Kentucky basketball and football negatives, University of Kentucky Archives.

Jim Line skies as Barker (23), Rollins (26) and Groza stand by. Courtesy of University of Kentucky basketball and football negatives, University of Kentucky Archives.

.A shot of Rupp's 1945-46 starters relaxing on the bench. From right: Coach Rupp, Jack Tingle, Jack Parkinson, Ralph Beard, "Wah" Jones, Wilber Schu and yes, that's Nick Englisis at the far left.

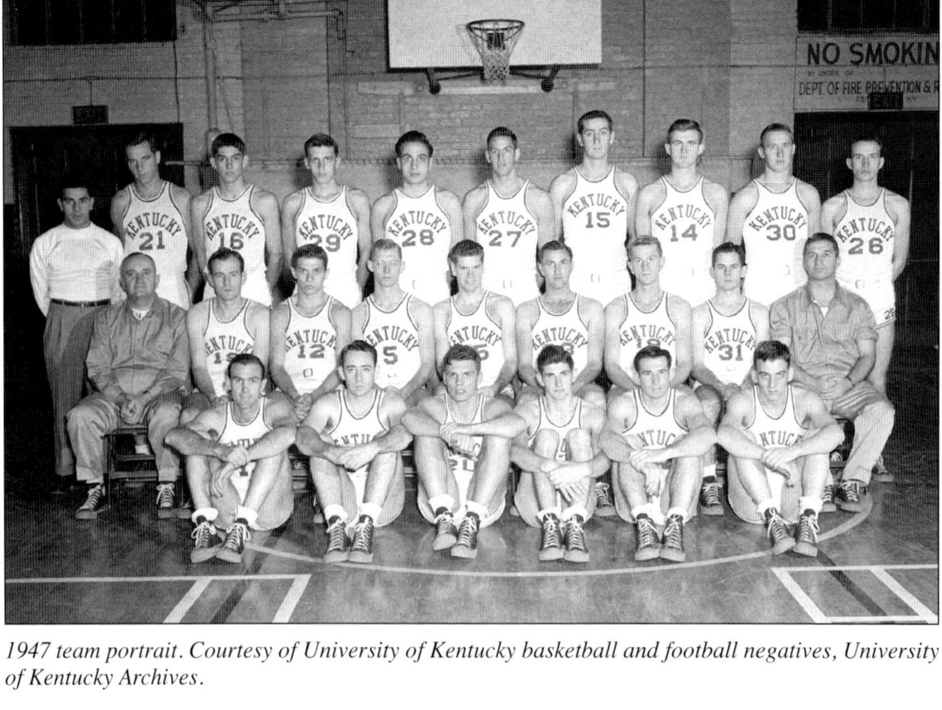

1947 team portrait. Courtesy of University of Kentucky basketball and football negatives, University of Kentucky Archives.

Bill Spivey maneuvers for his unstoppable hook shot. Courtesy of University of Kentucky basketball and football negatives, University of Kentucky Archives.

Baker (23), Jones (27) and Groza (15) in action against LSU. Courtesy of University of Kentucky basketball and football negatives, University of Kentucky Archives.

Bill Spivey. UK's first seven-footer would have put up some astounding numbers had he been allowed to finish out his career. Courtesy of University of Kentucky basketball and football negatives, University of Kentucky Archives.

"Wah" Jones has his UK jersey number 27 retired in both football and basketball. Courtesy of University of Kentucky basketball and football negatives, University of Kentucky Archives.

"Wah" Jones in his football jersey. Courtesy of University of Kentucky basketball and football negatives, University of Kentucky Archives.

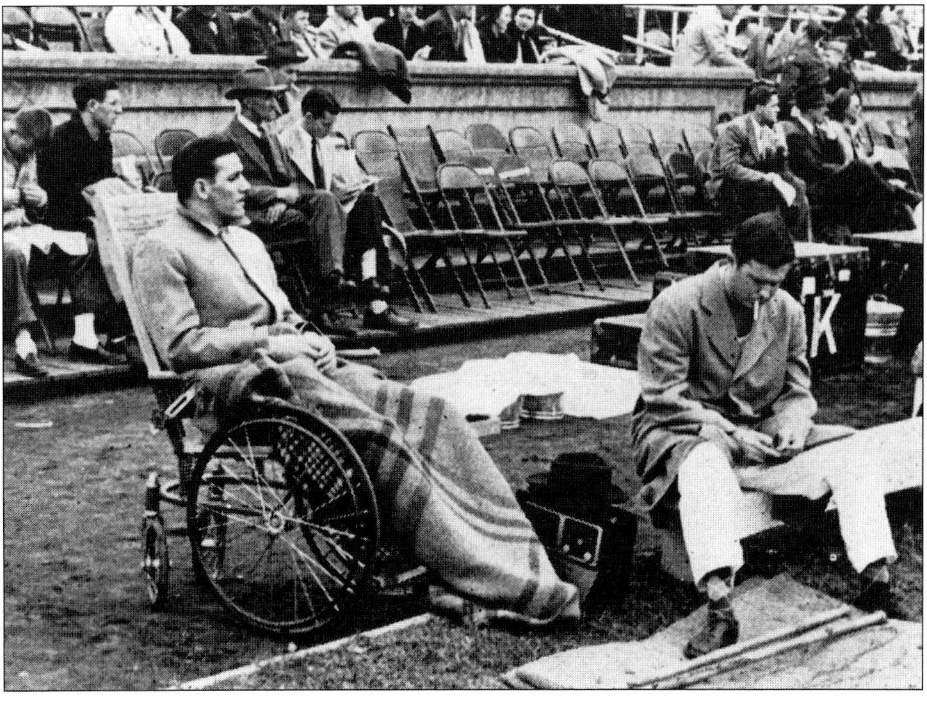

"Wah" Jones sits out a game at Stoll Field. Courtesy of University of Kentucky basketball and football negatives, University of Kentucky Archives.

Coaches Lancaster and Rupp and the team beam as Ralph Beard accepts the championship trophy. Courtesy of University of Kentucky basketball and football negatives, University of Kentucky Archives.

Coach Rupp accepts the National Championship Trophy. Courtesy of University of Kentucky basketball and football negatives, University of Kentucky Archives.

Wat Misaka. The 5'7" Utah player gained a pro contract after he "held" Ralph Beard to one point in the 1947 NIT Championship game.

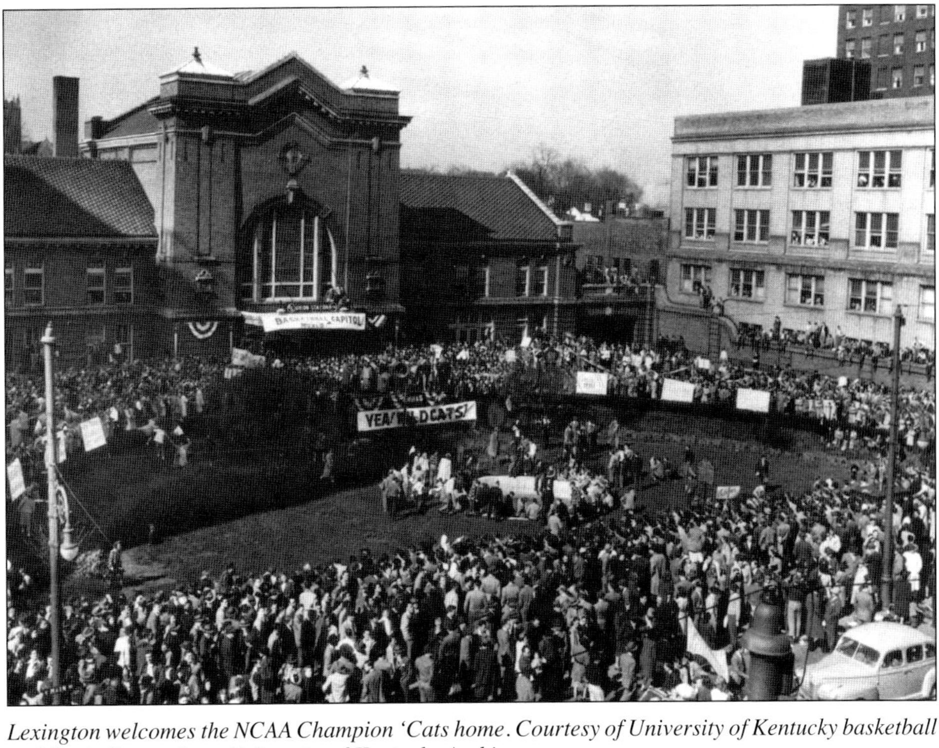

Lexington welcomes the NCAA Champion 'Cats home. Courtesy of University of Kentucky basketball and football negatives, University of Kentucky Archives.

Kentucky's Fabulous Five were instrumental in bringing the 1948 Olympic Gold Medal to the United States.

The Fabulous Five show off their Olympic uniforms. From left, Beard, Rollins, Barker, Jones, Groza and Rupp. Courtesy of University of Kentucky basketball and football negatives, University of Kentucky Archives.

Joe Holland joined his UK teammates to form the NBA's Indianapolis Olympians. Courtesy of University of Kentucky basketball and football negatives, University of Kentucky Archives.

UK's President and number one fan, Herman Donovan, congratulates Cliff Barker. Courtesy of University of Kentucky basketball and football negatives, University of Kentucky Archives.

Kentucky Favored Over Holy Cross 5

Wildcats Are Given 9-Point Edge In Encounter At Boston Tonight

As this newspaper headline from 1948 shows, finding the point spread was not difficult. Courtesy of The Courier-Journal.

The largest crowd ever to witness a basketball game in Kentucky showed up at UK's Stoll Field in July 1948 for the match between the Fabulous Five and the Phillips Oilers.

Kenny Rollins shows his defensive skills. Courtesy of University of Kentucky basketball and football negatives, University of Kentucky Archives.

Alumni Gym hosted UK's home games from 1924 to 1950. The 'Cats record was 262-25 in this building. Courtesy of University of Kentucky basketball and football negatives, University of Kentucky Archives.

Memorial Coliseum, home of the 'Cats from 1950 to 1975 is dedicated to Kentucky's WWII dead, but better known as "The House that Rupp Built." Courtesy of University of Kentucky basketball and football negatives, University of Kentucky Archives.

"Big Bill" shows off his form. Courtesy of The Kentuckian.

Coach Rupp congratulates Bill Spivey. Courtesy of University of Kentucky basketball and football negatives, University of Kentucky Archives.

UK's biggest fan, A. B. "Happy" Chandler, flashes the smile that won him his nickname. Courtesy of University of Kentucky basketball and football negatives, University of Kentucky Archives.

Former UK player, assistant and head coach Joe B. Hall. Courtesy of University of Kentucky basketball and football negatives, University of Kentucky Archives.

Alex Groza was college basketball's Player of the Year for the 1948-49 season. Courtesy of University of Kentucky basketball and football negatives, University of Kentucky Archives.

The inaugural issue of Sports Illustrated, published by Dell in February 1949, featured Ralph Beard on the cover.

Jim Line (25) and Cliff Barker fight for the ball. Courtesy of University of Kentucky basketball and football negatives, University of Kentucky Archives.

The 'Cats arrive in Seattle to battle for the 1949 NCAA Championship. Barker and Beard kneeling; Jones, Groza, Line and Rupp stand. Courtesy of University of Kentucky basketball and football negatives, University of Kentucky Archives.

Some history of the building is given by this plaque placed outside Alumni Gym by UK's Alumni Association in 1950. Courtesy of Ron Elliott.

total of eight present college athletes charged with accepting bribes to impact the outcome of games as well as several fixers. Hogan declined to explain how he had gotten onto the LIU players, but hinted that there were charges against more players and additional colleges yet to come.[234]

These developments got plenty of interest as lots of people now sat up and took notice. Tennessee's Democratic Senator Estes Kefauver said that the U.S. Senate would look into the matter of game fixing in other cities. "New York is not an isolated case," he observed. Dr. Hugh Willett, President of the NCAA, said the problem was of "great concern" and would be taken up at the NCAA meeting in Chicago in March. Ned Irish, Director at Madison Square Garden opined, "Gambling isn't confined to the Garden or New York City."[235]

The arrest of another former LIU player on February 26 added to the total. Nat Miller was accused of fixing LIU games against Bowling Green and Western Kentucky, bringing the total number of games in question to 15.[236] Two days later, Hogan nabbed CCNY's Floyd Lane. This latest development caused CCNY to join LIU in the drastic step of canceling the remainder of their games for the current season.[237]

No one at the University of Kentucky even considered cancelling their schedule—certainly not while that third NCAA Championship seemed within reach. The Wildcats took their sterling 24-1 record and number one rating into the SEC tournament at the beginning of March. They blew away Mississippi State, Auburn and Georgia Tech to face Vanderbilt in the final. Bill Spivey, down with tonsillitis, did not play in the first game, but came back to score 23 against Auburn and 19 on Georgia Tech. Evidently totally unimpressed with Kentucky's rating and record, and despite the fact that the 'Cats had defeated them roundly twice in the regular season, Vandy scored the first basket of the game and still led 22-19 with three minutes left in the first half. The 'Cats got hot at that point and went to the locker room leading 30-26. The Louisville Armory crowd sat back, content that the 'Cats would roar to victory in the second half. For a while it appeared that would be the case as UK was up 40-30 early in the second period. But then the Commodores got hot, hitting 42.1 percent in the final half including 10 of the last 13 attempts. When the smoke cleared Vanderbilt had pulled off "one of the most incredible surprises in recent sports history," winning by a count of 61-57 to garner their first SEC championship. The Commodores feat also broke Kentucky's seven-year reign atop the conference.[238]

Surprisingly, the loss did not cost Kentucky the number one rating, so it was on to the NCAA tournament, now expanded to sixteen teams, still atop the polls and hence the number one seed. The first round match-up was with a surprisingly tough Louisville squad in the East Regional at Raleigh, NC. When Bill Spivey fouled out with nearly 10 minutes to go and the Cards up 64-60, things looked bleak for the 'Cats. But Shelby Linville and Skippy Whitaker stepped up to help Kentucky win it 79-68.[239]

That brought up number nine rated St. John's in the regional semifinal in Madison Square Garden, still the prime venue in college basketball for a while longer yet. The Redmen were less troublesome than usual as Kentucky won going away 59-43 behind the scoring of Spivey, Watson and Linville.[240]

Two nights later, the Wildcats escaped number five rated Illinois in the regional final by a count of 76-74. Shelby Linville, in for the foul-plagued Spivey, was the hero once again, throwing in the winning goal with eighteen seconds remaining. Linville's total was 14, just half of Spivey's 28, which was four short of the tournament record.[241]

The championship game pitted a pair of Wildcat schools, number one Kentucky against number four Kansas State in Minneapolis. Despite Kentucky's number one rating and sterling record, the gamblers established K State as a four point favorite.[242] The purple clad Wildcats made it look like the gamblers knew what they were doing as they took a 29-27 lead at the half. After intermission, Spivey came to life for the Big Blue. Big Bill poured in 22 points and dominated both boards. His 21 rebounds were nearly as many as the entire Kansas State team pulled down. Cliff Hagan added plenty of help to bring UK the 68-58 win.[243] This was Kentucky's and Coach Rupp's third NCAA title in the last four years. As previously noted, the total might have been four but for his stubbornness. Bill Spivey was named to everybody's All-American team and was Helms' Player of the Year. With him and Cliff Hagan and Frank Ramsey returning, the Wildcats' future looked bright.

In the meanwhile, the Olympians were making a run at the NBA title. In early March, Commissioner Maurice Podoloff and several others hatched the idea of holding an NBA All-Star Game to offset the adverse publicity surrounding all the game fixing news. The pro league had been shuffled causing the divisions to be revamped in the off season. Indianapolis was now in the NBA West with Minneapolis, Rochester, Ft. Wayne (all good teams) and Tri-Cities. Ralph Beard, Alex Groza, George Mikan, Jim Pollard and Bob Davies were the starting team chosen to represent the West. They were opposed by the East's Bob Cousy, Ed Macauley, Joe Fulks, Andy Philip and Dolph Schayes. The East took the game, held at the Boston Gardens 111-94 behind Celtics star, "Easy" Ed Macauley. Groza led the losing scoring effort with 17.[244]

The Olympians made the play-offs, finishing fourth in the division with a disappointing 31-37 record. That paired them with the division champion Lakers, who had the home court advantage in the three game series. Despite an outstanding Olympian effort, the defending champion Lakers took the first game 95-81, behind their star, George Mikan's 41 points. In the second game in the Hoosier city, Mikan, having scored one goal, went to the bench with an injured ankle early in the game. With him out, Groza controlled the game, racking up 40 points. Ralph Beard added 23 as the Olympians romped to a 108-88 win to tie the series at one game each.[245]

The deciding game took place back in Minneapolis on March 25. Mikan, although still hobbled, put forth a heroic effort, scoring 30 in a back-and-forth battle that was tied 12 times. Groza also battled hard, posting 38. Beard added 24, but it was not enough as the Lakers advanced, winning 85-80.[246] Once again, the Olympians were disappointed, but the frustration was mitigated by the fact that both Alex Groza and Ralph Beard were named to the All-NBA first team along with Mikan, Davies and Macauley. Ralph Beard felt that the honor, plus being named to the very first NBA All-Star team, made him one of the five best players in the world and was proud of those accomplishments for the rest of his life.[247]

In late April, Rupp's 'Cats played an exhibition game against "an All-Star college team composed of players from eastern and central Kentucky" in Memorial Coliseum as an adjunct to the University's annual coaches clinic. UK won easily, handing the All-Stars a 92-49 setback.

With an eye toward the 1952 Olympics (and this time he intended to be the **head** coach), Adolph Rupp scheduled his team for a series of games in Puerto Rico to gain some experience in international competition. The Coach himself and his assistant Harry Lancaster had other commitments, so he sent the team away on August 21 under the watchful eye of acting coach Dale Barnstable. Barnstable, having graduated the year before, was the mentor at Louisville's Manual High School at the time. The Wildcats handily won all six games and returned to Lexington on September 5.[248]

Coach Rupp himself was at a coaching clinic at the University of Nebraska in Lincoln when his team left. Addressing the growing concern of game fixing, he declared, "Gamblers couldn't get at my boys with a 10 foot pole." He maintained that this was so because, "we all eat and sleep at the game hotel, phone lines to every room are plugged and the rooming lists are sealed to prevent the boys from being annoyed...." In firm words, he avowed, "None of my players, to the best of my knowledge, have ever been approached by gamblers or fixers."[249] The press would soon have a field day with those quotes.

In mid-September, the point shaving scandal got a little closer to home when a Peoria (IL) grand jury handed down an indictment against four Bradley players, including their star Gene Melchiorre, for accepting bribes to impact the outcome of games. Alert citizens of the Commonwealth eyes' widened when they read that the indictments also included, as fixers, former UK football player and basketball manager Nick Englisis and his brother, Tony.[250]

Adolph Rupp remained philosophical. "Basketball is the biggest sport in the nation. Biggest in attendance and active participation. We cannot expect it to remain completely untainted."[251] In an expansive mood, without reference to any particular case, Coach Rupp observed that "Ten million kids have been playing basketball for the last 58 years and only a few have strayed from the straight and narrow." When asked to compare the players involved in shaving points with baseball's famous Black Sox scandal, Rupp called for leniency. "The Black Sox threw games. These kids simply shaved points. There's a difference. Why forever condemn a boy for his one mistake of a lifetime?"[252]

Chapter Twelve

Scandal

Instead of the usual "plop", newspapers hit front porches all over Kentucky and Indiana on the crisp Saturday morning of October 20, 1951 with a sound more akin to the atomic blasts then being heard on Bikini Atoll.

"TWO FORMER UK CAGERS QUIZZED IN POINT FIX" screamed Louisville's *Courier-Journal* front page headline. The subhead identified the players in question as Ralph Beard and Alex Groza and detailed the apprehension of the players in Chicago the previous evening. The story recounted the highlights of the two stars' careers and stated that New York Assistant District Attorney (ADA) Vincent O'Conner had been in the Windy City for two previous days. The paper also noted that the point shaving scandal already involved 31 players and six colleges.[253]

Speculation was rife after the arrival of O'Conner and the detectives in Chicago. It was common knowledge that the New Yorkers were in town in conjunction with the still-developing scandal in the college game, and many thought that the players on the College All-Star team were the target. The newspaper's attempts to contact Coach Rupp were unsuccessful.[254]

Disbelief surrounding the accusation of Beard and Groza transcended the sports world. In addition to being NBA stars, in Indianapolis these two were considered to be outstanding citizens. Much in demand as public speakers at civic and corporate events, Beard and Groza held annual summer basketball camps to help young players learn from the pros. Additionally, Ralph and Alex participated in and sponsored many charitable fund-raisers.[255] "Well," many readers thought as the lay the paper aside, "let's not get too upset—the paper only said they'd been 'detained.' Perhaps they're not actually guilty."

Sunday's news burst the dam. GROZA, BEARD AND BARNSTABLE ADMIT TAKING $500 EACH TO SHAVE POINTS shouted the front page story filed by the Associated Press. Details revealed that after questioning, the three former Wildcats admitted accepting bribes to go under the point spread in the NIT Championship game versus Loyola in Madison Square Garden on March 19, 1949. "Loyola, a ten point underdog, whipped Kentucky 67 to 56 in a stunning upset," said the newspaper, also noting that if convicted the players would face a maximum penalty of five years in prison.[256]

The story said that after the players' apprehension, New York ADA O'Conner had taken Beard and Groza to Chicago's Criminal Courts Building where they were grilled for seven hours and detained for an additional eight hours after that. Both initially denied accepting any bribes, but gave in when Nick "The Greek" Englisis was brought into the room. Englisis, his brother Anthony and their cohorts, Saul Feinberg and Nat Brown were under indictment in New York, charged with game fixing.[257]

The story did not point out that the players were held without charges, not allowed legal representation or advised to remain silent. Had the Miranda rights rule been in effect, Beard and Groza would probably have just walked away as all O'Conner had was Englisis' word. In fact, discussing the investigation that led to the Kentucky player's involvement, O'Conner had previously said, "We could never take the word of a gambler on a thing like this." That would appear to be exactly what he did, as he possessed no other evidence. The ADA also defended his tactics: "…you've got to wait until you can catch the boys off guard. You've got to spring it on them suddenly and not give them a chance to be coached on what to say."[258]

There was worse news. O'Conner said that the fixers had indicated that there were other UK games involved. "Therefore," O'Conner noted, "practically every other game" played by Kentucky in the 1948-49 season would be investigated. Beard and Groza, however, only admitted to accepting bribes for the Loyola game. O'Conner's implication that his investigation "might spread as far south as Louisiana" immediately brought UK's Sugar Bowl losses to mind. The article also reported that Englisis had told Hogan that he paid Groza $1,000 and Beard and Barnstable $500 each for the Loyola game. The reporter evidently could not resist a jab at Coach Rupp by observing that "the fixers must have found an eleven foot pole."[259]

And there was worse news still. NBA Commissioner Maurice Podoloff flew to Chicago to announce that Groza and Beard, "now stock holders and mainstay players on the professional Indianapolis Olympians," were immediately and indefinitely suspended from professional basketball. On an inside page of the Sunday paper, *Courier-Journal* sports editor Earl Ruby reminded his readers that Podoloff was the "same fellow who flew to Lexington in a huff when Groza jumped a contract in Podoloff's BAA to join the other boys in forming the Indianapolis Olympians. He threatened to sue."[260] Mr. Podoloff told reporters that the NBA's directors would meet at 11 AM (October 22) "for a complete appraisal of the situation."[261] In light of developments, one wonders if "Poodles" was nursing a grudge.

Back in his UK office that Sunday morning, Adolph Rupp was asked if his plea for leniency earlier in the week meant that he knew what was about to happen. "Of course I had no idea of what was coming," the Coach roared. "Do you think that if I had known anything, I would have allowed one of those kids involved (Barnstable) to coach my team and take it to Puerto Rico?"[262]

University of Kentucky President Donovan said that the school "would in no way defend the boys" and then proceeded to defend them. "Anyone who knew these boys intimately will recognize that they are primarily victims of an unscrupulous syndicate of gamblers that apparently persuaded them that it was not a serious offense to reduce a point spread...."[263]

Earl Ruby, the *Courier's* sports editor, had some good questions. "One of the worst features of the scandal is that it may directly hurt many, many boys and men not involved in the point shaving. By accepting cash on the barrel head for point shaving during the season the Wildcats became professionals before the NCAA tournament. Will this mean that the championship will be taken away? Will the trophy have to go back?"[264]

According to the *Courier-Journal's* article concerning Dale Barnstable, after the detectives burst into his home about 11 PM, he confessed and told the detectives that Englisis paid the bribes to the three players in a mid-town New York hotel room where they were staying for the Loyola game. New York ADA William Sirignano said that Barnstable told him that the "sales talk" of the fixers was based on the fact that the players were not being asked to lose games, but only not to win by the expected margin.[265] Barnstable's comments would lead to a world of speculation concerning the relationship between UK's players and the "boosters." "The thing about it is that you convince yourself that you are doing no harm at the beginning, "he said. "You get $15 or $20 from the school for playing a good game and you figure that it won't hurt to take some bigger money for winning with something to spare." The ADA also said that Barnstable explained that receiving money from alumni was a "customary practice" at Kentucky. In contrast to Groza's and Beard's claims, Barnstable told Sirignano that he had accepted $100 from gamblers on "three or four" other occasions to go over the point spread.[266] Note that the New York statute did not make it a crime to accept bribes to go over the point spread, it only outlawed *limiting* the margin of victory.

"So you take the money," Barnstable went on, "and then you are offered some real money to shave the points. There's a lot of smooth talk and you talk yourself into the idea that it wouldn't hurt you or the school to win by a small score.

"You are a little confused and you don't know exactly what's going on, and the next thing you know, you are in it deep—too deep.

"I just hope the public won't judge us too harshly for our mistake," he pleaded.

The *Courier's* editors seemed to hear the appeal. "Nobody bothers to seduce the untalented player, the inconsistent team, the lads who get on varsity squads for sheer lack of better. Most players and schools are safe not because they are any more 'moral' than others, but because so few are in the big time...and thus less subject to temptation....

"And this goes back to the yapping demands of...the wild-eyed students and alumni who insist on victories.... We suppose this adds up to what more and more people these days are calling over-emphasis."[267]

Free on bail and perhaps unaware that they faced bigger problems than public opinion, Groza and Beard expressed similar sentiments the next day. "We realize what we did was wrong and we're sorry," said Ralph Beard from his home in Indianapolis. "If no other good comes out of this, it might help someone else to realize what will happen to them if they do take money." With a sigh, Beard added, "It's like a load has been lifted."[268]

Alex Groza commented, "It's our own fault. We should live it down ourselves. They shouldn't take it out on our families."[269] Also with a sigh, Alex added, "College athletics should not be made such a big business." Sound familiar? "Living it down" would prove to be a lifelong chore for all three men.

Groza and Beard declared that their entire NBA career had been "on the up and up" and expressed the hope that this situation would have no impact on their professional status.[270]

No such luck. On Tuesday, October 23, Maurice Podoloff announced that Beard and Groza were banned from the NBA for life and that they would be required to sell their interest in the Indianapolis Olympian franchise within 30 days. That order would, in all probability, entail a huge discount from the $1,000 each share of stock was worth initially.

By this time, both players had waived extradition and traveled to New York voluntarily (as had Barnstable) in the company of ADA O'Conner. O'Conner's boss, Frank Hogan said that all three would be arrested and charged with bribery and conspiracy.[271] Ford Frick, who had only a month before, succeeded Kentucky's A.B. Chandler as Commissioner of Major League Baseball, jumped on the bandwagon by banning Ralph Beard from playing professional baseball for life as well. One wonders what action, if any, "Happy"—the quintessential UK fan—would have taken had he still been in the Commissioner's office.

Beard, Groza and Barnstable appeared before Magistrate Ambrose Haddock for arraignment that same afternoon. He released them on $1,000 bail and set their hearing for November 7.[272] Addressing a crowd of reporters outside the courtroom, Ralph Beard admitted that he had accepted money in two other games (in addition to the Loyola game,) all in the 1948-49 season. He could not remember which games, but insisted, "I don't care what anybody says, there were only three games."[273] Beard would repeat that statement many times over the rest of his life. Asked why he did it, Ralph just shook his head. "I wish I knew," he lamented. After a moment's hesitation, he added, "The money was nothing." He was at the same loss for an explanation even 50 years later. A reporter then inquired if they "dumped" or intentionally lost any games. "Just shaving," Beard replied angrily. "It looked so easy. If we held the points down, we were promised $100 each for the two games...."[274]

Alex Groza joined Beard before the reporters. "Some day when I'm gray and this thing is done and I've lived it down, I'd like to tell the whole story about what it's all been like, about recruiting and playing and this."[275] It is unclear whether he meant "recruiting" as coming to play for UK or to being asked to shave points. If the story about him being upset because he received no offer from Ohio State (or anybody else) is true, which it evidently is, he must have meant being recruited to shave points. Although he lived to be old and gray, alas, he never did "tell the whole story."

While all this action was going on in New York, back in Louisville sports editor Earl Ruby had questions about ADA O'Conner's motives. "What is he trying to do—prove that kids from virtually every state have taken easy money, or is he sincerely attempting to gather evidence to break up the ring of New York criminals responsible for the scandal?

"If he is seeking evidence against the criminals, couldn't he do this without spectacular midnight raids on the homes of the already badly frightened kids?

"...So far, the only persons helped by the investigations have been the bookies, who have been 'taken' by the gambling syndicate."[276]

At the same time, back in Lexington, Adolph Rupp had to put his former players out of his mind as he prepared for the up-coming season. His plans suffered a serious set-back on October 18 when superstar Bill Spivey was admitted to Lexington's St. Joseph's Hospital, scheduled for surgery to remove cartilage from his right knee damaged while performing a "stunt" for a photographer. The doctors said it was "likely" would be able to play in the season opener December 8. Not to be outdone by the New York papers, the Kentucky paper suggested that Spivey might use Rupp's "ten foot pole" as a crutch.[277]

On October 25, the three ex-UK players testified before a New York Grand Jury. ADA O'Conner reported that during several hours of testimony, they confessed not only to the Loyola game, but to accepting $500 each "for keeping down their team's winning margin in a 1949 game against the University of Tennessee."[278] Something is amiss here! You may remember that is the game in which Groza established several new scoring records. Also, the "$500 each" does not match up with the amounts the players said they received.

Reports were more complete the next day. "Indictments were returned yesterday in General Sessions against three former University of Kentucky basketball players and five alleged fixers in conjunction with the rigging of a game played at Madison Square Garden against Loyola of Chicago on March 14, 1949." The "fixers" were Nick and Tony Englisis, Saul Feinberg, Marvin Mansberg and Nat (Lovey) Brown. O'Conner said that Brown had acted as "contact man" for the other four fixers and had traveled to various parts of the country where Kentucky was playing. O'Conner also disclosed that the three Kentucky players had received $100 each for running up their winning scores in games against DePaul in Chicago on January 22, 1949, Vanderbilt in Nashville on January 31, 1949, and St. John's in Madison Square Garden on December 18, 1948. Finally, O'Conner noted that the players had "failed to come through to the gamblers' satisfaction in games against Notre Dame, Bowling Green, Xavier and in two Sugar Bowl games played late in 1948 against Tulane and St. Louis University."[279]

It is worth noting that the number of games and the amount of money involved seemed to vary with each succeeding report. Also, keeping in mind that the only game in which the players admitted to having "shaved" points that was played in the State of New York—and hence subject to New York's jurisprudence—was the Loyola game. Also in view of the fact that "running up" the margin was not a crime, even in the Empire State, seems to hone Earl Ruby's questions concerning the District Attorney's motives to a fine point.

Chapter Thirteen

See Anything?

Here, in chorological order, are the complete newspaper write-ups and box scores for the five games in which New York ADA Vincent O'Conner alleged that Alex Groza, Ralph Beard and Dale Barnstable were guilty of accepting bribes. The indictment accused them of "going over" against DePaul, Vanderbilt and St. John's while shaving points against Tennessee and Loyola. The players admitted to accepting bribes for the games against DePaul, Tennessee and Loyola.

Through these summaries, we are able to see—through the writers' eyes—what happened in these games and draw our own conclusions. Keep in mind that at the time these were written, nobody had any suspicions about the games being fixed. Only with our historical perspective are we able, perhaps, to read unintended meanings into the sport's writers' words.

From the *Courier-Journal*, December 19, 1948:

Kentucky Routs St. John's 57-30
Groza and Jones lead 'Cats to Sixth Straight Victory
Special to the *Courier Journal*

New York, Dec.18 – The cage cyclone that ripped into this territory from the Bluegrass completed its devastation of the East tonight by wrecking the unbeaten record of another basketball team.

Kentucky this time blew St. John's from the ranks of the unbeaten, sweeping to an easy 57-30 triumph. The Wildcats had opened their invasion of the East Thursday night by smashing previously unbeaten Holy Cross. St. John's had won five in a row.

Thus, in the course of three days, the Bluegrass basketeers have destroyed the number 1 and number 2 rated Eastern quintets. And, meanwhile, they have rolled comparatively unhampered to their fifth and sixth victories of the season.

Their triumph tonight before 19,000 Madison Square Garden fans was their 19th in 26 appearances here and their 42nd in 45 games over the past two seasons.

Big Alex Groza and Wallace "Wah Wah" Jones again provided the whiplash to Kentucky's attack. Groza poured in 21 points and Jones hooped in 15. Ralph Beard and Cliff Barker were next high with six.

The NCAA and Olympic champions proved tonight that their defense is just as wicked as their offense. And, although the Wildcats were a little short of the brilliant game they have displayed in previous Garden appearances, they still showed themselves to be a powerhouse.

The Wildcats, fighting defense with defense, got off to a slow start. At the end of a sluggish, actionless first half, the sharp-shooting Wildcats had a comfortable but unimpressive 23-11 lead.

During that first half, UK's defense was so stout that St. John's was able to make only four field goals. And the Redmen added to their misery by missing nine of twelve free throws.

The Wildcats began to get hotter in the second half, however. St. John's, continuing to lag behind, abandoned its deliberate style of play and changed into a wild throwing outfit in the second period. That was playing right into Kentucky's hands, and the Wildcats enjoyed it—especially Groza and Jones.

Both had a scoring field day. And both played equally brilliant ball on the floor and off the boards. They were helped considerably, too, by All-American Ralph Beard, who cast off his role as a scorer tonight to set up plays and pass the ball to Jones and Groza when they were in scoring positions.

That trio sparked the second half action of the Wildcats who went out and scored 34 more points to add to the halftime margin. In the process, Groza completely outplayed the big centers assigned to guard him—Arthur Oldham and Igor Summer. Both fouled out attempting to bottle up Groza, who was recently named the nation's most outstanding basketball player.

The Wildcats showed little of their vaunted marksmanship and speed in the early minutes of the game. Slowed down by their own inaccuracy and by the deliberate style of play of the Redmen, the Wildcats had a meager 9-3 lead at the end of 10 minutes of play.

They warmed up considerably thereafter and began to slip by the close guarding Redmen. At the same time, their shooting began to sharpen.

The Wildcats came out in the second half and took advantage of nearly every St. John's lapse. They ran up a 40-20 bulge after 10 minutes in the second half of play. And the game, which had been advertised as an intersectional battle of two powerhouses, was no contest after that.

St. John's hit in the second half for only five field goals for a total of nine for the evening. Beard, meanwhile, brilliantly carried out his defensive assignment by stopping St. John's ace—Dick McGuire. He could only make one point in the first half and four in the second.

Kentucky	**fg**	**ft**	**pf**
Jones	7	1	4
Hirsh	0	2	2
Barnstable	0	1	2
Stough	0	2	2
Groza	7	7	3
Beard	2	2	4
Barker	3	0	3
Line	1	2	4
Totals	**20**	**17**	**26**
St. John's			
Dombrosky	1	0	1
Finn	1	1	3
Dalton	0	0	4
Calabrese	1	3	1
Wassmer	0	0	0
Summer	1	0	5
Oldham	2	1	5
Redding	1	3	3
D. McGuire	1	3	0
Buckley	0	0	0
Mulzoff	0	0	1
A. McGuire	1	1	1
Totals	**9**	**12**	**24**

From the *Courier-Journal* January 23, 1949:

UK Wins 56-45
Alex Groza paces Cats with 18
Barker, Beard Also Big Help To Blue Cause
By Larry Boeck
Courier-Journal Staff Writer

Chicago, Jan. 22 –This Windy City is accustomed to strong gusts, but a whirlwind out of the bluegrass swept it off its feet here tonight.

Kentucky, moving with speed and accuracy, captivated a crowd of 17, 350 as it handily blitzed past DePaul 56-45.

Strange as it may seem, the biggest stadium mob of the season was loudly pro-Kentucky here in the heart of DePaul territory.

The hospitable Chicagoans—fiercely booing decisions against Kentucky and generously applauding nifty shots by the Wildcats – were particularly appreciative of UK's Mutt and Jeff combination.

Mr. Mutt – six-foot eight Alex Groza and Mr. Jeff – five foot 10 inch Ralph Beard – combined for 34 of Kentucky's points. Groza hooped in 18 and Beard 16. And, outside of the scoring department, they were equally brilliant in other phases of play.

It was a rough game, too with 48 personals being called, 26 on UK and 22 on DePaul. After Barker, Jones and Line went out on personals near the game's end. And Beard played most of the second half with four on him.

Although it was a rough game, it was not one that got out of hand. The fouling characterized the aggressiveness and battling will of both teams.

Cliff Barker, who fouled out with nine minutes remaining was a handy guy in the clutches with 10 points. Wallace "Wah Wah" Jones tabbed seven and was, as you might expect, a man of dauntless aggression under the boards and on the floor.

Jack Phelan with 10 points and Bull Benson with nine led the scoring attack of a gallantly fighting, but outmanned and outplayed, DePaul.

The Demons, now twice defeated this season by the Wildcats, made a ball game out of it for 13 minutes. Then Kentucky, owning a scant 14-12 margin, started drawing away. The Wildcats led by a comfortable nine points at the half–32-23.

They boosted that advantage midway in the second half to 43-29 and that was enough. They coasted on from there to their 12th triumph in 13 games.

The Chicago crowd, which probably came out to see a champion and wanted to see it act like one, wasn't disappointed in the first half. The Wildcats outfought the determined, scrapping Demons in those first blistering 13 minutes, and sewed up the ball game there.

Barker, looping in seven points in 11 minutes, gave the Wildcats the initial scoring spark. From there, Beard, Groza and Jones took over.

Alert, spirited and driving, Kentucky hit for a hefty 37.1 percent of its shots in the first half. But, at the same time, it was guilty of frequent fouling. DePaul took advantage of that charity gesture and stayed in the game by sinking 11 of 13 free throws.

Kentucky continued its assault through 10 minutes of the second half. Then, prancing along merrily a few minutes later by 45-31, the Wildcats took it easy. After Barker fouled out, Coach Adolph Rupp started using his substitutes and in the ensuing wild, final minutes, the Kentucky offense was slowed.

As a result, the Wildcats had—on paper – another poor second half. They hit just 15.1 percent of their shot attempts. And, they outscored DePaul by just two points—24-22.

But as Coach Adolph Rupp has been saying for the past two weeks, during which UK hasn't been as keen in the second half as in the opening portion: "I just like the boys to win—that's all."

They did it tonight with a brilliant performance.

Kentucky (54)	**fg**	**ft**	**pf**
Barker	3	4	5
Line	0	0	5
Jones	3	1	5
Stough	0	1	1
Groza	5	8	2
Hirsh	1	2	2
Barnstable	0	0	2
Beard	6	4	4
Totals	**36**	**20**	**26**

DePaul (45)			
Benson	2	5	3
Kampa	1	0	3
Gillespie	2	2	1
Vukovich	0	1	0
Phelan	4	2	5
Govedarica	1	4	3
Allen	1	0	0
Leddy	0	2	2
Coorlas	0	2	2
Totals	**13**	**19**	**21**

From the *Courier-Journal* February 1, 1949:

Groza Hits 31 As UK Rips Vandy

Nashville, Tenn. Jan. 31 (AP)–Kentucky's cagey Wildcats won their 51st straight Southeastern Conference basketball game tonight, drubbing the Vanderbilt Commodores 72-50. Alex Groza, six-foot-seven center for the 'Cats, tossed in 31 points.

The Commodores were able to keep abreast of the Kentuckians for a little more than 10 minutes and then the fade began. Led by Groza's top effort in SEC competition, the Wildcats outplayed the locals with ease.

Billy Joe Adcock, Vanderbilt's high-scoring forward, who led the league last season, turned in his best performance of the current campaign, bucketing 22 points.

Vanderbilt matched the 'Cats basket-for-basket early in the game but Kentucky began taking advantage of every Vanderbilt miscue and the runaway grew more obvious midway in the second period.

With the score 22-21 in Kentucky's favor, Groza, Cliff Barker, Walter Hirsh and Ralph Beard drilled the hoop to put the visitors ahead 41-28 at halftime.

The defeat was the worst suffered by the Commodores this season. While the Wildcats were recording their 14th win in 15 starts, Vandy was losing its sixth in 14 games.

Kentucky	**fg**	**ft**	**pf**
Barker	3	1	2
Day	0	1	1
Hirsh	2	3	5
Line	0	0	2
Groza	11	9	4
Beard	8	0	0
Stough	0	1	1
Barnstable	4	1	3
Townes	0	0	1
Totals	**28**	**16**	**19**
Vanderbilt			
Adcock	8	6	3
Parks	0	1	0
Kelley	4	3	5
Robinson	2	1	4
Curtis	0	0	2
Craig	1	3	1
Duvker	3	0	4
Lane	0	0	1
Totals	**18**	**14**	**20**

Halftime score: Kentucky 41, Vanderbilt 28
Missed free throws: Vanderbilt – Adcock 4, Kelley 4, Lane.
Kentucky – Hirsh 1, Groza 2, Beard 1.

From the *Lexington Herald*, February 9, 1949:

ALEX GROZA SCORES 34 POINTS TO BREAK SEC RECORD AS CATS WHIP VOLS 71-56
Single Game Mark Smashed by Great Kentucky Pivotman
By Babe Kimbrough
Sports Editor, *The Herald*

Records fell—and so did the Tennessee Volunteers—while Capt. Alex Groza and his Kentucky Wildcats rose to new heights last night as they trounced their arch rivals from Knoxville, 71-56, in a thrilling but spotty cage contest on the Alumni gymnasium court.

A capacity crowd of yelling, screaming, whistling students all but lifted the roof from the building as they saw Groza chuck through a total of 34 points to establish a new Southeastern Conference scoring record, a new individual mark for a Kentucky player and a new high for Alumni gym.

When, late in the game, the Wildcats realized that their big pivotman had a chance to crack the scoring records, they began feeding him the ball at every opportunity and it was on a court-length pass from Cliff Barker in the last minute of play that Groza dropped through the field goal which gave him the crown.

After receiving the long toss from Barker, the Kentucky center – apparently nervous as he realized what the shot would mean – missed an easy crip, but took the ball off the backboard on the rebound and dropped it through to bring his total to 34.

Prior to last night, Groza held ties for the records which he shattered. His 33 points against Baylor in the finals of the Olympic trials last spring in New York made him share the individual scoring record for a Kentucky cager with "Big Ed" Edwards, while his 31 points at Nashville last week made him co-holder of the SEC record with Pinky Lipscomb, a former Commodore star.

Edwards tallied his 33 points against Creighton in Alumni gymnasium during the 1935 season while Lipscomb hit his 31 during the 1941 season.

Until last night, Paul Walther, Tennessee's star forward, was leading the scoring parade in the conference this season by three points over Groza. But Walther was limited to 21 while the Kentuckian was piling up his total to establish new records and take the loop lead as well.

Groza and Walther were the only men on the two teams to hit the double figures. Wallace (Wah Wah) Jones finished second for Kentucky with nine points while his brother Hugh, and Ed Montgomery, each got nine for the Volunteers.

Although the Wildcats sparkled at times—particularly when they needed the points—they had several lulls during the evening as the Tennesseans pressed forward in an attempt to overtake Coach Rupp's champions.

Then, too a little extra whistle tooting by the officials appeared to disrupt the Wildcats' attack on other occasions. The officiating, like the play of the two teams, was spotty.

The battle was a duplicate of the one between the Kentuckians and the Vols at Knoxville earlier in the season insofar as the margin of victory was concerned. In that game, however, the UK cagers sparkled in the first half and coasted in the second, while last night, they reversed the procedure to give their greatest exhibition in the final period.

After connecting for only 25.4 percent of their attempts from the field in the first period, the 'Cats leveled at the hoop in the second period to finish at 33.7 percent for the entire game. The Tennessee cagers also did slightly better in the final stanza, having a game average of 26.8 percent after connecting for only 21.4 percent in the opening half.

Little Ralph Beard, who was held out of the starting lineup because of an ankle injury received Saturday in the Bradley tilt at Owensboro, went into the battle with eight minutes remaining in the first period but lasted for only 15 minutes of play before he was ousted on personal fouls.

During his brief stay in the game, the All-American guard managed to give several spectacular ball-hawking demonstrations and toss in three field goals.

Sophomore Walt Hirsh, who took Beard's place on the starting five, accounted for a like number of points. His floor play, along with that of Jones, Barker and Dale Barnstable, had much to do with Groza's record-breaking performance.

Good ball handling on the part of these Wildcats gave the lanky pivot-man numerous opportunities while Jim Line, during his three and a half minutes of play, was a distinct asset to the cause. Line went in for Jones when the Harlan athlete turned his ankle in the final minutes of play.

The Kentuckians had easy sailing during the first ten minutes as they chalked up 24 points against 12 for the Volunteers and appeared to be headed for a lop-sided victory.

But in the next five minute period, both quintets went into a slump, the 'Cats hitting only two field goals and the Tennesseans one. In the final five minutes, before the rest period, a crip shot by Beard was the only mark on the score sheet for Kentucky while the Vols tossed in seven points to place the count at 30-21 at intermission.

As the second half opened, the Tennessee cagers continued to press and in the first ten minutes of play outscored the Ruppmen 14 points to 13, the score standing at 43-35. During the next five minutes, however, the Wildcats stepped on the gas to take an 11 point advantage at 54-43.

With less than a minute to play, Kentucky had an 18 point margin. But Hank Kinzel, substitute center, slapped in a rebound for the Vols, then hit a gratis shot after having been fouled by Barker to put the final score at 71-56.

Tennessee (56)	**FG**	**FT**	**PF**	**TP**
Walther	8	5	3	21
Keenan	1	0	0	2
Graham	2	0	1	4
Burris	4	0	3	8
Kinzel	1	1	0	3
H. Jones	3	3	2	9
Montgomery	3	3	3	9
Totals	**22**	**12**	**12**	**56**

Kentucky (71)				
W. Jones	4	1	4	9
Hirsh	3	0	0	6
Line	1	1	1	3
Groza	14	6	1	34
Barnstable	3	2	3	8
Barker	1	3	4	5
Beard	3	0	5	6
Totals	**9**	**13**	**18**	**71**

Halftime score: Kentucky 30, Tennessee 21
Free throws missed: Montgomery 5, Graham, Walther, Burris 2, Groza, and Barker 2.

From the *Courier-Journal*, March 15, 1949:

Inspired Loyola Stuns UK 67-56 in NIT
Bradley Topples Western From Meet 95-86
'Cats Hurt by Loss of Jones, Groza
All 4 Seeded Teams Lose As B.G. Rips St. Louis and San Francisco Nips Utah
By Larry Boeck, *Courier-Journal* Staff Writer.

New York, March 14. –Disappointing Kentucky was the victim of basketball's most fantastic and dramatic upset this afternoon as it crumpled 67-56 to Loyola of Chicago.

Considered as the only other certainty in life besides death, the first-seeded Wildcats were knocked out of the National Invitational Tournament by a poised and confident Loyola.

Few people here can believe yet what unfolded before their startled eyes in stunned Madison Square Garden.

The Wildcats loss added to the bleakness of the day here for bluegrass basketball fans. Western Kentucky bowed out of the tournament earlier in the afternoon, losing to Bradley 95-86.

Tonight's session saw the elimination of the other two seeded teams. San Francisco nosed out third-seeded Utah 64-63 on a basket in the last five seconds and Bowling Green toppled defending champion St. Louis 80-74.

Kentucky, seeking both the NIT and NCAA crowns and a prohibitive favorite to do it, staggered and reeled under the most punishing blows in basketball—the loss of key men via the foul route.

At the same time, the Wildcats were beaten at the free throw line. Although they tied Loyola on field goals with 21, they hit for just 14 of 22 free throws. Loyola provided its victory by linking 23 of 34. The difference was 11 important points, for Kentucky's margin of defeat was just – 11 points.

Wallace "Wah Wah" Jones, an aggressive inspirational leader, fouled out with 10:20 minutes to go and with Kentucky leading 47-46.

Approximately five minutes later, All-American Alex Groza fouled out. Inspired Loyola, gaining momentum, led 57-54 at the time in a nip-and-tuck game.

The departure of Groza, who scored 12 points in the first half but was blanked in the second, was the decisive wallop but it wasn't the last one for the fading, hard-pressed Kentuckians. The last of the three big men, Walter Hirsh, also left seconds later. Loyola had just a two-point lead—58-56—but it might as well have been 100.

Kentucky now could not get the rebounds. It was outmanned under the baskets and finally, outfought.

When it was all over, people streaming out of the Garden pinched themselves. What happened was unbelievable—a wild fantasy to neutral observers and a wild nightmare to Wildcat fans.

True, Kentucky was behind 31-32 at the half, principally because it could hit for seven of 15 free throws while Loyola was connecting on 14 of 16.

But that was just the first half. Surely, the champion Wildcats—the most acclaimed and power-laden basketball team of all time, it was said—would come back.

The Wildcats did, to no one's surprise, in the opening minutes of the second half. Jones sank a free throw to tie the score at 32. Ralph Beard, a plucky little guy who kept UK in the running, hit from out. Then Jones connected from the side.

Now it was Kentucky 36, Loyola 32. Yes, sir, this was it. The Wildcats were rolling. Loyola, a gallant and scrapping outfit, was fading.

It wasn't the case. It was, actually, the other way around. Jones and Groza both had four fouls on them, and Hirsh and Barnstable and Barker had their fair share of them.

So the Wildcats eased back.

Groza did not play his competing center, Jack Kerris, closely, but Kerris who turned in a brilliant performance with 23 points, also had four personals, all achieved in the first half. Still, he unleashed that spectacular hook shot of his. Groza, meanwhile, did not get the ball, although coaches yelled frantically from the bench for the boys to feed it to him.

The result was disaster for Kentucky. Kerris kept shooting; Groza, who played one of the poorest games of his career at Kentucky, fouled out.

After Groza left with five minutes to go, Kerris sank one free throw to push the fighting, poised and calm Loyola out front 58-56.

Cleric cashed a free throw and then Kerris came right back to hook in the clincher, the one that made it 61-56. Just three minutes were left, and Kentucky had Dale Barnstable, Cliff Barker, Roger Day, Jim Line and Ralph Beard in the game.

Outshot at the free throw line, a stale afternoon in firing from the field, the loss of Groza and Jones and an inspired, hard-working Loyola combined to beat the "unbeatables."

The Wildcats had a shooting percentage of 28.3; Loyola had 32.3.

Then there was the matter of the law of percentages. Victor in 21 straight games, the Wildcats were due for a poor effort.

Loyola gave the tip-off to what might happen—although few took it seriously—when it romped to a 4-0 lead. Kentucky charged back to lead 8-5, but Loyola tied it back at 9. From there, it was a close, tense battle.

The score was tied at 14, 16, 20, 25, 32, 37, 42 and 47.

The lead changed hands almost as much. Loyola led at 14-13, 17-16, 19-18, 24-23, 32-31 and 51-50.

Beard led Kentucky with 15, followed by Barker and Groza with 12.

Kentucky	**fg**	**ft**	**fta**	**pf**	**Pts**
Jones	2	2	3	5	6
Line	2	3	3	4	7
Barnstable	1	2	4	3	4
Hirsh	0	0	0	5	0
Groza	5	2	5	5	12
Day	0	0	0	2	0
Beard	6	3	3	1	15
Barker	5	2	4	4	12
Totals	**21**	**14**	**22**	**29**	**56**

Loyola					
Earle	3	3	4	3	9
O'Grady	0	1	2	2	1
Klaerich	1	5	5	2	7
Bluitt	3	3	4	0	9
Kerris	7	9	12	4	23
Dawson	1	0	0	1	2
Nicholl	1	3	3	2	5
Hildebrand	0	0	0	0	3
Nagel	5	1	4	3	11
Totals	**21**	**25**	**34**	**20**	**67**

Half time score: Loyola 32, Kentucky 31.
Free throws missed: Kentucky –Jones, Barnstable 2, Groza 3, Barker 2. Loyola –Bluitt, Kerris 3, Nagel 3, O'Grady.

From the *Courier-Journal*, March 15, 1949:

"Cats Were Flat" – Rupp
Kentucky Coach Has Hard Time Explaining Loss to Baffled New York Sportswriters
By Larry Boeck

New York, March 14—"What Happened?"

A sizeable group of New York sports writers, disbelief and bewilderment written in their faces, huddled outside the Kentucky dressing room to ask that question of Coach Adolph Rupp.

They themselves—the experts—did not trust even themselves to answer the question of how Loyola managed to upset Kentucky. What impressed you, when the interview got underway, was that they asked what happened to Kentucky, not how did Loyola do it.

Rupp, the rims of his eyes red, came to the door. The Wildcats, dressing in the background, were silent. There was only the splashing of water from the showers to be heard.

"We were flat, awful flat....That's all there was to it," said Rupp answering a question. "We didn't hit—not even the free throws. When you can't do that, you are going to be beat. And Loyola played well. They deserved the victory."

"What's that? Why were you flat?"

Rupp managed a wry smile, almost as if in sympathy for the interrogator. "Well, sir, I can't figure that out....I never could figure why teams go flat. You go out and get the answer to it and you'll get the academy award or whatever they give for basketball." There were hollow chuckles.

You had to admire the graying Kentucky Coach—disappointment deeply etched in his tired eyes, and face—for his poise, for his calm answers and occasional humor as he answered the volley of questions fired at him. You somehow felt that he, too, wondered what happened—and why it did when it did.

"Why didn't the boys feed the ball to Groza in the second half?" a reporter asked, relentlessly driving to see if there was an answer to one of basketball's most baffling questions.

"Jack Kerris had four fouls on him at the half, and it seemed logical that Groza would shoot and try to foul him out. Why didn't he get the ball?"

"That's another question I'd like answered," said Rupp.

"You mean you instructed the boys to feed him the ball?"

"Good Lord, man! Didn't you hear the whole bench yelling for the boys to do just that?" Rupp shot back.

Chapter Fourteen

Big Bill's Big Trouble

As the year 1951 drew to a close, many basketball fans in Kentucky and Indianapolis hoped the bad news would also close with it. Coach Rupp would have to begin his season with this star center, Bill Spivey, hobbled from his knee problems. The Olympians would try to carry on, but without their two star players, Ralph Beard and Alex Groza, they would be no factor in the NBA. In fact, the franchise would only last two more struggling seasons before folding after the 1952-53 campaign.

In the on-going point shaving scandal, not much appeared to be happening on the surface, but things were boiling behind the scenes. New York ADA Vincent O'Conner was not through with the University of Kentucky. O'Conner had visited with Kentucky's Governor Lawrence Wetherby sometime during the summer and, without publicly naming names, revealed that he "had the goods" on three additional UK players. O'Conner, who would not even say if the ones he was after were current or former players, wanted to question the three in private. Because he could not get their attorney's permission to do so, and as Wetherby was the Chairman of UK's Board of Trustees, O'Conner sought the Governor's help. Wetherby referred the matter to UK's President Herman Lee Donovan. Dr. Donovan, a huge supporter of his schools' athletic teams, was prone to stonewall the New Yorker's efforts and that fact may be the reason the players had sought a lawyer's protection.

In mid-December following a return trip to Frankfort by O'Conner, he allowed the *New York Times* to break the story. According to the *Times*, Wetherby said that if "the New York authorities were able to supply 'conclusive evidence' that any Kentucky player had been guilty of a disloyal act, he would favor action by the University that would prevent the player from participating in basketball in the future."[280] The newspaper quoted O'Conner as saying that the testimony of the three players was needed as proof that a bribe was paid in the latest "fix." Interestingly, O'Conner offered that the players, "would not be prosecuted as there was no sports bribery law in Kentucky."[281] Governor Wetherby decided to remedy that situation.

Rupp's 'Cats, pre-season rated number one based solely on having Spivey, Hagan and Ramsey on the floor (sound familiar?) had easily dispatched their first two opponents and then lost a close one at lightly-regarded Minnesota. Still atop the polls, they took the floor in Memorial Coliseum on December 17 against number two rated and unbeaten St. John's under a cloud of speculation about what would happen with UK's players. Amid the hype of the clash of the two top rated teams, hints began to surface that ailing Bill Spivey was one of the three on O'Conner's hit list.[282] In the swirl of controversy, the fact that the Wildcats embarrassed the Redmen 81-40 to log their 100th consecutive win on the home floor, seemed almost an afterthought.

A week later, Bill Spivey shocked the Big Blue Nation when he announced that he was voluntarily suspending himself from UK's basketball team "until I am cleared of any suspicion in connection with the current collegiate basketball scandal." In an open letter to President Donovan, Spivey said that he requested this action because he understood that he was the only member of the present team that "the New York District Attorney's office desires to question and I wish to stop the vicious rumors being circulated in regard to my teammates and to remove any suspicion from them." Using the letter as a forum, Spivey denied that he had ever been involved in fixing a basketball game, "in New York or any other state," and also denied that he "had any knowledge of point shaving that would be of any value to the New York authorities, or authorities of any other state, in the prosecution of gamblers or basketball players."[283] Donovan, UK's Dean of Men (and former football coach) A.D. Kirwan and Spivey's attorney, John Y. Brown Sr., were the men who advised the player to forgo his eligibility.[284] There have always been questions about just what their motives were and how "voluntarily" Spivey agreed. However that may be, the fact is that Spivey would never even don the UK uniform again. Spivey's action is made even more curious in view of O'Conner's offer of immunity.

On January 31, 1952, Nickolas and Anthony Englisis and Nathaniel Brown appeared before Judge Saul Streit in New York's General Sessions Court and withdrew their original "not guilty" pleas. Nick Englisis, painted by ADA O'Conner as the major figure in the fixing of college games involving Bradley University and the University of Kentucky, pleaded guilty to one count of bribery to cover the four indictments pending against him. The other two men pled guilty to lesser charges. All three were to reappear for sentencing on March 4 when Nick "The Greek" would face a possible $10,000 fine and up to five years in prison.[285]

Back in Frankfort, Governor Wetherby had been busy. On February 14, he signed into law a bill making fixing any amateur or professional sports event a crime in the Commonwealth of Kentucky.[286] Aside from a public relations gesture, that measure seemed to have small value (although it brings to mind one of my grandmother's favorite remarks concerning locking the barn door after the horse had been stolen.)

On the same day, the biggest news since the Kentucky players' involvement in the point shaving scandal broke when the March issue of True Magazine hit newsstands. The magazine contained an article entitled "How I Fixed Big-Time Basketball Games" authored by Nick Englisis, as told to Jimmy Breslin.

Englisis said that he was just "a small-time guy with big-time ideas," and that his goal in telling all was that "if coaches and college presidents know the details, they will be able to prevent bribery from corrupting their teams." He revealed that as a football player at UK in 1944 (when Kirwan was coach) and 1945 (Shively) he became acquainted with Alex Groza, Ralph Beard and Dale Barnstable. In the fall of 1948, Nick claimed, he and his brother, Tony, met, on UK's campus, with Beard and Groza, who were just back from the Olympics trip. Asked about the trip, according to Englisis, Beard snapped, "It was lousy. They gave me a fancy blue cardigan and white duck pants to wear—like I was a kid graduating from high school. They should have cut out that stuff and handed us some money...."[287]

Then, Englisis went on, Groza chimed in. "Money? Yeah, I sure made a lot of money out of all the headlines I made in England. I couldn't buy a beer with the dough I got in the Olympics." After stating he knew that Groza was aware that he (Nick) bet on games, Englisis implied that it was Groza who suggested that he and Beard might accept a bribe to shave points. "'Nick,' Groza continued, 'you're around New York a lot. You must know a guy someplace who can make some money for us. It's my last year here and my last chance to cash in on some basketball. I'm serious.'"[288]

Englisis said that he then returned to his home in Brooklyn and soon hooked up with friends Saul Feinberg and Nat Brown, who he said "knew the shady side of basketball." A few days after Brown was dispatched to Kentucky to negotiate with Groza, he reported back that Groza, Beard and Barnstable were willing to "do business." The fixers agreed to pay the players $100 for an "over" and $300 for an "under." The fixers would pick the game and agreed to let the players decide if they wanted to go over or under.[289]

For starters, Englisis says he chose Kentucky's game against DePaul in Louisville on December 8, 1948. Groza informed him that they'd go over. According to Englisis, Groza said that Beard was more willing to go over and Barnstable would go along with whatever the other two decided. On the phone, Groza said, "Man, will the little guy (Beard) go wild when I tell him this!" Englisis bet $250 with three different Brooklyn bookies that Kentucky would go over the 15 point spread published by the odds makers. After UK murdered DePaul 67-36, Englisis claimed he collected his winnings and, as agreed, paid Groza, Barnstable and Beard $100 each. This scenario was repeated for UK's games against Notre Dame, St. John's, Tulane, Vanderbilt and a return game with DePaul during December 1948 and January 1949. Nat Brown handled all the details, including the pay-offs, always meeting the players off campus.[290]

Englisis stated that he traveled to Lexington to be on hand for the rivalry match with Tennessee in February. Groza came to his room in the Phoenix Hotel the night before the game to say he wanted more money, so they'd go under against the Volunteers. Groza assured that he could talk Beard into shaving the points. "We'll be under Nick, don't worry." The 'Cats, favored by 18, won the game by 15, 71-56. Nick said he received a check for his $8,000 winnings and paid the players their $300 each.[291] It's difficult to imagine these transactions being paid by check!

Now, in March 1949, on to the NIT in Madison Square Garden where there was "some real money to be made". Englisis says the fixers headquartered at Hotel Paramount, where the teams stayed. Groza,

Barnstable and Beard came to the fixers' room, where Englisis offered them $500 each to go under against Loyola. Groza bragged that they'd go under in every tournament game and said, "This is where I make a killing." Englisis noticed that he didn't say "we," but the other two players did not take note of his pronoun usage. On his way out the door, Ralph Beard said, "…this will bust up my old man's 'make your money the hard way' lectures." Nick reports that Groza was back, alone, in a flash. He informed the fixers that he was "the big boy" and, as the game could not be fixed without his cooperation, he wanted an additional $500 and his teammates kept ignorant of the fact that Groza was to receive additional money. The fixers had no choice but to agree. With the fix in place, they bet $6,000 that Loyola would come closer than the 11-point spread.[292]

Watching from the stands as Loyola surged ahead, Englisis says he observed that Groza realized that his chance to make big money through the rest of the tournament was slipping away, so he stepped up his play, only to foul out. The fixers noticed Beard and Barnstable tried to pick up the slack, but "then Beard fouled out and walked off the court chewing his gum like a piston. He sat down and kept his head on his chest. I guess he also was counting all the dough he lost." The fixers collected big money on the Loyola win.[293]

With Kentucky eliminated from the tournament, the fixers turned their attention to Bradley's players, fixing their games for the rest of the NIT, buying off Gene Melchiorre and his teammates in the same fashion. Despite the fix, Bradley did not manage to get under against Bowling Green, so the fixers lost a bundle.

Well, back to Groza and Beard for Kentucky's run in the NCAA tournament. Englisis reports that even though Kentucky was a 14 point favorite over Villanova, Beard and Barnstable were afraid they might lose again if they tried to go under. He figured "Beard was a little less hungry for quick money." Hurt by the Bradley fiasco, they bet all their remaining money, $3,000, on Kentucky winning by more than 14. The 'Cats won 85-72, "one lousy point under the spread." Englisis says all he had left at that point was "a crisp ten dollar bill."[294]

Nick Englisis then went into great detail about how he became involved with big-time gamblers and stepped up his operation for the next season. Those activities led to his eventual arrest and incarceration. Before he ended the article, he could not resist a few parting shots, including how high the bidding had gone for Alex Groza's services when he was entering college. "One day he turned up on the Kentucky campus with a new car. I know he didn't buy it with pennies from his piggy bank."[295]

Ralph Beard and Alex Groza were quick to point out that Englisis' *True* story was not so true. Groza, back in Marin's Ferry and Beard, working in Louisville, both denied meeting with Englisis on UK's campus at any time, saying that their first contact with him was in New York in December 1948. "Englisis is nothing but a liar when he says I complained about the Olympic suit," Beard angrily declared. "Why, I'm prouder of having been in the Olympics than anything. It's been the thrill of my life and as for the suit, it's one of my most prized souvenirs...."[296]

Beard also derided the "quote" from his father about making money the hard way. "I've only seen my father three times since I was six years old," he declared. "We never talked about making money." As additional proof that the story was all lies, Beard pointed out (correctly) that he did not foul out of the Loyola game.[297]

Groza saw inconsistency in Englisis' claim that he (Groza) complained about not cashing in on his basketball fame while a bidding war was conducted for his services. "I didn't get anything promised but an athletic scholarship to go to UK," Groza said. "Yes, I had a lot of much better offers but I thought Coach Rupp could make a great player out of me." There was an inconsistency: Groza had previously said several times that UK's was the only offer he received coming out of high school. As for the car, "It was mine, and I paid for it. I borrowed a little over $1,000 from my brother Lou...."[298]

Alex Groza dismissed Englisis' entire statement. "That story is the greatest collection of lies I've ever heard. I never met Englisis at the Paramount Hotel...."[299]

At the same time, Adolph Rupp, with his 'Cats rated number one in the polls even without Bill Spivey, threatened to sue *Look Magazine* over a story in their January 29 issue entitled "How Basketball Players Are Bought." Written by *Look's* sports editor, Tim Cohane, the article begins by noting that Groza, Beard and Barnstable would soon stand trial and then quoting LIU's coach, Clair Bee, speaking at a clinic, criticizing Rupp's coaching. In losing to Loyola, Bee says, "He (Rupp) had the best ball club in the world, but he proved himself the worst coach."

When a reporter asked how the "worst coach" could have such a better record than himself, Bee snapped, "That's easy. We haven't the money to buy the horses." To prove the point, the magazine said that Rupp wanted a player named David Gotkin so badly that "Kentucky offered Gotkin everything except a half interest in Rupp's prize breeding bull, Domino."[300]

After describing the bidding wars for several players, Cohane took up the case of Tom Marshall, a six foot-four 200 pounder from Mt. Juliet, Tenn," who, after weighing all his offers, signed with Vanderbilt, making him off-limits to all other conference schools. "Rupp," declares Cohane, "worked openly to see that Tom got better offers from schools outside the SEC."[301]

Look then charged that Western Kentucky Coach Ed Diddle said that Rupp visited with Ralph Beard and Wallace Jones in their hotel room in Indianapolis the night before the 1945 Kentucky-Indiana High School All-Star game (Diddle coached the Kentuckians) in violation of NCAA rules.[302]

Coach Rupp demanded an apology and a retraction the day the magazine hit the streets. The newspaper write-up of Rupp's reaction reported that David Gotkin denied the "prize bull" comment and that Rupp was known, by two separate sources, to have been in Lexington the night he allegedly visited Beard and Jones in Indianapolis. It also said that Diddle denied making any statement about Rupp visiting Beard and Jones.[303]

Look responded with a letter to Louisville's WHAS radio station saying that the magazine was unconcerned. "In answer to your several questions: (a) we will definitely not print a retraction; (b) we do not anticipate any settlement out of court." A few days later, Rupp filed a suit in Lexington's U.S. District Court seeking $250,000 from the magazine for libel, which damaged his "reputation as a coach and a businessman."[304]

Look then asked the court to dismiss the suit, pointing out that the publisher, Cowles Magazines, Inc. was an Iowa corporation and hence "not subject to suit or to service of summons within the territorial limits of the State of Kentucky." Additionally, Cowles said it had no agent or office in Kentucky, had never done business in the state and there was "no cause of action alleged in the suit arising out of or connected with doing business in Kentucky."[305]

A lot of paperwork flew back and forth, but, in the end, the suit eventually came to nothing. On February 2, 1954, United States District Judge Church Ford dismissed it for "lack of jurisdiction."[306] As the saying goes, nobody wins but the lawyers.

The Wildcats, rated number one for most of the season, ended their year with a 57-64 loss to St. John's in the NCAA regional final at Raleigh, NC. The loss brought their record to a quite respectable 29 wins and 3 losses, not bad considering that All-American Bill Spivey had not played a minute or even suited up. What was going on with Spivey? the fans wondered. He'd been seen walking around campus without crutches and—despite the still-swirling rumors—had been charged with no crime. Soon the newspapers took up the cry: Why hadn't the University reinstated his eligibility?

Chapter Fifteen

THE EDICT

Of the select few who knew why Bill Spivey's eligibility had not been reinstated, UK President Herman Lee Donovan was the man on the hot seat. Because Governor Wetherby had involved him in New York ADA Vincent O'Conner's quest, Donovan knew that the three UK players O'Conner wanted to interview were Spivey and former players Walt Hirsh and Jim Line. While Spivey complained that he was being victimized and appealed for reinstatement and the public demanded to know why the All-American remained on the sidelines, Donovan, the man from whom answers were demanded, was pledged to silence.

In the spring of 1952, Donovan did not know that New York Assistant District Attorney O'Conner, at the behest of his boss, Frank Hogan, had located Walt Hirsh (who played for the 'Cats from 1947 through 1951) in his hometown of Dayton, Ohio and instituted extradition proceedings to bring him to New York to testify before a Grand Jury concerning his involvement with two fixers who were under indictment. Rather than wait for the papers to go through, Hirsh voluntarily flew to New York and testified that in the 1949-50 season, after Beard and Groza were gone, Dale Barnstable recruited him and Jim Line to shave points. Hirsh admitted that the three of them had accepted $500 each to go under the spread against DePaul on December 21, 1949 in Louisville (Kentucky won 49-47) and $1,000 each against Arkansas at Little Rock January 2, 1950.[307] UK won that one 57-53. As neither of those games was played in the State of New York, Hogan and O'Conner had no jurisdiction and could not touch the players, which is why they sought Wetherby's and Donovan's help. Post fact, O'Conner praised both Governor Wetherby and President Donovan as "sincere leaders and fine citizens." At the same time he disparaged their management of UK's athletic programs: "...In their enthusiasm for successful intercollegiate athletic competition...put an unfounded emphasis on victory and developed amateur sports into a big-time promotion," raved O'Conner.

Bill Spivey, assured that O'Conner only wanted his testimony against the fixers, agreed to go to New York to testify provided that his attorney be allowed to accompany him. Hogan didn't like the idea much, but agreed, so late in February, Spivey, his attorney Elmer Drake and UK's Dean of Men, A.D. Kirwan, traveled to the Big Apple. In what must have been some kind of a behind the scenes deal, Hogan allowed Kirwan to examine Hirsh's (secret) Grand Jury testimony in the DA's office. The Dean learned, and hurried to report to Donovan, that Hirsh told the Grand Jury that Spivey was involved in a conspiracy with Hirsh and Line to fix the Sugar Bowl game December 29, 1950. In a shocker, UK lost that game to St. John's 43-42.[308] That game, too, was beyond Hogan's purview.

At the same time Spivey arrived in New York, Ralph Beard, Dale Barnstable and Alex Groza were appearing before Judge Streit in General Sessions Court. They admitted they had conspired with gamblers to fix the game against Loyola in Madison Square Garden and pleaded guilty to a charge of conspiracy—a misdemeanor—to cover a two-count indictment that included a felony charge of accepting a bribe. In entering his plea, Ralph Beard told the court, "I took their money and I never did a thing to impact the outcome of a game. If taking the money makes me guilty, then I'm guilty."[309] Facing fines and prison terms, the three were scheduled for sentencing on March 28.[310] When that date rolled around, the Judge postponed sentencing until April 29.

On March 2, following Spivey's appearance before the Grand Jury, speaking for his client, attorney Drake told the press, "Bill came here to clear his name and as far as I'm concerned, he did. I can see no reason why the school will not permit him to play in the NCAA tournament."[311]

UK's athletic board saw reason, though. And, Hirsh's revelation solved Dr. Donovan's problem. Although Dr. Donovan was probably still pledged to silence, that same afternoon in response to this new information, the University's athletic board permanently barred Bill Spivey from participation on any of its teams. "Spivey's stout denial of this brings this evidence into issue," said the press release. "The board would have preferred to reserve judgment on this issue until it can be properly evaluated in the courts...."[312] So, there was no need to wait for proof, the accusation was good enough for the University of Kentucky officials.

Despite Spivey's adamant denials, when ADA O'Conner confronted him with evidence that he had, indeed, been approached by a fixer while employed at a Catskill's Mountains resort in the summer of 1949, Spivey admitted an encounter with a man who called himself "George." The man's name was actually Eli Klukofsky, aka Eli Kaye, an associate of Nick Englisis and Nat Brown. Spivey later said that he came to understand that a lot of the fixing took place in those resorts where many college players spent their summers. Spivey testified that "George" had told him that he might as well go along because his teammates were involved, gave him a couple of names and offered him $500 per game, but Spivey insisted that he had said "nothing doing." Then, sometime in October, Spivey continued, George showed up at his UK dorm room. Before he could make an offer, Spivey threw him out. "I didn't report those two attempted fixes because it would have affected my teammates and I wanted to protect them whether it was true or not—and I was sure it was not true—so I thought it best to just forget about it." But he didn't just forget it. After he returned to school in the fall, "I asked the teammate (presumably Hirsh) if he knew such a fellow and he said he didn't, although he looked a little startled when I mentioned the name. I told this teammate that "George" had mentioned knowing him and another teammate (Line) and he turned colors. I sort of suspected something then…."[313]

Spivey reported that O'Conner did not believe his sworn testimony and "insisted that I had accepted money to shave points against St. Louis in the 1950 Sugar Bowl." After O'Conner told him that he'd "see to it that he never played professional basketball" unless he confessed, Spivey shot back, "I was not approached by anyone to throw that game and I received no money from anyone. I certainly did everything I could to help the team win."[314]

As the New York DA had nothing other than Hirsh's and Line's accusations to balance against Spivey's unyielding denials and the game in question took place in Louisiana, Hogan and O'Conner had no choice to but let Spivey alone until they could come up with something else. Asked if Spivey's testimony cleared the player, O'Conner testily replied, "No comment. Gambling activities concerning Kentucky's games are still being inquired into."[315] Vincent O'Conner certainly sounded like a man with a mission.

Finally, the big day arrived for Barnstable, Groza and Beard. On April 29, 1952, the trio showed up for New York County's Court of General Sessions nattily attired and prepared to hear the court's sentence. The players sat quietly and unemotional through what was surely an ordeal as the Judge loosed his full barrage on the University of Kentucky's athletic programs in general and Coach Adolph Rupp in particular before he got around to the players.[316]

In a sixty-three page document (18 of which are devoted to Rupp) that took 80 minutes to read, Judge Streit began with an overall indictment: "I found that intercollegiate football and basketball at the University of Kentucky have been highly commercialized and systematized, allows covert subsidization of players, ruthless exploitation of athletes, cribbing at examinations, illegal recruiting, a reckless disregard of their physical welfare, matriculation of unqualified students, demoralization of athletes by the coach, alumni and townspeople and the most flagrant abuse of the athletic scholarship...." He then blasted UK's basketball and football programs as "the acme of commercialism and over-emphasis" and urged all colleges to "rid themselves of the disintegrating influences of money mad athletics" and to "eliminate the vices and evils existing in intercollegiate sports." In pointing up the over-emphasis, Judge Streit observed that UK spent money "far in excess of the normal and average costs of the operation and maintenance of a first rate *professional* football or basketball team."[317] (my emphasis.)

Specifically, he charged that UK:

1. Spent $107,000 on its basketball program in 1951, only $25,000 less than a professional team.
2. "Encouraged and tolerated 'cribbing'" by Groza, Beard and Barnstable.
3. Allowed "unqualified" students to enroll in school via athletic scholarships.
4. Used athletic scholarships as "barter and trade"...to give "so-called education" in exchange for four years of service for football or basketball.
5. Subsidized athletes in violation of amateur rules.
6. Allowed coaches, alumni and townspeople to contribute to "demoralizing" the athletes.[318]

If Judge Streit was still around to learn that, according to a *Courier-Journal* report, UK spent $342,716 on the use of private jets for Coach Calipari in the 2013-14 fiscal year, the shock might kill him.[319]

The Judge then hammered hard at his last two points. Citing the Grand Jury testimony of the players and Rupp (although no one knew that the Coach had testified or when), he charged that after each game the players received "$5 or $10 from Rupp if the coach thought he had played well" and an occasional $50 bonus. Additionally, the Judge revealed that Ralph Beard had received "$40 or $50 a month from Lexington druggist Owen Williams during the 1947-48 season," and that Groza was given a "job" by Lexington warehouse owner Owen Campbell. The job, which allowed Groza to "come in when he felt like it," paid $50 per month. Streit said that when Barnstable was asked if he received money when they lost, he told the Grand Jury, "No, sir. We'd be lucky to get something to eat." Barnstable also testified that after the Sugar Bowl game in January 1949, "Rupp came back and gave me the devil" over a missed shot, informing the player that his miss "cost (Rupp's) friend Burgess Carey $500."[320]

When the Grand Jury asked, Streit said, Coach Rupp admitted that he knew about Beard's and Groza's "jobs,"[321] but did not know if they were required to perform any services and that, following some games, he had, indeed, handed out $50 to each player in "left over money raised for the Olympic trip".

Thus vented on the program, the Judge warmed to his task as he turned his attention to Adolph Rupp. For his opening salvo, Streit described Rupp's demeanor: "His overbearing manner and 'it pays to win' policy mark him as foreman of a hard driven working squad rather than a teacher and an inspirational force worthy of the institution he represented."[322]

Next, the Judge examined Rupp's association with Lexington bookie Ed Curd. Rupp admitted having visited at Curd's home and explained that Curd, who was simply a bookie, not a gambler or a crook, often contributed to Rupp's efforts to raise money for the local Shiners' hospital. The Judge brought out Beard's testimony that Curd had dinner at the table with him, Rupp, UK Athletic Director Bernie Shively and "Happy" Chandler, former Kentucky Senator and Governor and then Commissioner of Major League Baseball at New York's famed Copacabana Restaurant. "Who paid the check?" the Judge wanted to know.

"I don't know," Rupp, who was known to be mighty tight with a dollar, replied, "I didn't."[323]

Testimony then revealed that Rupp often called Curd to learn the point spread on games and shared that information with his team before the games. Rupp admitted to that and said that he used the point spread as a motivational factor. Groza remembered an occasion when Rupp said, "I just called Curd and got the points. We are favored by 15. Now these guys will be tough, so let's really pour it on."[324] The Judge opined that Rupp had "failed in his duty to observe the amateur rules, to build character and to protect the morals and health of his charges," and thus both he and the University "must share in the responsibility for the plight of the three defendants as well as two other former members of Kentucky's team who have admitted accepting bribes to shave points".[325]

Having expended so much energy on that barrage, Judge Streit disposed of the players very quickly. As he had done for the LIU, Bradley and Manhattan and other players who had cooperated with the DA's investigations, he handed each of them a three-year suspended prison term and an indefinite probationary period.[326] The three players left the courtroom with crushed spirits.

As you might well imagine, Judge Streit's opinions played to mixed reactions in Lexington. From the Governor's office, Lawrence Wetherby side-stepped by proclaiming that "whether Coach Adolph Rupp will be asked to answer Judge Saul S. Streit's scathing criticism of him will be up to the University of Kentucky's athletic board…." The Governor did note that the news was no surprise to him as "the information disclosed in the past few days is what I received from Mr. O'Conner when he came to Frankfort."[327]

Dr. Donovan was out of town and could not be reached for comment. A.D. Kirwan, however, was on hand, but had no immediate statement. "Judge Streit had four months in which to prepare his opinions," Kirwan noted, "I feel the University should have at least a few days before commenting." Kirwan, UK's Dean of Men, who was deeply involved in the school's dealings with the New York authorities, also evaded answering whether Rupp would have to answer to school officials concerning Streit's charges of his violating amateur rules. Instead, he told reporters that Streit sent a long questionnaire to UK several months prior inquiring into several matters, including athletic recruiting and finances. Kirwan said that the athletic department did not want to answer the questions, but at the Dean's insistence, the questions were answered completely and forwarded to the Judge.[328] That would explain where Streit got his information on how much money UK spent on basketball.

Members of the athletic board were a bit less circumspect. "I do not believe that any one of the charges is justifiable," declared Dr. T.V. Terrell, Dean of the College of Engineering. "The board goes about its business very carefully and everything is done on the up and up."

A board member who was associated with Rupp's pending lawsuit against *Look Magazine* (probably William Townsend) challenged Streit. "I dare Judge Streit to come down to Rupp's hearing and testify to what he said today as not a word of it is admissible in court."[329]

Another board member who asked not to be identified addressed Streit's contention that athletes were allowed "cribbing." "It would be utterly fantastic to believe that any University official would condone such procedures."[330]

As concerned the issue of Burgess Carey's $500 loss, opinions were also mixed about exactly who said what. Carey himself, a member of some of Rupp's early teams and currently a Lexington building contractor, was amused. "There's some gross exaggeration somewhere. I rarely bet, and when I do, it's for small amounts. No, no it's not anywhere near $500."[331]

"I never saw any $50 bill," said a former player. "We usually got $5 after a game to eat and maybe go to a movie." He reported that after the Notre Dame game (in Chicago, UK won 71-66) Rupp had given each player $25 and said, "I want you to know that I'm proud of you. The season is over now. Here's some money to go out and have the biggest steak dinner you can find.... Go out and enjoy yourselves, you deserve it."[332] That comment makes little sense in view of the fact that the game was played on February 2, 1951—the middle of the season, not the end.

On the same day all this news hit the papers, ADA O'Conner announced that Bill Spivey had been indicted for perjury and a warrant was issued for the player's arrest. O'Conner maintained that Spivey had lied to the New York County Grand Jury during his testimony on February 27 when he said that he'd never accepted money to fix a game. In Lexington, Spivey, after conferring with his attorney, said he would make himself available as soon as the necessary paperwork arrived and continued to protest his innocence. "I still maintain my former position. If the other guys (Line and Hirsh) got money, I don't know anything about it. I certainly didn't get any."[333] If convicted, this charge could bring the player a five-year prison term or a $5,000 fine, or both. Interestingly, O'Conner said not one word about any of the fixers he had under his thumb implicating Spivey, which would certainly lead one to believe that they did not. It is difficult to find any justification, other than vindictiveness, for his indicting Spivey for perjury. How would sending Spivey to prison help convict the fixers?

Here's the *Courier-Journal's* write up of the game in question in Spivey's case:

ST. LOUIS SLIDES BY KENTUCKY IN OVERTIME
43-42 IN SUGAR
By Larry Boeck Staff Writer

New Orleans, La., Dec. 29 – The Sugar Bowl was filled only with bitterness for Kentucky Wildcats (sic) once again here tonight.

The battling St. Louis Billikins of Coach Ed Hickey blasted Kentucky from the ranks of the undefeated in a pulsating overtime 43-42.

It was Kentucky's first loss in seven games. And once again it was Hickey, "the spoiler," who ruined the Wildcats' hopes of winning the Sugar Bowl crown. Just two years ago, Hickey's Billikins, underdogs then as now, upset the "fabulous four" in the Sugar Bowl.

Cats Turned Cold

Kentucky turned cold in the last 16 minutes of the game and of the overtime collecting just five points in that frigid period. And the aroused Billikins, meanwhile, twice staved off what seemed to be certain defeat.

The teams fought a tense, tight first half, and they went into the dressing room knotted at 22-22.

Kentucky, however, began to sprint away in the opening minutes of the second half. It led by what looked to be a big nine points after eight minutes of this canto – 28-37.

However, St. Louis, a team glutted with courage, fought back valiantly. Slowly but surely it chiseled down the Kentucky lead.

The Billikins, with about two minutes left, took the lead at 39-38 but Kentucky went back out in front 41-39 on a free throw by Spivey and a bucket by the big guy.

With just one minute to play now, Kentucky froze the ball. However, Walt Hirsh, who with 20 seconds to go, threw the ball away and Ed Scott tied it up amid the tumult of 7,000.

Only one basket was scored in the overtime, a follow-up by Ray Sonnenberg with two minutes left. Spivey cashed a free throw. Walt Hirsh then missed two, and it was over.

High for Kentucky was Spivey with 16 points. Sonnenberg had 12 and Scott 11 for St. Louis.

Kentucky's cause was severely damaged when the dashing Frank Ramsey fouled out with five minutes of regulation play remaining. Ramsey had accrued 12 points, and he turned in a terrific game both on the floor and boards.

Refused to Crack

St. Louis tonight was a team of great spirit and relentless determination. It refused to crack when Kentucky hauled to a nine point margin, and its defense was tight throughout.

In the last quarter, for instance, Kentucky could get but five shots and one field goal. Meanwhile, Bob Koch was doing a good job of guarding Spivey, too.

In the Sugar Bowl opener tonight, Bradley had a tough time defeating Syracuse but pulled away 75-64 in the game's closing minutes.

Saturday night, Bradley will play St. Louisville (sic) and Kentucky will meet Syracuse in the consolation game.

Some hot Billiken shooting late in the half threatened to send Kentucky to the dressing room with a deficit. However, the 'Cats pulled even at 20-20 on Spivey's fielder and free throw and finished even with the Bills in the final minute.

Two Men On Spivey

Kentucky's game was hurt badly by Spivey's inability to get at the boards. With Koch in back of him and Sonnenberg in front, the big center was blocked out.

The lead changed hands nine times in this tense first half and was tied three times.

St. Louis took a 23-22 lead on a free throw, but Kentucky stormed back. Spivey's two free throws and a bat in and two fielders by Ramsey sent the Cats out front 30-25.

Hit Long Shot

Watson hit a set shot from out and now it's 32-25 – a lead of seven. The margin was boosted to eight on Hirsh's free throw, but Russell also cashed a charity toss for the Billikins.

Sonnenberg then hit a push, but Linville countered for Kentucky with a crip.

Watson again came through with a long shot to give Kentucky a nine point lead at 37-28. By now, Kentucky seemed to have reassembled its forces. Kentucky had lost its timing and smoothness after the slowdown of the game early when St. Louis employed a double post.

The Wildcats were dominating the boards now, too. Their fast break was working, and that brilliant Ramsey was maintaining his hot pace of the first half. When the third quarter ended – tonight's game was divided into quarters – Kentucky led 37-29 when Scott closed the quarter by sinking a free one.

Ranked No. 2 in the nation, Bradley had all it could handle for more than 30 minutes against sharp-shooting Syracuse.

Although Syracuse led only twice in the game, 3-2 and 42-41, the New Yorkers had the game tied up almost a dozen times but it was Bradley's general ball-handling finesse that turned a close game into a six point victory.

St. Louis	**fg**	**ft**	**pf**
Scott	5	1	1
Sonnenberg	5	2	2
Koch	2	0	5
Kovar	3	2	1
Steiner	1	1	1
Russell	1	1	1
McKenna	0	0	0
Gardiner	0	0	2
Lillis	1	0	2
Totals	**18**	**7**	**15**

Kentucky	**fg**	**ft**	**pf**
Hirsh	1	2	0
Linville	1	0	4
Spivey	4	8	1
Ramsey	5	2	5
Watson	4	0	1
Whitaker	0	0	1
Lansaw	0	0	1
Totals	**15**	**12**	**13**

Chapter Sixteen

Damned Yankees

Fallout from Judge Streit's opinions shook the Commonwealth from center to circumference. What that New Yorker had said was the topic of conversation around every water cooler, in every drug store and around the stove in every country store. And the consensus was, "Who the hell is he to criticize our beloved Wildcats?" While Coach Rupp had wisely decided to wait for some direction from the University, in speaking to the Winchester Kiwanis Club on April 30, he said that he was "willing for the citizens of Kentucky to be the judge" of his conduct.[334] Asked about Streit's recommendation for "de-emphasis," Rupp replied, "I'm a little tired of this de-emphasis business. Do they want de-emphasis on ability in sports, spectator interest or winning games?" With a sly grin, the Coach added, "I'm in favor of deemphasizing de-emphasis."[335] Pressed for a reply to Streit's blast, Rupp simply informed the press, "The only statement to be made will coming from Dr. Donovan's office."[336]

The current UK basketball team was quick to spring to their Coach's defense. In a statement released, "to protect ourselves and let the public know the truth," the players declared, "We feel Judge Streit's statements, besides being unfair to the present team, Coach Rupp, the University and all the people of Kentucky, are simply not true...." They also denied that Rupp ever discussed point spreads and that they received any money beyond what the scholarships allowed. Additionally, they said that their classroom attendance and performance was closely monitored and pointed out that the basketball team's academic standing was higher than for the school's men in general. Finally, they adamantly denied that the coaches, "ever sacrificed the physical welfare" of their athletes.[337]

In Chicago, the American Council on Education and the NCAA both called for an investigation into UK's programs.[338] The NCAA's statement said that Judge Streit's "indictment" was "of sufficient importance to prompt…an inquiry into the athletic policy and practices at the University of Kentucky."[339] Five days later, President Donovan locked the barn door again (as Grandma would say) by sending a telegram to the NCAA inviting an investigation. After informing that Judge Streit had attacked the integrity not only of Coach Rupp, but also UK's "administrative officials, alumni, trustees and faculty," the telegram "respectfully requested" that at its earliest convenience, "the NCAA send to our campus representatives to investigate the truth of these charges." Similar messages went to the SEC offices and the Southern Association of Colleges and Secondary Schools.[340]

While UK's President Donovan and New York's ADA O'Conner praised each other publically, the animosity between these two and Judge Streit ran deep. Donovan, who would brook no criticism of his beloved athletic programs, plotted with his ally, Happy Chandler, seeking some way to get back at Judge Streit and the New York DA's office. "We are outraged at the Judge's attempts to smear the university, its officials and coaches," raved Chandler.[341] When Donovan's efforts to procure the FBI's file on Streit failed, he asked his friend Harry Byrd, President of the University of Maryland for any derogatory material he could dig up on Streit. Byrd had the good judgment to advise Donovan to let it go, but Donovan rejected that advice and pressed UK's law school with the ludicrous idea of attempting to make a case for judicial misconduct.[342]

In response to all the criticism of Kentucky's athletics, football Coach Paul Bryant announced that he would try to "eliminate the evils attendant upon recruiting" by allowing no more than five non-Kentuckians on his team. "We have confidence in the ability of Kentucky boys to stand toe-to-toe with those of neighboring states," said Bryant.[343] His call for other schools to follow suit lasted about as long as the idea did at Kentucky.

On May 29, the Southeastern Conference executive committee announced that it had directed Commissioner Bernie Moore to launch a "complete and thorough" investigation into Kentucky's athletic programs.[344] Moore responded that the investigation would be "fair and impartial" and would not consider the fixing cases already adjudicated unless some reason to do so was uncovered.[345]

On the home front, things simmered down as May gave way to June and everyone waited, but Kentucky and Rupp came in for some additional national criticism for their response—or lack of it—to Streit's attack. "The official Kentucky answer was no answer at all. It even begged the issue on one point by saying that Judge Streit had failed to be critical of organized gambling in New York..." said the *New York Times*.[346] In the *Washington Post*, Shirley Povich was vicious. "When the Kentucky educators do come up with an answer, it ought to be an interesting one, explaining why and how they were so blind to the filthy goings-on, in which not only the players but Coach Rupp openly consorted with the gambling scum...."[347] Referencing Rupp's comment about point shaving being different from throwing games (made before he knew his players were involved), Povich noted that "The difference is that the basketball players didn't have to lose games to carry out their part of the fix.... In Rupp's view, it is only a slight case of conspiracy, apparently."[348] A Kansas City sports writer reported that he had talked with "several college men all of whom expressed surprise that Rupp had not resigned...and each expressed the opinion that he should."[349] From Atlanta, the *Journal's* Ed Danforth, a UK alumnus, said that Rupp should take his doctor's advice and "go back to his registered cattle and live in peace" as he could easily "clear up the whole matter by resigning."[350] Anyone who thought that Rupp would voluntarily retire or that Donovan would fire him did not know either man very well or understand the dynamics that drove Kentucky basketball.

On May 6, 1952, the University of Kentucky finally released its official response to Judge Streit's opinions and, as *The Washington Post* and others had predicted, it was indeed interesting. In what was termed a "preliminary statement" University officials "pledged to make such reforms in our athletic programs" as would make such scandals impossible in the future, but quickly noted "our policies will not be dictated by Judge Streit."[351] To drive that point home, the report noted that "... Much of Judge Streit's statement reflects only his personal opinions, based on meager and sometimes erroneous information....." Furthermore, the damned Yankee Judge had 'way overstepped his bounds, too. "...It was totally unnecessary to the accomplishment of the purposes of the court for him to attempt to shake the confidence of the people of Kentucky in the entire structure of their university." And, UK's officials also noted that the New Yorkers had failed to take their share of the blame, as in the entire 63-page document, "...not one reference is made to the organized gambling in New York and the criminals that produced this scandal." Judge Streit also failed to affix any responsibility to "those who have tolerated the unsavory environment in which Madison Square Garden operates." And, in that regard, "University administrators and coaches have erred in several respects, but one of their greatest errors was in ever permitting a basketball team to play in Madison Square Garden."[352] So there!

As for themselves, "For what has happened in respect to basketball, the administrative officials and the athletics staff are partially responsible and they are ready to acknowledge that responsibility." Fine, but be that as it may, they observed, there was still plenty of culpability left to go around. "But the blame for the tragic events of the past few months does not rest completely on any group or individual. It must be shared by the public that persists in gambling and in protecting gamblers, by over-zealous alumni, real and synthetic, who place athletic victories above all other considerations, by radio stations, newspapers and magazines which feature college sports out of all proportion to their importance and by college and university administrative officials and coaches throughout the land."[353]

Turning to specifics, the report addressed several of Streit's points:

1. "Streit attributes the athletic scandal at Kentucky to 'the inordinate desire by the trustees and alumni…for prestige and profit from sports.' The University of Kentucky Athletic Association is a non-profit agency…. The desire for winning teams is not a characteristic peculiar to the alumni of Kentucky."
2. As for unqualified students on athletic scholarships, Nicholas Englisis and Walter Hirsh in particular, "this statement was based on an erroneous remark made to him (Streit) by Dean Kirwan who did not know that an earlier admissions rule had been changed in 1943." Englisis had ranked 219th in his high school class of 230 students and was awarded a football scholarship during the war when players were scarce.[354]
3. In response to the Judge's "cribbing" accusations, the report pointed out that, as Beard, Barnstable and Groza had reported, they were allowed to make up examinations missed while the team was traveling. "They were permitted, in some cases, to take the same exam which had been previously given to the class," thereby creating the possibility "to converse with other students"

concerning the "nature of the exam." This same practice applied to non-athletes who missed an exam for legitimate reasons and, "sometimes the faculty's member's trust was betrayed."

4. To the charge that Rupp discussed point spreads with his team, the board pointed out that, "This information was published in every metropolitan newspaper in the land for all who were interested to read." Additionally, the athletics board could "appreciate that Coach Rupp (and others) would use this information to stir their team to greater efforts."
5. Lexington bookie Ed Curd was "not a member of Rupp's party," so his presence at Rupp's table in a nightclub was merely "a coincidence as Curd only called for a short time at Rupp's table." Rupp's visits to Curd's home "were for the purpose of securing contributions to the Shrine Crippled Children's Hospital (remember PC hadn't been invented yet.) While we certainly do not condone even a causal relationship between a university employee and a professional gambler, it appears to us that Judge Streit has taken a rather accidental affair and given it an appearance of evil that is not warranted."
6. Streit's contention that Rupp "sacrificed the welfare of his players," the board said, was based on a single incident that occurred in Madison Square Garden in 1948 when Ralph Beard had a sprained ankle. Beard "was taken by the team trainer to the official physician of Madison Square Garden who injected Novocain and taped the ankle" allowing Beard to play that evening. "Two of the most eminent surgeons in Kentucky explained that this was proper medication for the injury…and that in their opinion there could be no harmful results therefrom."
7. The board did not take issue with the fact that players had, on occasion, received sums of money beyond scholarship allowances. "Steps have been taken to eliminate such practices and we charge officials of the university to exercise such diligence to insure they will not recur."
8. In response to Barnstable's comment that 'we were lucky to get something to eat" when they lost, the board examined the financial records for every game and found that "in all instances, the same subsistence allowance was paid all players. We find that these amounts were adequate but not excessive…."

9. Addressing how much money was spent on the basketball program, the board listed some of the expenses and pointed out that every cent of the money was from gate receipts, so "not a dollar of taxpayers' money is spent on the athletics program."
10. The board declared that they were proud of the fact that the athletics programs were "highly systematized" and congratulated Judge Streit for recognizing it. As for "commercialized," well, the programs do have to support themselves, don't they?
11. Judge Streit is mistaken if he thinks recruiting is "illegal." The university, however, "is concerned with the problems attendant upon recruiting and...took strong affirmative action to see that undesirable practices not continue."
12. Players were not given money "left over from the Olympic fund." A separate fund was raised to allow the three Kentucky players (Barnstable, Holland and Line) not on the Olympic squad to travel with the team. Bonus money handed out to players was remaining from this fund.
13. Judge Streit was simply mistaken in his opinion that "the University of Kentucky has no scholarships for students who find it necessary to work their way through college." As a matter of fact, UK annually awarded "approximately 260 scholarships and fellowships—totaling in value more than $75,000, none of which has the slightest connection with athletics."

In summary, the board noted that, "This only argues that the University of Kentucky has been carrying out the policies of the conference of which it is a member, and that these policies have for years had the endorsement of the region who have been sufficiently concerned to express themselves. Every packed stadium and field house constitutes an endorsement of this athletics policy."[355]

So, it would seem that UK's official opinion was that those of Judge's Streit's points that weren't just plain wrong were based on insufficient or erroneous information, somebody else's fault or merely his uninformed personal opinion. The University promised to institute some minor adjustments but, aside from that, basically said that the New York courts should clean up their own house and let us Southerners alone. In essence, the university said "we'll be just fine, thank you very much." The report was "preliminary," though, indicating that there might be a follow-up. More than 60 years later, we're still waiting.

As summer warmed the air and turned the Bluegrass brown, representatives from both the SEC and the NCAA were snooping around UK's athletics programs. Perhaps in hopes of reducing the severity of the penalties sure to result from those investigations, the athletics board did dictate that UK would only play in on-campus arenas (sorry, Coach Cal, no more domes), limit out-of-state players to five per team per year (sorry Julius Randall) and reduce the size of some coaching staffs and traveling squads.[356]

On July 2, Judge Streit dropped another bombshell that did not bode well for college sports. While sentencing eleven fixers to prison terms ranging from six months to seven years, the Judge unloaded a four hour tirade denouncing "commercialism in college sports" and called for a law "making it a criminal offense for any person, be he alumnus, town booster or college official, to subsidize athletes." Labeling the fixers as "brazen and audacious brown rats," the Judge handed the stiffest penalty, a four to seven year sentence to Joseph Benintende. Jack West (of whom we will soon hear more) received two to three years, Nicholas Englisis received an indeterminate term of up to three years, and Anthony Englisis and Nathaniel Brown received six months. It probably didn't make UK officials feel any less picked on, but Judge Streit announced that "the activities of these defendants and two other fixers already sentenced by me involve 31 bribed college athletes, six colleges or universities and 86 intercollegiate basketball contests in 23 cities in 17 states."[357]

So, with that all squared away, the talk around the water coolers and stoves now turned to what would come out of the conference and NCAA investigations. Maybe the 'Cats wouldn't go back to Madison Square Garden any more, but even without Spivey, they still had Cliff Hagan and Frank Ramsey and should be capable of winning the national championship once again.

Chapter Seventeen

PROBATION

In the extreme heat of late July, the six-member Southeastern Conference executive committee gathered at conference headquarters in Birmingham to receive Commissioner Bernie Moore's report and decide Kentucky's fate. It was no secret that Moore had spent three days on the Lexington campus in late May and then retreated to his Birmingham office where he devoted three weeks assimilating the facts he'd uncovered. In the Commonwealth, everybody held their breath and hoped the *Courier-Journal's* Earl Ruby was right when he opined that, "the league will find no reason for punitive action against the school."[358]

Those hopes were mitigated by the fact that the committee had been called to hear the report, as the general feeling was that if only a simple fine was in order, Commissioner Moore could announce that without calling the committee into session. On July 25, President Donovan and Dean Kirwan were summoned to Conference headquarters in Alabama where they would, perhaps, be allowed to defend their athletics programs, and would certainly hear the results of the investigation and the committee's decision. Under the conference guidelines, penalties, if any were to be handed down, could range from fines (for recruiting violations) to expulsion for more serious offenses.[359] The fact that UK's administrators were called to the meeting did not bode well—they would not be asked there to hear that the committee found everything in order. The next day, Donovan and Kirwan filled a four-hour session attempting to defend UK's athletic policies. Big Blue Nation's optimism sank even farther when Dr. John Gallalee, President of the University of Alabama and chairman of the committee, announced that a decision would be delayed because, "the charges against Kentucky are too serious to reach a decision without study of materials which are not available at this time."[360] Exactly what that material might be was the cause of much speculation.

The nature of that material is still a mystery, but the committee apparently got it as, on August 9, Earl Ruby gathered national attention when he used his *Courier-Journal* column to announce that the decision had been reached and that he had advance knowledge that the committee "suggested pretty strongly" that Kentucky might get off lightly if they would fire Coach Rupp. According to the *Courier-Journal's* sports editor, the committee was highly resentful that Rupp had failed even to condescend to apologize to the conference and his fellow coaches for the scandal and embarrassment brought on by his players. Feathers were also ruffled by the feeling that Rupp could have and should have known about Ralph Beard's and Alex Groza's jobs that paid them money in excess of allowable limits. If UK failed fire Rupp, Ruby predicted, the result would be suspension from the conference. He also predicted that suspension was exactly what was going to happen as UK "hardly could be expected to accede to a request or suggestion that Rupp be dropped. To do so would be an admission that he (and Kentucky) had been guilty of rules infractions that other coaches and schools in the league had not been guilty of…."[361] The next day, Dr. Gallalee refused to comment on Ruby's report, causing additional speculation.

On the eve of the conference's announcement, in a move that has been suggested many times before and since, *Lexington Leader* sports editor Larry Shropshire noted that as the days and weeks passed with no word from Birmingham, the best thing UK could do would be to say "nuts to you" and drop out of the SEC because, "the local school suffers more as each day drops off the calendar."[362] Abandoning the SEC for greener pastures has been discussed many times in the Commonwealth Kentucky. The general feeling among Wildcat fans has always been that the 'Cats would dominate any conference in basketball, so they should find one in which they could be competitive in football.

At the request of Dr. Donovan, the committee met on Monday (August 11) to reconsider. Donovan's pleas went unheeded and, unfortunately for the Wildcat faithful, Earl Ruby's prediction was correct; that afternoon, the Southeastern Conference banned Kentucky from playing any SEC basketball games for the 1952-53 season. The announcement simply said, "The executive committee of the Southeastern Conference, having investigated the athletic program at the University of Kentucky, finds that between October 1946 and the close of the 1951 season, the University of Kentucky participated in intercollegiate games and tournaments in violation of the rules and regulations of the Southeastern Conference...."[363] Dr. Donovan said that while he was "impressed with the honesty and sincerity" of the committee, he nevertheless felt "that the punishment we have received is excessive for the violations for which we have been charged...and which have been committed by other members of the Southeastern Conference in recent years."[364] Or, in other words, Dr. Donovan said, "we're no worse than the rest of 'em." Sound familiar?

Commissioner Moore ruled two of Bear Bryant's football players (Gene Donaldson and Chester Lukswaki) ineligible for further competition for having received unallowable benefits and fined the school $500 for each of them. At the same time, some of the investigation's findings were released. Among them was the fact that Bill Spivey (who was already suspended) unallowably received $25 per month from Lexington's Sleepy Head House. Other players ruled ineligible, all for having received excess money were: Alex Groza for his entire career at UK; Ralph Beard, Wallace Jones, Jim Line and Dale Barnstable for 1947 to 1949 and Walter Hirsh, Frank Ramsey, Shelby Linville, Bobby Watson and "Skippy" Whitaker for part of the 1950-51 season.[365]

Being banned from conference play meant that UK suddenly had fourteen open dates on its schedule. Non-conference games already scheduled against St. Louis, Minnesota, DePaul, Notre Dame and Xavier were unaffected. "Well", Kentucky fans thought, "this gives us the option to play a stronger schedule as we won't have to take on the traditionally weak sisters of conference basketball title for the first time in ten years. The Wildcats have ruled the loop and been an outstanding national power during most of the 21 years the SEC". The typical Kentucky fan's attitude was that this action had been taken simply because the conference was tired of being dominated. An Alabama newspaper said it, quite eloquently, for Big Blue Nation: "Kentucky's removal means another team will win for the first time since Adolph Rupp has been their coach."[366] The *Lexington Herald's* Ed Ashford was more succinct, "if you can't beat 'em, suspend 'em."[367]

More mature thought analyzed the penalty beyond the obvious. The lost revenue from ticket sales for conference games was calculated to be equivalent to a fine of $103,000—the gross income from conference games the previous season. Furthermore, it constituted a ban on post-season play. As a part of its new program, UK had ruled out the NIT in Madison Square Garden (which, incidentally, was the last nail in the coffin of that tournament as the more prestigious), and, as only conference champions were eligible for the NCAA tournament, Kentucky would not be eligible to participate in that event, either.

At the moment, Big Blue Nation, being involved with Coach Bryant's football season, pushed the basketball sanctions to the back of its collective mind, until, on November 3, the other shoe dropped, when the NCAA released the results of its investigation.

Only of passing interest was the fact that Bradley University, while allowed to play its regular season games, was banned from upcoming NCAA tournament because some of their players had received unallowable subsidies. Of much greater concern in the Bluegrass, the NCAA council announced that Kentucky was found guilty of allowing its athletes to receive pay in violation of NCAA rules and allowing athletes to participate in NCAA events when the coaches had knowledge of the facts (that the players were being paid) which made the players ineligible. The council announced that at its annual convention, to be held in Washington in January, it would recommend that Kentucky be put on probation for all sports for the 1952-53 season.[368] The University of Kentucky holds the honor of receiving the very first "death penalty" ever handed down by the NCAA!

Specifically, the NCAA found that:

1. In the spring of 1948, upon departure for the NCAA tournament, each member of the basketball team was given $50 by boosters not connected with the university.
2. The same violation occurred in the spring of 1949.
3. Each member of the team was given $50 before the team departed for New York to play St. John's in December 1950.
4. Players were given amounts ranging from $25 to $50 following the Sugar Bowl in January 1951.
5. Between October 1947 and December 1950, two members of the basketball team (Beard and Groza) had received monthly stipends of $50 from boosters not connected with the university.[369]

UK's reaction was swift and decisive. Of some relief was the fact that, as the ruling would not take effect until the football season was over, the gridiron 'Cats were not affected. The school immediately announced, however, that it had canceled its entire basketball schedule for the 1952-53 season. They then notified each scheduled opponent of the NCAA's ruling and asked to be relieved of the commitment. President Donovan said, "It is the opinion of our athletics board that the penalty inflicted…is unduly severe and is far more harsh than any penalty that has ever been inflicted on a member for violation of NCAA rules in the past." Nevertheless, he added, the school did not plan to appeal.[370] Coach Rupp, who had kept a low profile throughout, refused to comment. His players however, had plenty to say. "It is a gross injustice to punish us for something former players did," commented Frank Ramsey. "They're taking it out on the wrong people." Cliff Hagan added, "This makes me more determined to stay at Kentucky. This is no time to desert."[371] It is interesting to note there is no mention of the point shaving business, a fact, it would seem, that made the players more "professionals" that a mere $50 here and there.

While some clamored for Coach Rupp's head, UK vice-president Leo Chamberlin announced that "the university has no thought" of firing Coach Rupp. Attorney William Townsend, president of the UK Alumni Association (and Rupp's personal attorney,) blasted the NCAA. "We contend that no man or set of men reeking with athletic halitosis has any right to point an accusing finger at a speck on Kentucky's vest," he virtually roared. Townsend went on to deride the NCAA's decision as it "seriously damaged, if not actually destroyed" the careers of current players who were perfectly innocent and that it condoned paying football players $250 for a bowl game (which the SEC had OK'ed) but condemned basketballers over $50. Townsend then published a litany of offenses committed by other schools "that belong to the SEC and NCAA and whose representatives sit in judgment of Kentucky." According to Townsend, these offenses were much worse than those committed by Kentucky but yet were "winked at" by both the conference and the NCAA. His final comments did sound a more rational note: "It may be said that the guilt of others has nothing to do with Kentucky's guilt. I say it has a great deal to do with it. If Kentucky has violated any rules or regulations…she ought to be punished and no representative of Kentucky…has ever said otherwise, but we do contend that the punishment ought to fit the offense…."[372]

A few days later, UK President Donovan announced that he had conducted an investigation of "Coach Adolph Rupp after the basketball scandals and, from all we could learn, Coach Rupp is an honorable man who did not knowingly violate athletic rules." Lending some credence to Townsend's statements, Donovan said, "When we first appeared in football bowls, we learned it was customary…to give players extraordinary expense money.[373] When we went to the Orange Bowl (1949), we asked the SEC about expense money and received permission to award each player $200. When we went to the Sugar Bowl (1950), we received permission to give the players $250. From that, we reasoned it would be within the rules to award basketball players $50 expense money after the Sugar Bowl basketball tournaments." It is interesting to note that they "reasoned" rather than asked. Dr. Donovan also failed to mention all the other occasions when players had been handed extra money.

You can almost hear the sigh of resignation in Dr. Donovan's voice as he told the Alumni Association, "If we can help athletics by being victims and by making sacrifices that will put college athletics on an honest, amateur basis, then I, personally, feel that it is well worth it for the school to go through the valley of shadows."[374]

Speaking to the Lexington Rotary Club in mid-November, Rupp broke his long public silence. "I'm not retiring, he announced, "and I'll not retire until the man who said Kentucky can't play in the NCAA hands me the national championship trophy." The Coach indicated that he had considered retirement several years earlier—before the scandal broke—but now was determined to ride out the storm. He noted that causes for the conference's and NCAA's actions were "completely beyond our control" and "we do not seek sympathy and have no apologies to make."[375]

Banned from official competition for the 1952-53 season, Rupp continued to hold daily practices and those sessions were probably long and brutal. Fans were allowed a look at what was going on through a series of intra-squad exhibition games held before packed houses in Memorial Coliseum in December 1952 and January and February 1953. In those games, old hands Cliff Hagan, Frank Ramsey and Lou Tsiropoulos performed well, while freshmen Jerry Bird and Phil Grawemeyer were impressive and gave hope for the future. Worth noting is that, as NCAA rules allow every player five calendar years in which to play four seasons (a red shirt year), the penalty would not cost any player any eligibility.

Chapter Eighteen

Where There's Life, There's Hope

While the University of Kentucky was battling its troubles with the Southeastern Conference and the NCAA, several former Wildcats had plenty of troubles of their own. Dale Barnstable had lost his job as a Louisville high school basketball coach, while Ralph Beard and Alexander John Groza had not only lost their jobs, but were forced to sell their interest in the Indianapolis Olympians franchise and thereby deprived of their investment as well as their opportunity to earn a living doing what they knew best.

In July, Groza and Beard, who had been given suspended sentences and banned from professional basketball for their point shaving activities, applied to the NBA for reinstatement. One can almost hear the chuckle in NBA Commissioner Maurice Podoloff's voice as he notified Groza that the league's board of governors had "decided to let things stand as they now are."[376]

A glimmer of hope, however, appeared on October 7, 1952, when both players received an offer from the Jersey City team of the American Basketball League.[377] The ABL had exisited, off and on, since the mid-1920's but had never made much of a splash in the professional basketball world and certianly posed no threat to the NBA at this time. At the same time, the Jersey City team made an offer to Sherman White, the Long Island University star who was also implicated in the point shaving. With the exception of the Kentucky players, White was the biggest name involved in the scandals. When he was arrested on February 20, 1951, he was the nation's leading scorer and had just been named Player of the Year by *The Sporting News*. Despite the fact that White had turned in all the money he'd received from the fixers, Judge Saul Streit came down hard on the only black player indicted for point shaving. Streit had given all the other players who cooperated suspended sentences, but handed White a one year prison term.

After serving nearly nine months, White was released and snapped right up by Jersey City. Although the offers were subject to league approval, with these three stars on the court, Jersey City figured to give the NBA teams a run for their money. Although the perjury charge was still hanging over Bill Spivey's head, the Elmira Colonels, also of the ABL, signed him the same week. Speculation among the sports community was that if the league allowed these "tainted" men to play and they were accepted by the fans, they'd be playing in the NBA the next season.

In view of the fact that a major portion of the ABL teams' reveunes were generated from exibition games against NBA teams, as soon as NBA commissioner Maurice Podoloff got wind of the signing Groza and Spivey, perhaps as a preventive measures, decreed that NBA teams schedule no games against Jersey City or Elmira.[378] Maybe he feared that the "taint" on these players could transfer into the NBA by physical contact.

As the October 23 ABL's annual owner's meeting approched, the general impression was that these players participation would be approved. League President John J. O'Brien, however, was opposed. "I'll help any one of them find a job," he announced, "just not in basketball."[379] As the owners gathered in New York, Jersey City and Elmira got together for an exibition game in the latter city. Groza had 22, Beard added 17 and White scored 13 in Jersey City's winning cause, but Spivey led all scorers with 32 as Jersey City won 95-87.[380] That would be the last ABL game. When the owners voted to not allow Spivey, Groza, Beard and White to play in their league, Jersey City and Elmira announced they would withdraw from the league, whereupon the reminder of the owners decided to disband.[381] The newspapers noted that these players "who had made no effort to rehabilitae themselves had put the league out of business."[382]

A few days later, Groza and Beard appeared in Judge Striet's chambers to appeal their suspension. They might as well appeal to hurricane winds not to blow. "You have betrayed your honor, your colleagues, your college and the public. You have forfeited the right to participate in public sports, amateur or professional," the Judge pontificated. He then told the players that the "indefinite probation" he had previously assigned was now definite—three years. "One of the terms of your probation is that you do not directly or indirectly engage in any public sports activity."

"Does that mean we can't play basketball?" pleaded Groza.

"It means exactly that," answered Striet.[383]

Ralph Beard would later say that the Judge told him that if he "so much as touched a basketball in a YMCA, he'd throw my ass in jail."[384] It would seem the Judge overstepped his bounds again—under what authority could he make such a pronouncement?

As 1952 gave way to a new year, Bill Spivey's case returned to the forefront. Spivey, who had been under indictment for some six months was eager to have his day in court. Back in May, New York's Governor Thomas Dewey signed an extradition warrant for Spivey, which District Attorney Hogan forwarded to Kentucky's Governor Wetherby. When the papers were received in Frankfort, Wetherby announced he'd wait a few days before deciding whether to grant the request.[385] Two days later, Fayette County Judge W. E. Nichols held that "the perjury indictment returned against Spivey in New York had no validity" and dismissed the warrant.[386] Spivey's attorney, John Y. Brown (Sr.) said that this development "left it up to Governor Wetherby to decide if New York officials get Spivey." Brown also indicated that his client was willing to go to New York for trial "under his own conditions and not in the custody of New York detectives." Understandably, Brown also asserted that Spivey did not want to be tried before Judge Streit. "Certainly they have Judges who have not prejudged Bill Spivey and spouted off to the press about the case," said Brown.[387]

In the end Spivey, now living in Macon, Georgia, went to New York of his own accord for trial. January 14, 1953 was a busy day in the New York County courthouse. In one courtroom, Judge Louis Capozzoli threatened convicted fixer Jack West with contempt if he continued to refuse to testify against Spivey. West, the man ADA O'Conner insisted had paid off Spivey, was currently serving the two to three year term to which he'd previously been sentenced. He angrily asked the Judge, "Why do I have to testify? My case is settled and I'm doing my time. What do I have to do with this case? I take no sides. What do I care if Bill Spivey is guilty or not? I'm fed up."[388] Following that outburst, Judge Capazzoli slapped a contempt citation, which would bring West and additional six years and a $10,000 fine, on the convicted gambler.[389] West did not testify in the Spivey case and a couple of months later, O'Conner dismissed West's contempt citation while requesting that the

State Parole Commission deny any application made by West.[390] How can an Assistant District Attorney nullify a court order?

Down the hall on the same day, jury selection began in the Spivey case. If you guessed Brown's appeal for a different judge had any effect, you're wrong. General Sessions Judge Saul Streit sat nodding in agreement as prosecutor O'Conner asked the talesmen, "If you believe he (Spivey) is guilty beyond a reasonable doubt, would you hesitate to convict him because of the fact that he has a great deal to lose or because of sympathy?"[391] Eight men and four women were selected to hear the case.

Opening arguments began on Friday, January 16, 1953. ADA O'Conner read the indictment, which charged that Spivey had lied to the grand jury on seven separate instances and told the jury that the chairman of the grand jury (to whom he contended Spivey had lied) would give damming testimony, as would Spivey's former teammates (Line and Hirsh).[392] Brown revealed that Hirsh and Line had initially given testimony "denying that Bill was in on the fix. Then later, they made a complete turn-around." His defense, he said, would bring in a witness—a basketball expert—who saw the games in question and would testify that "Spivey never, ever held back in a game." In conclusion, Brown asserted, "In the Sugar Bowl game against St. Louis University (the game O'Conner claimed Spivey and West had fixed), Spivey was the high scorer of both teams with 16 points. He made eight of eleven free throws, not bad for a man charged with shaving points."[393]

On Monday, O'Conner called the court stenographer to the stand to certify that the Grand Jury testimony of Jack West and two other fixers was real and accurate. Judge Streit called a recess to give him time to study the transcript, after which he ruled that the jury did not need to hear it as the testimony did not involve Spivey. O'Conner objected, to no avail, pointing out that the testimony provided "background matter" on the fixing process.[394]

O'Conner then called his star witness, Spivey's ex-teammate and confessed fixer Walter Hirsh. Hirsh began by explaining that Dale Barnstable had pulled him and Jim Line into the point shaving business after Beard and Groza left UK. He then admitted that he had accepted bribes for "working" the scores in games in the 1949-50 season. Spivey came to him, he said, shortly before the 1950 season saying that a gambler (Eli Kaye) had told him that Hirsh and Line were being paid for shaving points. When Spivey demanded to know if what that was true, Hirsh told his teammate that it was. Hirsh asserted that Spivey wanted in on it, so, with Line as a go-between, they agreed with Jack West to accept $5,000 to go under the point spread in the Sugar Bowl game against St. Louis. Hirsh explained that the game got out of hand and when Kentucky lost 43-42, West was quite upset and gave Line only $2,600…$800 each for Hirsh and Line and $1,000 for Spivey. O'Conner sat down, apparently satisfied with the testimony.[395]

Defense attorney John Y. Brown sprang to his feet for cross-examination. "Didn't you tell the grand jury that Spivey had never met West?" he demanded.

"Yes, that's true," Hirsh said, softly.

"Didn't you tell the grand jury that you didn't think Spivey ever got money for a fix?"

"Yes. I failed to tell the grand jury the complete truth on some occasions." After a pause, he added, "But Spivey did get $1,000 for his part in the Sugar Bowl fix, and that's a fact."[396]

Next up was Jim Line, who testified that Jack West became very angry with him and Hirsh and Spivey when they failed to go under the point spread in a game against Notre Dame on January 15, 1951. He then admitted that he had acted as go-between for Hirsh and Spivey to fix the Sugar Bowl game. Line basically repeated Hirsh's story and reiterated the $800/$800/$1,000 split. Judge Streit asked how they arrived at that arrangement. "West dictated it," Line answered. He explained that he and Hirsh and Spivey had met with West at the Little Inn in Lexington and agreed to the split.[397]

On cross-examination, Line admitted that he had told the grand jury that the amount of money involved in the Sugar Bowl fix was $1,600. He said that he had tried to get Spivey to "come clean," but "Bill said he would lose friends if he changed his story because the people of Kentucky believed him to be innocent." Spivey was "hungrier for glory than for money," Line said, so he refused to fix games against Kansas and St. John's because they had All-American centers and Spivey wanted to outplay them.[398] At that point, the prosecution rested. It seems strange that Spivey would worry about "losing friends" with all the other, and more important, issues he had at stake.

On January 22, big Bill Spivey folded his seven-foot frame into the witness chair. He adamantly denied that he had ever accepted any money from a gambler, agreed to shave points or even discussed such matters with gamblers. He also declared that he had been "entirely truthful" with the grand jury. In answer to Brown's question, he admitted that he had lied to Dean Kirwan when asked if he knew of any game fixers. He knew, he admitted, about Hirsh and Line, but lied to protect his teammates.[399] All in all, he painted himself as a man whose honor had been besmirched by his teammates who had lied about his involvement in an apparent attempt to militate their own culpability.

On cross-examination, he reiterated his story about being approached by "George" the summer he worked in the Catskills. He said that was his only contact with a fixer and that he refused the $500 per game "George" offered. When they parted, "George" had said, "I'll see you again."[400]

"I was lying in my bed in the dorm that fall," the player testified. "There was a knock at my door and there was this fellow standing there. I told him to get out, but he just stood there in the doorway. I started to get up and he ran. That's my entire experience with the gamblers."[401]

O'Conner identified "George" as Eli Kaye, who was now dead and hence not available to confirm or deny Spivey's account of their meetings. Spivey was forced to admit that he had not told Dean Kirwan of Kaye's offer, even though Kaye had told him about Hirsh and Line. "You mean that you were willing to forget that your teammates were crooked?" O'Conner demanded.

"I didn't believe it," Spivey calmly answered.

Asked if he came to know the truth, Spivey said that he remembered a game in which he thought Hirsh "double-crossed him." "Hirsh was supposed to be the feeder in a game against Arkansas," Spivey testified, "and he is, as a rule, an excellent feeder. That night, he threw the ball around my feet which is not good for a fellow of my height." Concerning the Sugar Bowl game, Spivey told the jury, "Every time I was in the clear, they did not throw me the ball until someone from the opposing team was on top of me."[402]

Before the next witness was called, Brown petitioned Judge Streit to dismiss the charge as all the prosecution had presented was "only testimony of two self-confessed perjurers." Not surprisingly, the Judge denied the motion, saying there was a question of fact, "but it is for the jury, not the court, to decide."[403]

John Y. Brown's "basketball expert" witness turned out to be none other than Kentucky's own Albert B. "Happy" Chandler. In addition to having been Kentucky's Governor and Senator, Chandler was a former commissioner of Major League Baseball and a basketball coach for a short time. He also served on UK's athletic board and fancied himself to be Coach Rupp's best friend. Calling on him to defend a Kentucky basketball player was equivalent to calling a fish to defend water.

Chandler said that he was present at the Sugar Bowl game against St. Louis and that Spivey played "sensationally." In fact, Chandler went on, Spivey was "better than anyone else on the floor." Following a number of character witnesses who testified as to Spivey's honesty, Brown rested the defense's case. As it was Friday afternoon, court adjourned until Monday.[404]

January 26 brought final arguments. Brown reminded the jury that Hirsh admitted lying twice to the grand jury and Line did the same three times. "You can believe Walt and Jim, self-confessed fixers and self-confessed liars under oath before the grand jury, or you can believe Bill, who from the start has maintained his innocence.

"Let it be your memory that you allowed a boy to go back to his university to get his degree and be a man instead of destroying him."[405]

Vincent O'Conner stood to face the jury. He told them that corruption of basketball by gamblers was a cancer. He declared that fixers offered as much as $1,000 a night to boys who did not come from wealthy families and "it is no wonder that they took it." He conceded inconsistencies in Hirsh's and Line's testimonies, but quickly added that they "showed character and rehabilitation by coming here and telling the truth."[406]

"If Spivey is made to realize that there is more in life than pro basketball," he said in conclusion, "if he is made to realize that there is more in life than money and if he is made to see that there are higher values than lying to get out of trouble, then he will have a good start."[407] With that, the case then went to the jury.

At 1:28 AM on January 27, Judge Streit called the jury back to the courtroom and pointed out that the fourteen hours they had been deliberating was "a long time to settle a small question." The jury foreman informed the judge that the jury was "hopelessly deadlocked." Assured that further deliberation was pointless, Judge Streit thanked the jury and dismissed them.[408]

One of the jurors told a *New York Times* reporter that the final vote was 9-3 for acquittal, as had been the case since the first poll. She said that the nine that favored acquittal "did not think there was sufficient evidence for conviction," but that the other three stubbornly held out for conviction.[409]

No date was set for a retrial. Spivey's attorney said he would formally move for dismissal. Bill Spivey said that he was disappointed that he was not cleared, but was "satisfied" that the majority were for acquittal. Evidently O'Conner either gave up or decided he'd made his point; the case never came before the court again.

On April 23, 1953, the NBA owners gathered in Boston for their annual meeting. With Commissioner Maurice Podoloff presiding, the top items on the agenda were what was to be done with the struggling Indianapolis Olympians franchise and whether Bill Spivey would be eligible for their upcoming draft. On the first question the league voted to let the Indianapolis management "do as they pleased," which meant the franchise would fold. Spivey had asked for permission to be present with his lawyer at this meeting, but was refused after Podoloff read O'Conner's report to Judge Streit, furnished by the Assistant District Attorney. O'Conner was as good as his word about ensuring Spivey would not play professionally, which is the only explanation of his providing court correspondence to Podoloff. With that information in hand, the owners decided that Spivey would be barred from playing in the NBA "in the best interest of the league."[410]

An extremely distressed Bill Spivey told reporters, "It certainly doesn't look as if a man is innocent until proven guilty anymore."[411]

Chapter Nineteen

Adolph Rupp

Perhaps the final chapter of the 1951 point shaving scandals was written in the spring of 1953, when Lexington attorney J.A. Edge filed a suit on behalf of Mrs. Lucille Chumbly Bradberry of Athens, Georgia in Federal District Court. Naming UK Coach Adolph Rupp, former Lexington bookmaker Ed Curd and New York racket boss Frank Costello as defendants, the suit charged the trio with "concocting a fraudulent and debasing scheme of gambling in schools, colleges and university sports and athletics."

Mrs. Bradberry said that she was the sister of Mr. George Chumbly, formerly of Richmond, Kentucky, who was "one of the losers to gambling operations conducted by Curd and his conspirators." The suit sought $573,257 from the defendants, that amount being triple the sum of Mr. Chumbly's gambling losses for the years 1948 through 1951.

Among the allegations was that "the defendants organized and are members of, and participants in, an illegal confederation, combination and conspiracy to set up, maintain and operate gaming and gambling places in Lexington and Madison County (KY.)"[412]

When pressed, attorney Edge said Rupp was made a party to the suit "because his association with Curd is known to be close."

The Associated Press reported that under Kentucky law, an out-of-state relative could file suit in the Commonwealth for recovery of gambling losses. Nonetheless, Rupp was outraged. "It's all a fantastic lie," he roared. "Of all the smear campaigns that have ever been conducted against anyone, this is the rottenest. It is evidently a well-organized campaign aimed entirely to discredit me."[413]

Rupp's attorney, William Townsend, also squealed. "I don't know exactly what the next step will be, but it will be prompt," promised Townsend. "The tragedy of this thing is that, while the allegations will be proved to be wholly and basically scandalous, that doesn't prevent the headlines and publicity." Townsend cited Rule 11 of Federal procedures which provides that "the signature of an attorney to a complaint filed in the district court of the United States constitutes a certificate by him that he has read the pleading and, to the best of his knowledge, information and belief, there is sufficient ground to support the complaint." Furthermore, Townsend went on, filing a complaint without such basis, "shall subject the attorney to appropriate disciplinary action and the complaint shall be stricken form the record as 'sham and false.'"[414] Townsend vowed that Edge would regret beginning this bogus legal action.

Courier-Journal sports editor, Earl Ruby, perhaps speaking for many UK fans, opined that if this suit was designed to injure Rupp, it would boomerang. Ruby noted that while Rupp had been on a hot seat of public opinion since the scandals broke, "he might be many things, and I feel he's made a lot of mistakes in public and school relations, but I know he's not a crook."[415]

Almost immediately, Mrs. Bradberry chimed in from Georgia to say that she had no knowledge of the case and was surprised to read her name in the newspaper. She added that she had previously filed a suit against Curd (which was dismissed without prejudice) and she thought this must be a continuation of the same action. Attorney Townsend said that regardless of what Mrs. Bradberry did, he and Rupp would press on. Again citing Rule 11, he said he could have the case dismissed on that basis, but "we do not want to win this case that way." Rupp waived his right to take 20 days to file an answer and Townsend filed a notice that depositions would be taken the next day. "They better be able to support the allegations against Coach Rupp with cold facts," he threatened.[416]

Two days later, Mrs. Bradberry announced that she had ordered attorney Edge to drop the case. Through her Georgia attorney, she said, "I know nothing of the charges made, and for that reason, I insist on the current suit's dismissal." Again noting that this must be an offshoot of the previous action against Curd, her attorney added that Mrs. Bradberry had not intended to continue that action and certainly had not intended to sue Coach Rupp.[417]

The next day, attorney Edge filed a motion for dismissal of the suit against Rupp. On April 15, 1953 Federal Judge Church Ford dismissed the action and ordered Rupp's name stricken from the suit on the grounds that the allegations in it were "false and made without authority"[418] As a final note on that action, Townsend did insist that the Kentucky Bar Association investigate attorney Edge's actions. The ensuing probe resulted in a one-year suspension for Edge.[419] Thus, with that whimper, the college basketball point shaving scandals began to fade into history.

The scandals did not fade from the fans' memory very quickly, though. Rupp and Lancaster made good use of the punishment year to hone the skills of their star players and polish their offensive and defensive patterns. As a result, the 'Cats breezed through the 1953-54 season with a perfect 25-0 record, and visions of another national championship danced in the fans heads'. But, because Cliff Hagan and Frank Ramsey had graduated the previous year, they were not eligible to participate in the NCAA tournament. Kentucky won the conference title that year and hence the team was eligible for the NCAA tournament. The team voted to accept the invitation, but Rupp evoked his 51 percent of the vote to override the players' wishes. Hence, Kentucky declined to play in the 1954 post-season without its stars.

The memories of the 1951 scandals certainly did not fade quickly from the consciences' of those most impacted. Adolph Rupp weathered the storm, as he had—and would—survive many other controversies and remained as Kentucky's basketball coach. On March 22, 1958, he was vindicated in his vow to "make the man who said Kentucky couldn't play" hand him the national championship trophy when his "Fiddlin' Five" defeated Seattle 84-72 for UK's unprecedented (at the time) fourth NCAA title.

Under Rupp's guidance, Kentucky would not "win it all" again, although they did finish as runners-up in 1966 with "Rupp's Runts," perhaps his most famous team since the Fabulous Five. In April 1969, Adolph Rupp was honored by being inducted into college basketball's Naismith Hall of Fame. As coach, Rupp would last another three years after that until the University forced him out at the mandatory retirement age of 70. In 42 years at UK, he had outlasted 56 SEC basketball coaches, many of whom had said he wouldn't last, and seven UK football coaches, including the legendary "Bear" Bryant. Overall, Rupp posted an impressive record of 876 wins against 190 losses before turning the reins over to Joe B. Hall for the 1972-73 season.[420]

A story, which I am assured is true, is illustrative of Rupp's wit and cannot be omitted. At a reception, a waiter offered a tray of drinks to the Coach. Rupp took a glass of bourbon, his favorite libation. The waiter then turned to UK's athletics director, Bernie Shively, who always railed against the evils of strong drink. "No thank you," said Shive, his voice laced with contempt. "I'd rather commit adultery than drink alcohol." Without hesitation, Rupp replaced his glass on the tray. "Me, too," he said with a grin, "nobody told me we had a choice." Rupp liked his bourbon. When the doctor ordered him to "lay off the hard stuff," he reluctantly switched to vodka.

Although he was allowed to maintain his old office in Memorial Coliseum after his forced retirement, his association with UK was at a bitter end. Over the next few years, he turned down several jobs, then finally accepted executive positions with the Memphis Tams and then the Kentucky Colonels, both of the American Basketball Association (ABA.) In failing health, he found no satisfaction in either job. "The man who built the biggest basketball empire of them all sits alone at home and forgotten," he lamented.[421]

Rupp left UK's Albert B. Chandler Medical Center in November 1976 to witness the first game in the arena in downtown Lexington that bears his name. He was also present for the official Rupp Arena dedication ceremonies on December 11, but would never attend another game.

A year later, he lay dying of cancer in the Medical Center at UK while Coach Hall's 'Cats played Rupp's alma mater, Kansas in Lawrence. Kentucky won 73-66, but the old coach did not live to hear the final score. Late in the coach's life, Lexington sportswriter John McGill asked Rupp if someone were to sum up his life in one sentence, what Rupp would have him say. After some thought, he answered, "He proved that a boy could come from immigrant parents unable to speak English until he was six years old and become a success, doing the job as he saw he should do it."[422] Much nearer the end, Rupp biographer, Russell Rice, asked Adolph for a summary of his life. "Just say I did the best I could," said Rupp. "That's good enough for me."[423]

Chapter Twenty

Alex Groza

When the NBA forced Alex Groza to sell his interest in the Indianapolis Olympians NBA franchise, after a short stint working at General Electric in Louisville, he returned to his family home in Martin's Ferry, Ohio. He went to work tending bar in the family tavern, and soon married the lady he'd been seeing there before the scandal broke. The couple would eventually have four children: Alex, Lisa, Leslie and Lee.

When his Streit-imposed probationary period ended in 1955, he started playing basketball for the Eastern Professional Basketball League's team in nearby Wheeling, West Virginia and also hosting a local television sports program there. Additionally, he did some scouting for ex-Olympians teammate Bruce Hale, now the basketball coach at Miami (OH) University. "Every time I applied for a job," said Groza, "they'd say, 'you've got no experience in this and none in that.' So, I finally said to myself, 'you've got experience in basketball, so it's about time to try that.'"[424]

At Hale's urging, in April 1959 Groza applied for the basketball coaching vacancy at Loyola of the South, a small Catholic school in New Orleans. Alex did not get that job, but the fact that he had filed an application attracted the attention of every newspaper in the country. At that time, in response to a reporter's question about the point shaving, Groza said, "I'll never be able to figure out why we did it. I guess we just got caught up in the times. We knew it was being done by other teams, so we just went along."[425]

Although Groza was not hired for the Loyola job, a month later, his name was again in the national news when he was hired as the basketball coach at Louisville's Bellarmine College. "Everything about Mr. Groza has impressed us very much and we think he's the kind of man we want for our team," said Bellarmine's President, the

Right Reverend Ralph Horrigan in announcing Groza's hiring.[426] Groza's employment made him the first of all the men involved in the point shaving scandals to return to college basketball in any capacity, a fact in which he surely found satisfaction. In the first team meeting, Coach Groza told his players, "You are all old enough to know what happened to me. Let's make sure it doesn't happen to you."[427]

Groza was right about knowing basketball and he could teach it, too. He proved himself to be a good coach. In the 1962-63 season, he led the Knights to the Kentucky Intercollegiate Athletic Conference championship with a 20-5 record while earning Coach of the Years honors for himself.

In a surprise move, Groza resigned his job at Bellarmine and took a job in industry after the 1966 season, having posted an 87 wins and 74 losses record as coach. Around the same time, Louisville got their long-sought after professional basketball team in the shape of the Kentucky Colonels of the newly-founded American Basketball Association (ABA). Groza took a front-office job with the Colonel's organization and was named the team's business manager for the 1967-68 season. In November 1970, when Gene Rhodes was fired as the Colonel's coach and his replacement, Frank Ramsey would not be available for a short time, Groza was named interim coach. In that capacity, he coached two games, winning both.

In 1972, the ABA expanded, creating the San Diego Conquistadors. Aware of Groza's work with the Colonels, one of the Conquistador's first actions was to hire Alex Groza as general manager. Groza served in that capacity until the franchise folded in 1975. He served a brief stint as coach in 1974, posting a 17-23 record, and hung around as the revamped franchise became the Sails for a short time the next season.

After that, Groza became the general manager of a San Diego professional volleyball team for one season and then joined Reynolds Metals as manager of the west coast chemical division.

Alex Groza was a sure-fire NBA Hall of Famer had his career not been cut short and belongs in the Naismith Hall of Fame.* He was inducted into the Kentucky Athletic Hall of Fame in 1992 and his retired jersey, number 15, hangs in the Rupp Arena rafters with UK's

*See Appendix B for Groza's statistics.

other greats. Referencing the Fabulous Five, Groza said, "The biggest part of my life was being a member of that team. It's something you can't replace, something that didn't cost a nickel."[120]

The first of the Fabulous Five to pass away, Alex Groza died of cancer in San Diego on January 21, 1995.

Chapter Twenty-One

Bill Spivey

Bill Spivey was devastated when the University of Kentucky cancelled his scholarship. "I went hungry for three days," he said. Things only got worse as the damming testimony of two college teammates resulted in his being dragged before the New York Grand Jury in the point shaving scandals. When he refused to admit that he'd accepted bribes to fix games, New York Assistant District Attorney Vincent O'Conner threatened that Spivey "would never pay a minute of professional basketball" unless he confessed. In the face of Spivey's adamant and persistent denials, O'Conner spitefully indicted Spivey for perjury. When that effort failed to make the player confess and did not produce a conviction, O'Conner made good on his threat, providing what little impetus may have been necessary to induce NBA Commissioner Maurice Podoloff to ban Spivey from the NBA.

Spivey signed on with the Washington Generals, a team that toured the country providing nightly competition for the famous Harlem Globetrotters. Little attention was paid to the score or statistics of those highly entertaining games, but Spivey routinely poured in 50 or more points and was acknowledged by teammates and opposing players as one of the best basketball players in the country.

National newspaper headlines trumpeted the fact that Spivey decided to return to UK to finish up his degree early in 1955. The University of Kentucky did its former star no favors—he was required to pay out-of-state tuition and ordered to stay away from the college athletes.[429] He continued to play with the Generals (and also teams called the New York Olympians and Kentucky Colonels) against the Globetrotters on weekends while he was in school. He took a weekend off in November 1955 to marry Miss Audrey Brenneman. The Spivey's had one son, Cashman. Bill Spivey reported one of the greatest moments of his life was during his UK graduation. As he stepped across the stage in UK's Memorial Coliseum for Doctor Donovan to hand him his diploma, the crowd of some 5,000 persons gave him a standing ovation. "I knew the people of Kentucky were for me," he exulted.[430]

Bill continued to play against the Globetrotters until early in 1958 when he signed with the Wilkes-Barre Barons in the Eastern League. He excelled in that environment, leading the league in nearly every offensive category and guiding his team to the league championship in 1959. His 1,004 points in 28 games that year set a new league standard, and he was named the Eastern league's Most Valuable Player.[431]

Spivey was again in the national news later that year when the Baltimore Bullets, formerly of the NBA but now in the Eastern League, bought his contract. He was probably excited to learn that he'd be teamed with Sherman White, the former LIU star also banned from the NBA. White, who had starred with several other Eastern League teams, was also bought by the Bullets evidently in an attempt to buy a championship ala the New York Yankees' of George Steinbrenner's day.

The biggest headlines so far, however, hit the papers on January 4, 1960. "BILL SPIVEY SUES NBA, PRESIDENT" screamed the banners. The suit, filed in Hamilton County (OH) where Spivey was living, charged that the NBA and Commissioner Maurice Podoloff had "conspired and confederated with owners of franchises"[432] to prevent him from playing in that league. Spivey sought $810,000 damages, although he claimed the amount of lost revenue was more like "two or three million." Adding Vincent O'Conner and Judge Saul Streit as defendants would have been a good idea.

The pending lawsuit did not hinder Spivey's play. He finished the season with Baltimore with an amazing 35.5 points per game average. After season's end, Spivey had a chance to match up with the other biggest man in the game at that time, Wilt Chamberlain, who was touring with a group of All-Stars. Wilt's team won 91-72 behind Chamberlain's 31 points and 28 rebounds, but Spivey held his own against Wilt, nearly matching his numbers with 30 points and 23 rebounds.[433]

At the end of April, Spivey rocked the sports world with the announcement that he'd signed a contract with the NBA's Cincinnati Royals, who had moved the franchise from Rochester. The Royals offered the big man $10,000 per season. Speculation about whether Podoloff would allow him to play and the status of Spivey's pending suit ran rampant in the press. The fact that the Royals had also signed the great Oscar Robertson had the fans licking their chops.

At the first of July, a spokesman for the John E. Reid law firm of Chicago announced that Spivey had taken a lie detector test and convinced "a group of polygraph experts that he was not involved in shaving points or fixing games while at Kentucky."[434] "I've done everything humanly possible to remove the cloud over my name," said Spivey. "This should clear everything with the man on the street and that's the most important thing to me."[435] Clearing everything with Podoloff would be another matter. That gentleman issued a terse "No comment," when advised that the polygraph results were being forwarded to him and New York ADA Vincent O'Conner.

On September 1, even though Spivey had offered to drop his lawsuit if allowed to play with the Royals, Podoloff announced that he would not allow Spivey to fulfill his contract with the Cincinnati team. "After a review of the facts, I have come to the conclusion that Mr. Spivey does not qualify as a player in the National Basketball Association...." said the press release.[436] Bill Spivey quickly sent a letter to Podoloff and the NBA board of governors asking them to appoint a three-man committee to hear his case. "...in the opinion of myself and Mr. Price (his attorney), it is impossible for the NBA board to rule objectively on my appeal," said Spivey's note. The letter also implied that the NBA's action was simply an effort on the part of the NBA owners to ensure that the Royals, deprived of Spivey on the floor, would not become a championship contender.[437] Through the press, Podoloff answered that he wasn't interested in Spivey's opinion. Spivey quietly went back to the Baltimore Bullets where he continued his assault on the record books and bided his time.

Early in 1961, Spivey announced that he had settled the lawsuit with Podoloff and the NBA out of court for $10,000. He indicated that he thought he could eventually win the legal action, but he would be too old to play by the time he did. With perhaps a touch of triumph, he told reporters, "as far as I'm concerned, the settlement and the league's action are an admission in my favor. I took a lie detector test. If they want to be fair, let Mr. Podoloff and everybody else in the NBA do the same...."[438]

After the end of the Eastern League's season, Spivey signed a contract to play with the Cleveland Pipers of the newly formed American

Basketball League. The Pipers were headed by none other than George Steinbrenner, who told the press that he had conducted a complete investigation and was "convinced that Bill is innocent."[439] The Baltimore Bullets did not take kindly to that arrangement and promptly instituted legal action against Steinbrenner over the rights to the seven-footer. That argument became moot when Spivey was traded to the ABL's Los Angeles Jets before the season began. When the Jets folded in January 1962, Spivey was dealt to the Honolulu ABL franchise, the Chiefs.

Throughout the early to mid-'60s Bill knocked around playing in various less-than-prime time venues and leagues. He retired and came back several times until he announced his final retirement from playing basketball in 1966. Then, in February 1968, Spivey received the only break he ever got. Due to the fact that the Baltimore Bullets were an NBA franchise both before and after Spivey played with the same outfit in the Eastern League, he was allowed to play in a Bullets "NBA old-timers" game. His team lost the 20-minute contest, but Spivey led all scorers with 12. When an NBA owner was quoted as saying Spivey would have won the MVP award had there been one in that game, Spivey responded, "That's ironic. It's the first time any NBA owner ever voted for me."[440]

After a few years with a building materials firm in Pennsylvania, Spivey returned to Kentucky in 1969 where he worked as a Lexington real estate and insurance agent. In 1976, he became State Deputy Commissioner of Insurance in Governor Julian Carroll's administration. Popular with all he met, Spivey made an unsuccessful run for Kentucky's Lieutenant Governor's nomination in 1983.

Bill Spivey died on May 8, 1995 having never reconciled with the fate that had befallen him. Maintaining his innocence every day of his life, he would always point out that he was never convicted of anything. Still, he was not bitter. "I think I would have had an era all my own in the NBA," he suggested. "George Mikan was at the end of his career and Wilt Chamberlain hadn't started. I was the biggest and best in the country and I think I would have dominated the game as those two did."[441] He's probably right—Bill Spivey is another sure-fire NBA Hall of Famer had he been allowed to play.*

In 2000, UK's Athletics Director, C.M. Newton, who had been Spivey's roommate when they were Wildcat players, led a successful cam-

*See Appendix C for Spivey's statistics.

paign to have Bill Spivey's jersey retired. Today, Bill Spivey's big number 77 banner hangs in the Rupp Arena rafters along with the other Kentucky greats.

Despite the heartbreak, Bill Spivey retained a sense of humor. Asked on the campaign trail if he'd be willing to compromise with another candidate, Bill's face lit up with a wry smile. "I didn't make deals back in '51 and I still don't," he informed the voter.

Chapter Twenty-Two

Ralph Beard

History would have us combine the names and stories of Bill Spivey, and especially Alex Groza and Ralph Beard into a single entity. That would be an easy thing to do as they have much in common: all were great players, all attended UK and were all caught up in the point shaving scandals of 1951. Beard and Groza do share a close association in that they were a part of one of the greatest college teams that ever existed, and the two men remained friends throughout their lifetimes.

But there the similarity ends. As heartbreaking as the tragedies that befell Spivey and Groza are, Ralph Beard's entire world caved in on him on October 19, 1951. Since his high school days, Beard had never given even a single thought to earning a living doing anything other than playing ball, and his every effort had been toward becoming a professional athlete. He fully intended to play professional basketball in the winter and professional baseball in the summer until "my legs fell off." When he confessed to accepting gambler's money, NBA Commissioner Podoloff and Major League Baseball Commissioner Ford Frick abruptly ended his dreams by banning Beard from their respective leagues. In the space of one day, Ralph Beard went from being on top of the world to lower depths than he could have imagined.

Forced to sell his financial interest in the Indianapolis Olympians and with no marketable skills, Beard moved from one unfulfilling job to another. "Drifting in a fog," he worked fitting pipe, selling cars and loading trucks.[442] Agonizing under Judge Streit's edict that he play no organized sports, he found no purpose in any activity. Then, his wife, Marilyn, filed for divorce. She left, taking three-year-old Ralph Beard III with her. "It wasn't her fault at all," said Beard, "I lived in a void and I thought of myself as a complete failure. I just wanted to go away and die. I was an absolutely unbearable person to live with."

Slowly, Ralph Beard began to realize that even though his world was shattered, the globe kept right on spinning. Because he had ended his academic career a few hours shy of a college degree, he re-enrolled at UK. Under the same admonition to avoid all contact with the Wildcat players that the University placed on Bill Spivey, Beard earned his degree. He also met a woman named Bettye Scott. "She made me realize that life goes on," he said. "That I couldn't keep on doing nothing other than mourn that same mistake. She taught me that I had to live." Bettye became Mrs. Ralph Beard on March 18, 1955.

Around the same time, Beard's (and Groza's) probationary period ended. "I don't know how they knew," says Beard, but he received his military draft notice practically on the very day the probation expired.[443] Allowed, once again, to play basketball, Beard fell into the familiar patterns of practice, training and playing games. With that and Bettye's encouragement, he began to come alive again. The Army shipped the Beards to Japan, where he played for Camp Zama. Showing no effects of the hiatus, he played Army ball with the same fervor he'd displayed at every other level. In 1956 Ralph Beard was named to the Armed Forces Press Service All-Star team. Incidentally, Cliff Hagan, serving in the Air Force, was also named to that same team.[444]

Honorably discharged in 1957, Beard returned to Louisville to look for a job. Totally past his youthful stuttering problem, he found that he liked talking to people and eventually landed a job as a travelling salesman for a wholesale pharmaceutical firm. He soon discovered that his travels to the East Coast would allow him to play professionally in the Eastern League. His signing a contract with the Baltimore Bullets made national headlines in October 1958.[445]

Slowly, some aspects of Beard's life became normal. By 1961 he and Bettye had a daughter, Jill, and a son, Scott. He spent his time in Louisville with his family, working and playing golf with the same intensity he brought to every other activity. In the summer, his memories of 1951 faded, but resurfaced with each autumn. "It wouldn't bother me if another basketball season never came around," Beard says with great sincerity.[446]

That attitude may have changed a little when the Kentucky Colonels of the American Basketball Association came to town and Beard's old friend and teammate, Alex Groza, became general manager. Beard became a regular at the Colonels games. After he was promoted to sales manager of his company in 1973, his attitude softened a bit more when he began scouting for the Colonels on weekends. Life was good, but, still, he could not shake the distress. "I took the money," he said many, many times, "but I never did a thing to affect the outcome of a game. I swear on my children's eyes. No matter what anyone says, the Lord and I know the truth."[447] When you see and hear the sincerity with which Ralph Beard tells his story, you cannot doubt his word.

When Beard heard that Coach Rupp was on his death bed, he called Mrs. Rupp to ask if it would be all right for him to pay a visit. "Of course," she replied, "you know, Ralph, that you were always his favorite player."[448] That answers a question that Rupp would never respond to in public and gave the aging player and his old coach a chance to reconcile their differences and say their goodbyes.

The exemplary way Ralph Beard lived his life, his humble attitude and his natural charm won Ralph Beard many friends and advanced his career. He retired as vice-president and general manager of his pharmaceutical firm. At the time, he looked like he could still beat everybody down the floor on the fast break.

Eventually, a measure of redemption came Beard's way. In 1985, he was inducted into the Kentucky Athletic Hall of Fame. Never forgetting the long hard road he'd traveled, at the end of an emotional acceptance speech, Ralph Beard turned his face skyward and said, "Mom, I finally made it!"[449]

When C.M. Newton, who had been a freshman at UK in 1948-49 when Beard and Groza were seniors, became the school's athletics director in 1989, he went out of his way to honor the Fabulous Five whenever possible. On several occasions, contrary to Ralph's being told to stay from the team when he re-enrolled, Newton asked Beard to address the basketball team. Beard willingly complied and unabashedly told the modern players how he had ruined his life for $700. Newton also joined forces with journalists Dave Kindred and Billy Reed and that ESPN announcer who formerly coached Indiana in an unsuccessful effort to get Beard admitted to the Naismith Hall of Fame.[450] Like Spivey and Groza. Ralph Beard would have, beyond doubt, been an NBA Hall of famer.*

Every one of the many who knew and admired Ralph Beard felt that he was a wonderful person who paid an inappropriately substantial penalty for a youthful indiscretion. And he did it without complaint.

*See Appendix D for Beard's statistics.

Ralph Beard died November 29, 2007, three days short of his 80th birthday. Two things certainly went to his grave with him: He was proud of having been national collegiate and Olympic champion and he rued the mistake he'd made. "Sometimes I go as long as ten or fifteen minutes without thinking about the point-shaving."

Chapter Twenty-Three

The Yardstick

Those Kentucky fans of 1951 who felt that Judge Saul Streit was picking on UK—and many certainly did—had not bothered to learn how he treated the other schools involved in the point shaving business. Judge Streit's pronouncements on Bradley University, Long Island University, Manhattan College and City College of New York are every bit as strident as what he had to say about Kentucky. And, if he picked on anybody, it unquestionably was LIU's Sherman White. After White pleaded guilty to fixing three games before Judge Streit in July 1951, he appeared, as ordered, for sentencing on October 2. Despite the fact that White's attorney did not bother to show up, Judge Streit proceeded to flay away at the only black player involved in the scandals at that time. Streit used several racial slurs, called White a "semi-moron," pronounced that White had no business in college and sentenced him to a year in prison.[451] That year was the longest sentence handed to any player for shaving points. Relative to White's treatment, the Kentucky players got off (from the legal standpoint) lightly, so it would seem that Judge Streit's grudge was against college sports in general and not with any particular bias toward UK.

Adolph Rupp had an interesting theory on why Judge Streit was so vocal about college athletics. Rupp opined that Streit was just after the publicity; that he liked seeing his name in the newspaper and perhaps hoped that if he spewed out enough criticism, along with suggested remedies, he'd be appointed as commissioner of the NCAA.

New York's Assistant District Attorney Vincent O'Conner may be another story when it comes to ulterior motives. It is certainly possible to consider that his vigorous pursuit of Groza, Beard and Barnstable was just performing his assigned chores as one of their admitted point shaving activities—the highest profile one, in fact—had taken place within his purview. We can even let him off on his quest after Line and Hirsh, though none of their point shaving games took place in New York, if we take his word that he needed their testimony to get at the gamblers involved. But, his treatment of Bill Spivey seems nothing less than mean-spirited. Even though he already had Line's and Hirsh's testimony, which should have been enough for his stated purpose, he threatened that Spivey "would never play a minute" of professional basketball unless he confessed. O'Conner went out of his way to make good on that threat when Spivey would not give in. Additionally, it is impossible to see how indicting Spivey for perjury and going all-out to convict him would have any bearing on helping catch any New York gamblers.

Ralph Beard had a theory about O'Conner's exuberance as concerned the Kentucky players. Beard believed with all his heart that O'Conner acted as he did because his boss, District Attorney Frank Hogan, had directed him to make scapegoats out of the Wildcats. Beard thought that Francis Cardinal Spellman had approached Hogan demanding that the New England Catholic schools and their players be protected. Beard's theory then, was that Hogan had acted as a broker between Spellman and NBA Commissioner Maurice Podoloff and that O'Conner dutifully carried out Hogan's directives.[452] The fact that O'Conner supplied the correspondence between himself and Judge Streit in the Spivey case to Podoloff surely indicates that some sort of relationship existed among these seemingly unrelated officials.

While Ralph Beard carried on his life with honor and integrity and never whined, he did harbor one deep-seated grudge. He said that he knew for a fact, and that the league also knew, that several other players who had done the same as he did—or worse—were in the NBA Hall of Fame.[453]

And, then there's Maurice "Poodles" Podoloff, who may very well have had his own motives. In May 1949, the newspapers reported that, Podoloff, fighting at that time for the survival of his BAA, was highly agitated when the Kentucky players announced that they'd be going to the rival NBL as a unit. Podoloff said that he was willing to let them do the same in his league and would even allow them play in Louisville, as that city was petitioning.[454] His anger was apparent when he said that he understood that the NBL had promised them each a $10,000 bonus, an aggregate salary of $50,000 and a start-up loan of the same amount. Those figures are all inflated, probably purposefully. Then when Alex

Groza reneged on his pledge to play for, and become the savior of, the BAA's Indianapolis Jets, on May 17, Podoloff was not the only person who was angry. "The action of the BAA president in signing a player to a contact after he'd been previously signed by another league is unprecedented in professional basketball," barked Olympians President "Babe" Kimbrough, while noting that Podoloff had "made every effort to tear down our Indianapolis structure."[455] In June, when the BAA's Indianapolis Jets franchise went into receivership, Podoloff issued an angry denial that the league would fold. While he did not cite the Kentuckians by name, he indicated that had they joined his league, this controversy would never have occurred.[456] That discussion became moot the next month when the leagues merged to form the NBA. Although Podoloff was named commissioner of the new league, it may be that he held hard feelings against the Kentucky players and saw his chance to get back at them when the point shaving came to light. Nobody would dismiss consorting with gamblers to fix the outcome of a game as a trivial matter, but if we consider banishment for life, as was Podoloff's decision, a harsh sentence for a youthful indiscretion, then we must consider that there might be factors beyond "the good of the league" at work. Adding that his initial ban on Spivey was based on nothing more than O'Conner's vengeance and that he ignored all Spivey's attempts to pacify the NBA, other factors of influence are indicated.

Podoloff defended his decisions: "You must remember that we have a definite interest in the spectators who are paying the freight," he solemnly told a group of reporters. "We are morally bound to present a sport that is beyond any criticism of conduct on the playing court. This would not be so if we allowed these players to return. We can survive the loss of a number of players, no matter what their status is, but we cannot survive doubt of the honesty of the sport." In closing, he thanked the New York officials, Hogan, O'Conner and Streit, for their help in "cleansing professional basketball from the taint of fixes."[457]

There would be other scandals in college sports, some involving UK. In what would become known as the "$100 handshake" scandal, in October 1985, the *Lexington Herald-Leader* ran a wide-ranging story which said that 26 former Kentucky basketball players admitted having accepted cash, clothing, car tires, meals or other gifts during their careers.[458] Both the University and the NCAA investigated but the *Herald-Leader* contended that UK's investigation was conducted "with a wink and a smile," which made a proper NCAA probe impossible. The major result of all the fuss was that many UK fans canceled their subscriptions to the Lexington newspaper.

Then, in April 1988 the *Los Angeles Daily News* reported that an envelope sent from the UK basketball office to California recruit Chris Mills popped open in a processing facility revealing $1000 in cash evidently offered to Mills as an illegal recruiting bonus. A few days later, veteran journalist Billy Reed, writing for the *Herald-Leader*, noted that while the fans cried that Kentucky was, once again, being picked on, "...for dispassionate observers, the obvious conclusion is that nothing much has changed in Lexington over the decades. Coaches, players and fans have come and gone, but the mentality has remained the same."[459] Contrasting UK's responses to the scandals of 1951 and 1988, it indeed seems that about the only difference is the cast of characters.

So, did Rupp know what was going on back in 1948-51? Should he have known? A case can certainly be made that the answer to the latter question is "yes," but all available evidence indicates that he did not know his players were shaving points. Russell Rice reports that on the day Judge Streit published his attacks on UK and Rupp—April 30, 1952—the Coach was sharing a room in Chicago with Sewanee coach Lou Varnell. Varnell heard the news on the radio while Rupp was out and called several newspapers and radio stations to verify it before he told Rupp. "Oh, my God," exclaimed Rupp. Then he stretched out on the bed and sobbed.[460] As soon as Rupp got back to campus, the pictures of Ralph Beard and Alex Groza vanished from their places of honor on the Coliseum's concourse wall.[461] Many years would pass before Rupp and Beard came to terms; evidently he and Groza never did.

Late in his life, when someone asked Rupp if he knew his players were shaving points, the frail old man mustered his strength. "Hell," he roared, "we won the NCAA and the NIT and we sent the team to the Olympics with those same players. They did every single damn thing I ever asked of them. If I was supposed to know what was going on when a team like that is winning, why doesn't a coach of a losing team ever think his players are fixing games?"[462] An excellent question.

That brings up the question of whether the Kentucky the players actually made any effort to impact the point spreads. Hirsh and Line admitted that they did; Barnstable never publically said anything. As those three had little professional potential, they faded from the headlines, leaving Beard, Groza and Spivey to garner all the ink.* Groza seldom made any public statements, so we only have his record as evidence. Beard said he took the money but would not have known how to shave points as he was too competitive to play less than all out. Not to mention, he said, that with two All-American guards on the bench, Rupp would have yanked him from the game had he made many errors.[463] Spivey repeatedly vowed that his only sin was in not reporting that he had been approached by a gambler.

Cliff Barker had an opinion on his teammates. "I don't think Beard, Groza and Barnstable ever did throw a game. I think it's just the way the score came out. I don't deny that they took the money, but I don't think they tried to lose the game on purpose. They were just poor country boys who weren't used to seeing a bunch of money fanned under their noses like that."[464] Barker's wife had another story from many years later. "Alex called out of the blue and asked us to meet him in Denver. We didn't know it at the time, but he was very, very ill. And he knew he was.... He felt that he might have ruined our lives by his actions and he wanted to get it off his chest.... He told us about meeting with the gamblers and how he took the money. Then he said to us in confidence, 'Never did I throw a game. Never!' Six months later he died."[465]

Kenny Rollins, who said that gamblers never approached him, as Captain of the team echoed Coach Rupp's comment. "They did everything I ever asked of them."[466]

What happened in the NIT game with Loyola? One theory is that the UK players did try to hold the point spread down and the game got out of hand. Maybe so. The fact that Beard had but two points at halftime and turned it on in the second to lead the team in scoring lends a little credence to that idea, if you care to view it that way. Beard said he did everything in his power to win and the box score bears that out, if you care to take that view. Groza, for a fact, did not have a good game and that could be on purpose or it could have just been a bad night. Asked, many years later, to explain the loss, Ralph Beard simply shrugged. "We just got beat."[467]

Raise your hand if you remember when Billy Gillispie's Wildcats were shockingly trounced by Gardner-Webb 84-68 in 2007, a loss no

*Walt Hirsh was playing minor league baseball when he was implicated in the point shaving. He was banned from any further participation in professional baseball.

less improbable than the 1949 NIT loss to Loyola. Keep your hand raised if it even crossed your mind that Patrick Patterson and Jodie Meeks were shaving points. As Beard said, "sometimes you just get beat."

Among the questions remaining unanswered is why Kentucky was allowed to retain the SEC and NCAA Championships won in 1949 when the players admitted to being paid, making them professionals. The SEC ruled several of the UK players ineligible for various periods, so it would seem that any games played during those times would be forfeit.

Why did they do it? The gamblers undoubtedly talked a good line. "Nobody gets hurt but other gamblers," "nobody will ever know," "everybody else is doing it," "easy money." It is doubtful that the players knew that point shaving was illegal, and perhaps they would have acted differently had they known. Nonetheless, it is easy to see why college students from impoverished background would take the money. But, both Groza and Beard said that the money was no factor. In his one public statement, when he was hired at Bellarmine, Alex Groza simply said he didn't know why he did it. Beard, on a television interview, said, "I never had two dimes to rub together. My mother cleaned six apartments so we'd have one to live in. Why did I take the money?" Here the man who said that he'd thought about it "every ten or fifteen minutes" for more than 50 years was at a loss for words. He shrugged and softly said, "I don't know," as his voice tailed off.[468]

Finally, is UK's Fabulous Five the best team ever to play college basketball? Now there's a question sure to start an argument. UCLA fans will tell you that whoever the best college team is, it would have to have Lew Alcindor on it. The Jayhawks would say Chamberlain, the Tar Heels would say Jordan. Hoosier fans will tell you that IU's 1975-76 that won the National Championship while going 32-0 was pretty good. Michigan supporters will point out their Fab Five of 1991-93 were not too shabby, and there are many other legitimate contenders for the title. Kentucky fans can point to the only college team to win an Olympic good metal, but had the method by which the USA Olympic team is chosen remained the same, some other school would probably have matched that feat.

For a fact, the Fabulous Five are the yardstick by which all Kentucky teams will be measured, at least until all who saw them play are gone.

As one who has read many, many sports pages while researching this book, I can tell you that for many years after 1949, national sportswriters compared every great team to "those Kentucky aggregations featuring Beard and Groza." At a fiftieth anniversary celebration of the 1948 season, in addressing this very issue, Ralph Beard said it best: "It's tough to compare. All you can do is dominate your era and leave the rest up to speculation."[469]

APPENDIX A

1948 USA Olympic Statistics

Name	Games	FGM	FTA	FTM	PCT	Fouls	points	PPG
Groza	7	35	14	8	57.1	19	78	11.1
Kurland	7	27	15	11	73.3	17	65	9.3
Barksdale	6	20	19	14	73.7	16	54	9.0
Pitts	4	13	6	5	83.3	3	31	7.8
Lumpp	5	14	10	8	80.0	11	36	7.2
Jones	6	19	9	5	55.6	11	43	7.2
Carpenter	5	13	12	9	75.0	6	35	7.0
Boryla	5	11	10	6	60.0	11	28	5.6
Renick	7	17	7	5	71.4	13	39	5.6
Beck	7	13	11	7	63.6	3	33	4.7
Rollins	6	10	5	4	80.0	5	24	4.0
Barker	5	7	12	5	41.7	13	19	3.8
Beard	7	10	12	6	50.0	7	26	3.7
Robinson	5	6	3	1	33.3	6	13	2.6
Total	**8**	**215**	**145**	**94**	**64.8**	**141**	**524**	**65.5**
Opponents	8	81	166	94	56.6	132	256	32.0

source: www.usab.com

Appendix B

Statistics for Alex Groza

1944-45: Drafted into military after 10 games

1946-47: Consensus First Team All-American, All-SEC Second Team, All SEC Tournament Team

1947-48: Consensus Second Team All-American, NCAA Final Four Most Valuable Player, NCAA Regional Most Valuable Player, All SEC First Team, All SEC Tournament Team

1948-49: Consensus All-American First Team, Helms National Player of the Year, NCAA Final Four Most Valuable Player, NCAA Regional Most Valuable Player, All SEC First Team, All SEC Tournament Team

Retired Jersey #15 hangs in Rupp Arena

UK Statistics:

Season	**Games**	**FG**	**FT**	**FTA**	**PF**	**Pts**
1944-45	10	62	41	57	?	165
1946-47	37	146	101	160	85	393
1947-48	39	200	88	140	87	488
1948-49	34	259	180	248	103	698
Totals	**120**	**667**	**410**	**605**	**275**	**1744**

Groza's career 1744 points topped UK's all-time scorer's list in 1949 and still ranks tenth.

Indianapolis Olympians Statistics:

1949-50	64	521	454	623	212	1496
1950-51	66	492	445	566	237	1429
Totals	**130**	**1013**	**899**	**1189**	**458**	**2925**

1949-50: Led the NBA in field goal percentage, second in scoring

1950-51: Led the NBA in field goal percentage in, second in scoring and fifth in rebounding, Named to the first NBA All-Star Team

Appendix C

Statistics for Bill Spivey

1949-50: Consensus Second Team All-American, All-SEC First Team, All SEC Tournament Team

1950-51: Consensus All-American First Team, Helms National Player of the Year, NCAA Final Four Team, NCAA Regional Team, All SEC First Team, All SEC Tournament Team
Retired Jersey #77 hangs in Rupp Arena

UK Statistics:

Season	Games	FG	FT	FTA	PF	Pts
1949-50	30	225	128	176	93	578
1950-51	33	252	131	211	91	635
Totals	**63**	**477**	**259**	**387**	**184**	**1213**

Appendix D

Statistics for Ralph Beard

1945-46: All-SEC First Team, All-SEC Tournament Team

1946-47: Consensus First Team All-American, All-SEC First Team, All SEC Tournament Team

1947-48: Consensus First Team All-American, All SEC First Team, All SEC Tournament Team

1948-49: Consensus All-American First Team, All SEC First Team, All SEC Tournament Team

Retired Jersey #12 hangs in Rupp Arena

UK Statistics:

Season	Games	FG	FT	FTA	PF	Pts
1945-46	30	111	57	110	69	279
1946-47	37	157	78	115	71	392
1947-48	38	194	88	149	80	476
1948-49	34	144	82	115	55	370
Totals	**139**	**606**	**305**	**489**	**275**	**1517**

Beard's career 1517 points ranked second on UK's all-time scorer's list in 1949 and still ranks twelfth.

Indianapolis Olympians Statistics:

Season	Games	FG	FT	FTA	PF	Pts
1949-50	60	340	215	282	132	895
1950-51	66	409	293	378	96	1111
Totals	**126**	**749**	**508**	**660**	**228**	**2006**

Endnotes

[1]*Lexington Herald-Leader,* Oct. 21, 1951.

[2]Gould, Todd, Pioneers of the Hardwood, Indiana University Press, Bloomington, 1998. 190.

[3]*Herald-Leader,* Oct. 21, 1951.

[4]*Louisville Courier-Journal,* Oct. 21, 1951.

[5]www.bigbluehistory.net/bb/statistics/Players/Groza_Alex.html

[6]www.bigbluehistory.net/bb/Statistics/Players/Beard_Ralph.html

[7]Gould, Pioneers. 189-190.

[8]*Courier-Journal,* Oct. 23, 1951.

[9]Ibid.

[10]*Herald-Leader,* Oct. 21, 1951.

[11]*Courier-Journal,* Oct. 21, 1951.

[12]Gould, Pioneers. 194.

[13]Commonwealth of Kentucky, Directory of Births and Deaths 1926-1930, Series 4, Vol. I. 456.

[14]Walton, Luke, Basketball's Fabulous Five, Greenberg Publishers, New York, 1950.

[15]Ibid. 12.

[16]Beard, Ralph, interview by Shelley Wilkie, June 6, 1998, Henderson County High School Oral History Project, Louie B. Nunn Center for Oral History, University of Kentucky Libraries.

[17]Walton, Fabulous Five. 11.

[18]Beard, Ralph, interview by Maurice Clay, May 6, 1986, Interscholastic Athletics Oral History Project. Louie B. Nunn Center for Oral History, University of Kentucky Libraries.

[19]Ibid.

[20]Ibid. Ralph remembered his time as 2:08, which he said "would not win a women's meet today."

[21]Walton, Fabulous Five. 13-14.

[22]Beard, Ralph, interview by Maurice Clay, May 1, 1989, Interscholastic Athletics Oral History Project. Louie B. Nunn Center for Oral History, University of Kentucky Libraries.

[23]Walton, Fabulous Five. 16.

[24]www.kyallstars.net

[25]Beard, 1986 Clay interview. Louie B. Nunn Center for Oral History, University of Kentucky Libraries.

[26]Rupp, Adolph, Interview by Russell Rice, undated, Charles T. Wethington Oral History Project, Louie B. Nunn Center for Oral Histories, University of Kentucky Libraries.

[27]*Courier-Journal*, Sept. 2, 1970.

[28]Kleber, John (Ed.), The Kentucky Encyclopedia, University Press of Kentucky, Lexington, 1992. 787

[29]Rupp, Rice interview. Louie B. Nann Center for Oral History, University of Kentucky Libraries.

[30]Ibid.

[31]The Rupp Tape, WHAS Productions, 1992.

[32]Rupp, Rice interview. Louie B. Nann Center for Oral History, University of Kentucky Libraries.

[33]Ibid.

[34]Rup, Rice interview, May 1, 1977. Louie B. Nann Center for Oral History, University of Kentucky Libraries.

[35]Ibid.

[36]Rupp, Rice interview, undated. At that time, UK played in Alumni Gym built in 1924 with a seating capacity of 2800. Louie B. Nann Center for Oral History, University of Kentucky Libraries.

[37]Ibid.

[38]Ibid.

[39]Nelli, Bert and Steve, The Winning Tradition, University Press of Kentucky, Lexington, 1998.

[40]Beard, Clay interview. Louie B. Nann Center for Oral History, University of Kentucky Libraries.

[41]Rupp, Rice interview. Louie B. Nann Center for Oral History, University of Kentucky Libraries.

[42]Ibid.

[43]www.wikipedia.org/wiki/Southeastern_Conference#Founding_and_former_members

[44]Ibid.

[45]*Courier-Journal*, Jan. 14, 1951.

[46]www.wikipedia.org

[47]Rice, Russell, Adolph Rupp, Kentucky's Basketball Baron, Sagamore Publishing, Champaign, IL, 1994. 88.

[48]*New York Times*, September 28, 2010.

[49]*Courier-Journal*, November 11, 1945.

[50]Beard, Wilkie interview. Louie B. Nann Center for Oral History, University of Kentucky Libraries.

[51]Ibid.

[52]*Courier-Journal*, February 1, 1998.

[53]Beard, Wilkie interview. Louie B. Nann Center for Oral History, University of Kentucky Libraries.

[54]*Courier-Journal*, December 2, 1945.

[55]*Courier-Journal*, December 19, 1945.

[56]Beard, Ralph, unknown interviewer, 2002.
[57]Walton, Fabulous Five, 18.
[58]*Courier-Journal*, March 1-3, 1946.
[59]The NIT would remain the more prestigious event until the point shaving activity at Madison Square Garden came to light in 1952.
[60]Beard, Ralph, Unknown interviewer, 2002.
[61]Ibid.
[62]Ibid.
[63]Rice, Adolph Rupp. 93.
[64]*Courier-Journal*, February 1, 1998.
[65]*Courier-Journal*, March 21, 1946.
[66]Rice, Adolph Rupp, 90.
[67]www.bigbluehistory.net
[68]Walton, Fabulous Five, 25-26.
[69]www.wickipedia.com
[70]Walton, Fabulous Five, 28-30.
[71]Ibid. 30
[72]Rice, Adolph Rupp. 82.
[73]Ibid. 83.
[74]*Courier-Journal*, January 2, 1945.
[75]*Courier-Journal*, January 9, 1945.
[76]*Courier-Journal*, January 14, 1945.
[77]Walton, Fabulous Five. 31.
[78]Rice, Adolph Rupp. 94.
[79]Ibid. 85.
[80]Nelli, Winning Tradition. 63.
[81]Walton, Fabulous Five. 37.
[82]Walton, Fabulous Five. 36- 46.
[83]Ibid. 46-47.
[84]*Courier-Journal*, February 2, 1998.
[85]Rice, Adolph Rupp. 45-46.
[86]Beard, Ralph. Unknown Interviewer, 2002.
[87]*Courier-Journal*, November 29, 1946.
[88]Nelli, Winning Tradition. 64.
[89]New York Times, December 23, 1946.
[90]*Courier-Journal*, December 29, 1946.
[91]*Courier-Journal*, January 1, 1947.
[92]Ibid.
[93]Ibid.
[94]Ibid.
[95]Rice, Adolph Rupp. 97.
[96]*Courier-Journal*, February 2, 1947.
[97]*Courier-Journal*, February 9, 1947.
[98]Rice, Adolph Rupp. 97-98.
[99]*Courier-Journal*, March 2, 1947.

[100]Ibid.
[101]*Courier-Journal*, March 25, 1947.
[102]Beard, Ralph, Unknown interviewer, 2002.
[103]*New York Times*, January 5, 2005.
[104]Rice, Adolph Rupp, 97.
[105]*Courier-Journal*, February 2, 1998.
[106]Rice, Adolph Rupp, 99. Rice, Adolph Rupp. 102.
[107]Ibid.
[108]Nelli, Winning Tradition. 41.
[109]*Courier-Journal*, December 21, 1947.
[110]Ibid.
[111]Rice, Adolph Rupp. 102.
[112]*Courier-Journal*, December 27, 1947.
[113]Rice, Adolph Rupp. 102.
[114]Nelli, Winning Tradition. 65.
[115]*Courier-Journal*, January 10, 1948.
[116]*Courier-Journal*, February 1, 1948.
[117]Ibid.
[118]*Courier-Journal*, February 3, 1948.
[119]*Courier-Journal*, March 7, 1948.
[120]Rice, Adolph Rupp. 105.
[121]*Courier-Journal*, March 21, 1948.
[122]*Courier-Journal*, March 24, 1948.
[123]Rice, Adolph Rupp. 105.
[124]http://en.wikipedia.org/wiki/Bob_Kurland
[125]*Courier-Journal*, April 1, 1948.
[126]*New York Times*, April 1, 1948.
[127]*Courier-Journal*, April 1, 1948.
[128]Waco (TX) News-Tribune, April 2, 1948.
[129]Beard, Ralph, unknown interviewer, 2002.
[130]*Lexington Herald Leader*, April 3, 1948.
[131]Rice, Adolph Rupp. 106.
[132]*Lawton (OK) Constitution*, July 1, 1948.
[133]*Courier-Journal*, July 9, 1948.
[134]Waukesha (WI) Daily Freeman, July 3, 1948.
[135]*Courier-Journal*, July 9, 1948.
[136]*Courier-Journal*, July 10, 1948.
[137]Ibid.
[138]Ibid.
[139]Ibid.
[140]*Syracuse (NY) Post-Standard*, July 13, 948.
[141]Beard, Ralph, unknown interviewer, 2002. Mr. Beard said he used the term "refurbished" loosely.
[142]Idid.
[143]Ibid.

[144]Beard, Ralph, unknown interviewer, 2002. Mr. Beard would not say who made the decision. "I just played," he commented.
[145]*Courier-Journal*, August 4, 1948.
[146]Rice, Adolph Rupp. 118-119.
[147]*Milwaukee (WI) Journal*, January 24, 1950.
[148]*Courier-Journal*, Aug 4-13, 1948.
[149]*Courier-Journal*, November 30, 1948,
[150]*Harrisburg (PA) Evening News*, December 9, 1948.
[151]North Adams (MA) Transcript, December 17, 1948.
[152]*Joplin (MO) Globe*, December 19, 1948.
[153]*Courier-Journal*, December 31, 1948.
[154]*Middlesboro (KY) Daily News*, January 12, 1949.
[155]*Austin (TX) American-Statesman*, January 23, 1949.
[156]Ibid.
[157]Walton, Fabulous Five. 94.
[158]*Tipton (IN) Tribune*, February 9, 1949.
[159]*Delta Democrat-Times* (Greenville, MS) March 6, 1949.
[160]*Courier-Journal*, March 14, 1949.
[161]*Courier-Journal*, March 15, 1949.
[162]Ibid.
[163]*New York Times*, March 15, 1949.
[164]*Courier-Journal*, March 15, 1949.
[165]Ibid.
[166]*New York Times*, March 22, 1949.
[167]*New York Times*, March 23, 1949.
[168]Ibid.
[169]*Courier-Journal*, March 27, 1949.
[170]*Courier-Journal*, April 5, 1949.
[171]*Middlesboro (KY) Daily News*, April 5, 1949.
[172]*New York Times*, April 5, 1949.
[173]*Middlesboro (KY) Daily News*, April 2, 1949.
[174]*Daily News*, April 8, 1949.
[175]*Daily News*, April 18, 1949.
[176]*Daily News*, April 23, 1949.
[177]Ibid.
[178]*Hagerstown (MD) Daily Mail*, April 29, 1949.
[179]Walton, Fabulous Five. 112-113.
[180]*New York Times*, May 11, 1948.
[181]*Indianapolis Star*, June 12, 1947.
[182]Gould, Pioneers. 158.
[183]Walton, Fabulous Five. 115-116.
[184]*Logansport (IN) Phoras-Tribune*, May 5, 1949.
[185]Walton, Fabulous Five. 116.
[186]*Muscatine (IA) Journal*, May 27, 1949.
[187]Ibid.

[188]*Sandusky (OH) Register,* May 28, 1949.
[189]*New York Times*, August 4, 1949.
[190]*Courier-Journal*, October 27, 1949.
[191]Walton, Fabulous Five. 128.
[192]*Syracuse (NY) Post-Standard*, November 1, 1949.
[193]*Kansas City (MO) Star*, November 2, 1949.
[194]*Kokomo (IN) Tribune*, November 9, 149.
[195]*Hagerstown (MD) Daily Mail*, November 11, 1949.
[196]*Dixon (IL) Evening Telegram*, November 21, 1949.
[197]Walton, Fabulous Five, 136.
[198]*Dixon (IL) Evening Telegram*, December 2, 1949.
[199]Beard, Ralph, unknown interviewer, 2002.
[200]*Kokomo (IN) Tribune*, December 23, 1949.
[201]Gould, Pioneers, 170.
[202]Curran, Nick (Ed.) Official NBA Guide, *The Sporting News*, St. Louis, 1969, 238.
[203]www.basketballreference.com
[204]Ibid.
[205]Gould, Pioneers, 173.
[206]www.basketballreference.com
[207]Walton, Fabulous Five, 143.
[208]Ibid., 144.
[209]Ibid., 22.
[210]*Lincoln (NE) Star*, August 16, 1951.
[211]*Brooklyn (NY) Daily Eagle*, December 16, 1949.
[212]*Alton (IL) Evening Telegraph*, December 30, 1949.
[213]*Kokomo (IN) Tribune,* December 31, 1949.
[214]Rice, Adolph Rupp. 119.
[215]*Burlington (NC) Daily Times-News*, January 10, 1950.
[216]*Hope (AK) Star*, January 24, 1950.
[217]*Kingsport (TN) Times-News,* February 26, 1950.
[218]So says the plaque on the building placed there by the UK Alumni Association on December 9, 1950. However, www.bigbluehistory.net says the count is 249-24. The UK 2013-2014 Men's Basketball Media Guide lists it as 247-24.
[219]*Kingsport (TN) Times-News*, March 5, 1950.
[220]Rupp, Adolph, Rice interview, undated.
[221]Rice, Adolph Rupp, 120.
[222]*San Mateo (CA) Times*, March 14, 1950.
[223]*Sandusky (OH) Register*, March 15, 1950.
[224]Ibid.
[225]Rice, Adolph Rupp. 121.
[226]Ibid. 120.
[227]*Courier-Journal*, December 30, 1950.
[228]Gould, Pioneers, 184-185. The other was between the Ft. Wayne Pistons and the Minneapolis Lakers on November 22, 1950. Ft. Wayne won 19-18 in the lowest scoring game in NBA history.

[229]*New York Times*, January 18, 1951.
[230]Ibid.
[231]Ibid.
[232]*Tucson (AZ) Daily Citizen*, January 18, 1951.
[233]*High Point (NC) Enterprise*, February 19, 1951.
[234]*Jefferson City (MO) Post Tribune*, February 20, 1951.
[235]*High Point Enterprise,* February 19, 1951.
[236]*Valparaiso (IN) Vidette Messenger*, February 27, 1951.
[237]*Traverse City (MI) Record-Eagle*, February 28, 1951.
[238]*Courier-Journal*, March 4, 1951.
[239]*Middlesboro (KY) Daily Mail*, March 21, 1951.
[240]*Brooklyn (NY) Daily Eagle,* March 23, 1951.
[241]*Zanesville (OH) Times Recorder*, March 25, 1951.
[242]*Courier-Journal*, March 28, 1951.
[243]Ibid.
[244]*Troy (NY) Times Record*, March 3, 1951.
[245]*Dixon (IL) Evening Telegram*, March 24, 1951.
[246]Ibid. March 26, 1951.
[247]Beard, Ralph, unknown interviewer, 2002.
[248]*Courier-Journal*, August 22, 1951.
[249]*Lincoln (NE) Star*, August 16, 1951.
[250]*New York Times*, September 15, 1951.
[251]*Lincoln (NE) Star*, August 16, 1951.
[252]*Alton (IL) Evening Telegram*, October 16, 1951.
[253]*Lincoln (NE) Evening Journal*, July 25, 1951. Three Toledo University players admitted accepting $1,750 for fixing Toledo's game against Niagara on December 14, 1950.
[254]*Courier-Journal,* October 20,1951.
[255]Gould, Pioneers, 189.
[256]*Courier-Journal*, October 21, 1951.
[257]Ibid.
[258]Ibid.
[259]*New York Times*, October 22, 1951.
[260]*Courier-Journal*, October 21, 1951.
[261]*New York Times*, October 21, 1951.
[262]*Courier-Journal*, October 21, 1951.
[263]Ibid.
[264]Ibid.
[265]Ibid.
[266]Ibid.
[267]Ibid.
[268]*Courier-Journal*, October 22, 1951.
[269]Ibid.
[270]Ibid.
[271]*New York Times*, October 23, 1951.

[272]Ibid.
[273]*Jacksonville (IL) Daily Journal*, October 24, 1951.
[274]Ibid.
[275]Ibid.
[276]*Courier-Journal*, October 23, 1951.
[277]*Middlesboro (KY) Daily News*, October 19, 1951.
[278]*New York Times*, October 26, 1951.
[279]*New York Times*, October 27, 1951.
[280]*New York Times*, December 16, 1951.
[281]Ibid.
[282]*Indiana (PA) Gazette*, December 17, 1951.
[283]*New York Times*, December 25, 1951.
[284]Ellison, Betty Boles, Kentucky's Domain of Power, Greed and Corruption, Writers Club Press, Lincoln, NE, 2001. 49-50.
[285]*New York Times*, February 1, 1952.
[286]*Courier-Journal*, February 15, 1952.
[287]Englisis, Nick, *True Magazine*, March 1952. 68.
[288]Ibid.
[289]Ibid.
[290]Ibid. 69.
[291]Ibid.
[292]Ibid.
[293]Ibid. 70.
[294]Ibid. 71.
[295]Ibid. 72.
[296]*Courier-Journal*, February 16, 1952.
[297]Ibid.
[298]Ibid.
[299]Ibid.
[300]*Look*, Vol. 16, No. 3., January 29, 1952. 58.
[301]Ibid. 60.
[302]Ibid.
[303]*Courier-Journal*, January 29, 1952.
[304]*Courier-Journal*, February 15, 1952.
[305]*Courier-Journal*, March 13, 1952.
[306]*Courier-Journal*, February 3, 1954.
[307]*New York Times*, February 20, 1952.
[308]*New York Times*, March 3, 1952.
[309]Beard, Ralph, unknown interviewer, 2002.
[310]*New York Times*, February 27, 1952.
[311]*Leavenworth (KS) Times*, March 2, 1952.
[312]*New York Times*, March 3, 1952.
[313]*Courier-Journal*, March 2, 1952
[314]Ibid.
[315]*New York Times*, February 28, 1952.

[316]*New York Times*, April 30, 1952.
[317]Court of General Sessions, County of New York, People v Ralph Beard, Indictment 2819-51, April 29, 1952.
[318]Ibid.
[319]*Courier-Journal*, July 27, 2014.
[320]*Courier-Journal*, April 30, 1952.
[321]Ibid.
[322]Ibid.
[323]Court of General Sessions, County of New York, People v Ralph Beard, Indictment 2819-51, April 29, 1952.
[324]Court of General Sessions, County of New York, People v Alex Groza, Indictment 2820-51, April 29, 1952.
[325]*New York Times,* April 30, 1952.
[326]Ibid.
[327]*Courier-Journal*, April 30, 1952.
[328]Ibid.
[329]Ibid
[330]Ibid.
[331]Ibid.
[332]Ibid.
[333]*El Paso (TX) Herald-Post*, April 30, 1952.
[334]*New York Times*, May 1, 1952.
[335]*Troy (NY) Record*, May 1, 1952.
[336]*Courier-Journal*, May 1, 1952.
[337]*Courier-Journal*, May 3, 1952.
[338]*New York Times*, May 1, 1952.
[339]*Courier-Journal*, May 1, 1952.
[340]*Courier-Journal*, May 6, 1952.
[341]Ellison, Kentucky's Domain, 53.
[342]Ibid.
[343]*Odessa (TX) American*, January 4, 1952.
[344]*Baytown (TX) Sun*, May 19, 1952.
[345]*The Daily Tar Heel*, (Chapel Hill, NC) May 20, 1952.
[346]*New York Times,* June 9, 1952.
[347]*Washington (DC) Post*, May 5, 1952.
[348]Ibid.
[349]*Kansas City (MO) Star,* June 24, 1952.
[350]*Atlanta (GA) Journal*, July 31, 1952.
[351]*Courier-Journal*, May 7, 1952.
[352]Ibid.
[353]Ibid.
[354]Ellison, Kentucky's Domain, 48.
[355]Ibid.
[356]Ellison, Kentucky's Domain, 53.
[357]*Courier-Journal*, New York Times, July 3, 1952.

[358]*Courier-Journal,* July 17, 1952.
[359]*Courier-Journal,* July 26, 1952.
[360]*Matoon (IL) Daily Journal-Gazette,* July 28, 1952.
[361]*Courier-Journal,* August 9, 1952.
[362]*Eau Claire (WI) Daily Telegram,* August 9, 1952.
[363]*Courier-Journal,* August 12, 1952.
[364]Ibid.
[365]Ellison, Kentucky's Domain, 54.
[366]*Anniston (AL) Evening Telegraph,* August 12, 1952.
[367]*Lexington Herald,* August 12, 1952.
[368]*New York Times,* November 4, 1952.
[369]*Albuquerque (NM) Journal,* November 4, 1952.
[370]*Traverse City (MI) Record-Eagle,* November 4, 1952.
[371]Ibid.
[372]*Courier-Journal,* November 5, 1952.
[373]*Courier-Journal,* November 7, 1952.
[374]Ibid.
[375]*Courier-Journal,* November 14, 1952.
[376]*Eau Claire (WI) Daily Telegram,* July 16, 1952.
[377]*Indiana (PA) Gazette,* October 7, 1952.
[378]*Traverse City (MI) Record-Eagle,* October 11, 1952.
[379]*Kokomo (IN) Tribune,* October 22, 1952.
[380]*New York Times,* October 24, 1952.
[381]Ibid.
[382]*Burlington (NC) Daily Times-News,* October 27, 1952.
[383]*Kokomo Tribune,* November 6, 1952.
[384]Beard, Ralph, unknown interviewer, 2002.
[385]*New York Times,* May 24, 1952.
[386]Ibid. May 28, 1952.
[387]*Troy (NY) Record,* May 28, 1952.
[388]*New York Times,* January 15, 1953.
[389]*Courier-Journal,* January 16, 1953.
[390]*Lincoln (NE) Star,* March 12, 1935.
[391]*Courier-Journal,* January 16, 1953.
[392]*New York Times,* January 17, 1953.
[393]*Courier-Journal,* January 17, 1953.
[394]*Brooklyn (NY),* January 19, 1953.
[395]*Courier-Journal,* January 21, 1953.
[396]Ibid. *New York Times,* January 20, 1953.
[397]*Courier-Journal,* New York Times, January 22, 1953.
[398]Ibid.
[399]*Courier-Journal,* New York Times, January 23, 1953.
[400]Ibid.
[401]Ibid.
[402]Ibid.

[403]Ibid.
[404]Ibid.
[405]*Courier-Journal*, January 24, 1953.
[406]Ibid.
[407]Ibid.
[408]*Courier-Journal*, January 27, 1953.
[409]*New York Times*, January 27, 1953.
[410]*Cumberland (MD) News*, April 24, 1953.
[411]*Brownsville (TX) Herald*, April 26, 1953.
[412]*Courier-Journal*, March 21, 1953.
[413]Ibid.
[414]Ibid.
[415]*Courier-Journal*, March 22, 1953.
[416]Ibid.
[417]Ibid.
[418]*Anniston (AL) Star*, April 16, 1953.
[419]*Hopkinsville (KY) New Era*, August 27, 1953.
[420]Rice, Adolph Rupp. 200.
[421]McGill, John, John McGill Presents Kentucky Sports, Host and Associates, Lexington, KY, 1978. 7.
[422]Ibid. 17.
[423]Rice, Adolph Rupp. 204-205.
[424]*Charleston (WV) Gazette-Mail*, December 6, 1959.
[425]*Freeport (IL) Journal-Standard*, April 16, 1959.
[426]*East Liverpool (OH) Evening Review*, November 27, 1959.
[427]*Charleston (WV) Gazette-Mail*, December 6, 1959.
[428]*Lexington Herald-Leader*, January 22, 1995.
[429]*Troy (NY) Times Record*, March 10, 1955.
[430]*Lexington Herald-Leader*, September 4, 1977.
[431]*Gettysburg (PA) Times*, March 20, 1959.
[432]*Anderson (IN) Daily Bulletin*, January 4, 1960.
[433]*Bridgeport (CT) Telegram*, April 7, 1960.
[434]*Anderson (IN) Herald*, July 2, 1960.
[435]Ibid.
[436]*Ogden (UT) Standard Examiner*, September 1, 1960.
[437]T*erre Haute (IN) Star*, September 6, 1960.
[438]Ibid. January 16, 1961,
[439]*Sandusky (OH) Register*, June 28, 1961.
[440]*New York Times*, February 13, 1968,
[441]*New York Times*, March 1, 1983.
[442]Beard, Ralph, Unknown interviewer, 2002.
[443]Ibid.
[444]*Cumberland (MD) Evening Times*, April 6, 1956.
[445]Ibid. October 15, 1958.
[446]Beard, Ralph, unknown interviewer, 2002.

[447]Ibid.
[448]Ibid.
[449]*Terre Haute (IN) Star*, November 17, 1985
[450]Reed, William, SportsIllustrated.com, November 30, 2007.
[451]*New York Times*, December 13, 1951.
[452]Reed, William, SportsIllustrated.com, November 30, 2007.
[453]Beard, Ralph, unknown interviewer, 2002. Gould, Pioneers, 196.
[454]*New York Times*, December 13, 1951.
[455]Ibid. May 26, 1949.
[456]*Syracuse (NY) Post-Standard*, June 25, 1949.
[457]Gould, Pioneers, 194.
[458]*Lexington (KY) Herald-Leader*, October 27, 1985.
[459]*Lexington (KY) Herald-Leader,* April 20, 1988.
[460]Rice, Adolph Rupp, 125.
[461]Ibid. 128.
[462]*Troy (NY) Record*, March 24, 1972.
[463]Beard, Ralph, unknown interviewer, 2002.
[464]Gould, Pioneers, 191-192.
[465]Ibid. 200.
[466]*Courier-Journal*, October 21, 1951.
[467]Beard, Ralph, unknown interviewer, 2002
[468]Ibid.
[469]*Courier-Journal,* February 1, 1998.

About the Author

Ron Elliott, a native of Lincoln County, Kentucky, is a graduate of Stanford High School, Eastern Kentucky University and the University of Kentucky.

Ron's background includes working on the historic Apollo missions and a stint on Kentucky's community college system faculty. Having a relative involved in the assassination of Kentucky's would-be governor, William Goebel, piqued his interest in history and launched a writing career.

A much-in-demand member of the Kentucky Humanities Council Speakers Bureau, Ron is the author of several books, including *Inside the Beverly Hills Supper Club Fire*, *Through the Eyes of Lincoln*, *From Hilltop to Mountaintop: The Life and Legacy of One Iwo Jima Flag Raiser* and *American El Dorado: The Great Diamond Hoax of 1872*. His work is also featured in numerous magazine articles. He is the 2012 DAR Literary Award recipient and recently appeared in an episode of "Mysteries at the Museum."

Retired, Ron and his wife, Carol, currently live in Nelson County, Kentucky.

INDEX

A

Adcock, Billy Joe 144, 145
Alabama 34, 58
Alcindor, Lew 212
Alford, Steve 21
Allen 144
Allen, Forrest (Phog) 23, 62, 96
Alumni Gym 27, 28, 33, 40, 42, 53, 55, 57, 63, 71, 91, 106, 120, 128
Amateur Athletics Union (AAU) 60, 63, 64
American Basketball Association (ABA) 194, 196, 204
American Basketball League (ABL) 183, 200
American Olympic Basketball Committee 60
Anderson, Dwight 20
Anderson Packers 81
Appalachian League 82
Arizin, Paul 74
Arizona 36, 96
Arkansas 33, 69, 91, 160, 188
Arkansas Teachers College 41
Ashford, Ed 179
Ashman, Allen 8
Athens 91
Atlanta 91
Auburn 34, 49, 72, 129

B

Baker, Floyd 38, 111
Baltimore Bullets 81, 199, 200, 201
Barker, Cliff 13, 14, 17, 44, 51, 52, 55, 56, 58, 59, 61, 62, 65, 67, 68, 69, 71, 73, 74, 75, 77, 79, 80, 82, 83, 84, 85, 87, 89, 94, 97, 102, 109, 116, 117, 126, 127, 141, 142, 143, 144, 145, 146, 147, 149, 150, 211, 214
Barksdale, Don 62, 64, 65, 214
Barnhorst, Leo 94
Barnstable, Dale 8, 15, 16, 17, 44, 45, 51, 52, 57, 59, 68, 69, 75, 89, 90, 104, 123, 132, 134, 135, 136, 137, 140, 142, 144, 145, 147, 149, 150, 154, 155, 156, 160, 161, 163, 164, 173, 174, 175, 179, 183, 186, 207, 210, 211
Basketball Association of America (BAA) 68, 79
Bauer, Marilyn 82
Baylor 58, 59, 60, 61, 62, 146
Beard, Marvin 18
Beard, Ralph 7, 9, 13, 14, 15, 16, 17, 18, 19, 20, 21, 22, 26, 28, 29, 30, 31, 32, 33, 34, 35, 36, 37, 43, 45, 46, 47, 48, 49, 50, 51, 52, 54, 55, 56, 57, 58, 59, 61, 62, 63, 64, 65, 67, 68, 69, 71, 72, 73, 74, 75, 76, 77, 79, 80, 81, 82, 83, 84, 85, 86, 87, 89, 94, 95, 97, 100, 106, 107, 110, 114, 116, 123, 126, 127, 131, 133, 134, 135, 136, 137, 138, 140, 141, 142, 143, 144, 145, 146, 147, 149, 150, 152, 154, 155, 156, 157, 158, 161, 163, 164, 173, 174, 178, 179, 180, 183, 185, 186, 203, 204, 205, 206, 207, 208, 210, 211, 212, 213, 214, 217
Beard, Ralph M., Sr. 18
Beard, Sue Anna (Moorman) 18, 19
Beck, Lewis 62, 64, 214
Bee, Clair 157
Benintende, Joseph 176
Benson, Bull 143, 144
Benson, Kent 21
Bigos, Adolph 96
Bird, Jerry 182
Blanda, George 30, 31
Bluefield, West Virginia 82
Bluitt 150
Boeck, Larry 142, 148, 150, 167
Boryla, Vincent (Vince) 62, 64, 65, 82, 83, 214
Boston 69, 190
Boston Braves 19, 82
Boston Celtics 59, 70, 81
Boston College 96
Bowling Green 71, 73, 129, 139, 148, 156
Boykoff, Harry 46
Bradberry, Lucille Chumbly 191
Bradley University 71, 72, 91, 132, 146, 148, 154, 156, 165, 168, 169, 180, 207
Brannum, Bob 39, 42, 43, 45, 48, 49, 57
Brenneman, Audrey 198
Breslin, Jimmy 154
Brewer, Melvin 42
Brooklyn College 16
Browning, Omar (Bud) 61, 64, 65, 66
Brown, John Y., Sr. 153, 185, 186, 187, 189
Brown, Nathaniel (Nat) 134, 139, 154, 155, 162, 176
Bryant, Paul (Bear) 30, 31, 43, 171, 179, 180, 194
Bryant, Ron 9
Buckley 142
Buffalo, NY 40
Bullets, Baltimore 204
Burris 147
Butler University Field House 21, 82, 84, 86, 87
Byrd, Harry 171
Byrnes, John 95

C

Calabrese 142
Calipari, John 22, 51, 67, 68, 164

Calverly, Ernie 36
Campbell, Kenton 42, 43, 45
Campbell, Owen 164
Camp Zama 204
Canavan, James 14
Capozzoli, Louis 185
Carey, Burgess 164, 166
Carnevale, Ben 50
Carpenter, Gordon 62, 66, 214
Carroll, Julian 201
Case, Everett 92
Chamberlain, Wilt 79, 199, 201, 212
Chamberlin, Leo 181
Chandler, Albert B. (Happy) 57, 124, 137, 164, 171, 189
Chapman, Rex 21
Chicago 13, 57, 71, 82, 89, 139, 142, 166
Chicago Stags 68, 80, 81, 85
Chicago Tribune 16
Chicago White Sox 16
Chiefs 201
Chumbly, George 191
Cincinnati 31, 53, 57
Cincinnati Reds 16
Cincinnati Royals 199
City College of New York (CCNY) 92, 93, 96, 129
Cleveland, Ohio 46, 71
Cleveland Pipers 200
Cohane, Tim 157, 158
Coleman, Kelly 21
Columbia 58
Cook County Courthouse 17
Coorlas 144
Costello, Frank 191
Courier-Journal 47, 64, 118, 133, 135, 140, 142, 144, 148, 150, 164, 167, 177, 178, 192
Cousy, Bob 58, 59, 69, 70, 131
Craig 145
Creighton 54
Curd, Ed 164, 165, 174, 191
Curtis 145
Czechoslovakia 65

D

Dalton 142
Danforth, Ed 172
Davies, Bob 79, 131
Davis, Mulford (Muff) 43
Dawson 150
Day, Roger 68, 145, 149, 150
Denver Nuggets 81, 84
DePaul 46, 48, 53, 57, 69, 71, 90,
91, 95, 139, 140, 142, 143, 155, 160
Dewey, Thomas 185
Diddle, Ed 21, 22, 28, 158
Dombrosky 142
Donaldson, Gene 179
Donovan, Herman 30, 31, 75, 76, 117, 135, 152, 153, 160, 161, 165, 170, 171, 172, 177, 178, 179, 181, 182, 199
Dorpinghaus, Sarah 8
Drake, Elmer 161
Duffy, Ike 87
DuPont Manual High School 15,
20
Duquesne 50
Duvker 145

E

Earle 150
Eastern League 195, 199, 200, 201, 204
East Lansing 31, 57
Edge, J.A. 191, 192, 193
Edwards, Leroy (Ed) 28, 146
Egypt 66
Elmira Colonels 184
England, Kenny 42
Englisis, Anthony (Tony) 132, 134, 139, 154, 176
Englisis, Nicholas (Nick) 30, 33, 110, 123, 132, 134, 135, 139, 154, 155, 156, 157, 162, 173, 176
Evans, Bob 84
Evansville Braves 87

F

Fabulous Five 7, 13, 55, 57, 84, 91, 97, 116, 118, 197, 205,
212
Farmer, Richie 35
Feinberg, Saul 134, 139, 155
Feldhaus, Deron 35
Ferris, Leo 79, 81
Fiddlin' Five 193
Finn 142
Florida 34, 58, 72
Ford, Church 159, 192
France 66, 67
Freeport High School 24
Freeport, IL 24
Frick, Ford 137, 203
Ft. Knox Army team 53
Ft. Wayne 131
Ft. Wayne Pistons 81
Fulks, Joe 131

G

Gallalee, John 177, 178
Gamage, Harry 25
Games of the XIV Olympiad 64
Gardiner 169
Gardner-Webb 211
Georgia 31, 57, 91, 92
Georgia Tech 49, 57, 58, 91, 129
Gillespie 144
Gillispie, Billy 211
Globetrotters 199
Goforth, Jim 42
Goldstein, Ruby 74
Gotkin, David 158
Govedarica 144
Graham 147
Grawemeyer, Phil 182
Great Lakes Bowl 46
Griffith, Darrell 21
Groza, Alex 8, 9, 13, 14, 15, 16, 17, 38, 39, 40, 41, 42, 45, 46, 48, 49, 50, 51, 52, 55, 56, 57, 58, 59, 61, 62, 63, 64, 65, 66, 67, 68, 69, 70, 71, 72, 73, 74, 75, 76, 77, 80, 81, 82, 83, 84, 85, 86, 87, 89, 90, 94, 97, 99, 106, 109, 111, 116, 123, 125, 127, 131, 133, 134, 135, 136, 137, 138, 140, 141, 142, 143, 144, 145, 146, 147, 148, 149, 150, 151, 152, 154, 155, 156, 157, 161, 163, 164, 165, 173, 178, 179, 180, 183, 184, 185, 186, 195, 196, 197, 203, 204, 207,

208, 210, 211, 212, 213, 214, 215
Groza, Frank 39
Groza, Lou 38

H

Haddock, Ambrose 137
Hagan, Cliff 94, 130, 153, 176, 181, 182, 193, 204
Hale, Bruce 84, 195
Hale, Dick 36
Hall, Joe B. 68, 124, 194
Hardesty, Joe 8
Hardinsburg, KY 18, 19
Harlan, KY 21
Harlem Globetrotters 198
Harringay Arena 65
Harrogate, TN 77
Hawkins, Marshall 84
Herald-American All-Star game 13
Herald-Tribune's East-West All-Star 75
Hickey, Ed 167
Hickman, Peck 22, 31, 60
Hildebrand 150
Hirsh, Walter (Walt) 68, 73, 89, 90, 91, 93, 95, 123, 142, 144, 145, 147, 148, 149, 150, 160, 161, 162, 167, 168, 169, 173, 179, 186, 187, 188, 208, 210
Hitler, Adolf 60
Hogan, Frank 16, 96, 129, 137, 160, 185, 208
Holland, Joe 13, 14, 17, 32, 40, 43, 45, 46, 49, 51, 52, 54, 55, 59, 61, 63, 64, 68, 76, 80, 82, 87, 94, 108, 117, 175
Holy Cross 58, 59, 69, 70, 140
Horrigan, Ralph 196

I

Iba, Henry (Hank) 47, 75
Illinois 74, 130
Indiana Central 45, 53, 69, 90
Indianapolis Jets 80, 209
Indianapolis Olympians 14, 82, 83, 84, 86, 87, 94, 95, 130, 131, 135, 137, 152, 183, 190, 195, 203
Indianapolis Star 21
International Olympics Games 60
Irish, Ned 129

J

James, LeBron 79
Jenkins, Paul 20
Jersey City team 183
Johnson, Ellis 25
Johnson, Walter 42
Jones, Hugh 146, 147
Jones, Wallace (Wah Wah) 13, 17, 21, 29, 30, 31, 32, 33, 34, 36, 37, 43, 44, 45, 46, 48, 49, 50, 51, 52, 53, 54, 55, 56, 57, 58, 59, 61, 62, 65, 66, 67, 68, 69, 70, 71, 72, 73, 75, 76, 80, 82, 83, 84, 85, 86, 87, 89, 94, 97, 98, 110, 111, 113, 116, 127, 140, 141, 142, 143, 144, 146, 147, 148, 149, 150, 158, 179, 214
Jordan 212
Jordan, Jim 44, 45, 51, 52, 106
Jordan, Michael 79
Journal 172

K

Kampa 144
Kansas State 13, 58, 70, 96, 130
Kaye, Eli 162, 186, 188
Keenan 147
Kefauver, Estes 129
Kelley 145
Kellogg, Junius 95
Kentucky 21, 26, 27, 34, 36, 37, 40, 41, 47, 48, 49, 53, 54, 58, 61, 62, 63, 67, 69, 70, 71, 72, 73, 74, 75, 76, 90, 91, 92, 94, 130
Kentucky Athletic Hall of Fame 205
Kentucky Colonels 194, 196, 198, 204
Kentucky Intercollegiate Athletic Conference 196
Kerris, Jack 73, 74, 82, 149, 150, 151
Kimbrough, J.R. (Babe) 76, 78, 79, 80, 82, 145, 209
Kindred, Dave 205
King, Jim 42
Kinzel, Hank 147
Kirwan, Dean A.D. 153, 154, 161, 165, 173, 177, 188
Klaerich 150
Klukofsky, Eli 162
Knoxville 43, 145, 146
Koch, Bob 168, 169
Kovar 169
Kurland, Bob 60, 61, 62, 63, 64, 65, 66, 75, 90, 214

L

Lancaster, Harry 34, 43, 52, 66, 104, 108, 114, 131, 193
Lane 145
Lane, Floyd 129
Lansaw 169
Lapchick, Joe 50
Leddy 144
Ledford, Cawood 20, 44
Lehman, Lou 70, 71
Lexington 31, 40, 41, 42, 45, 69, 71, 75, 91, 94, 115, 164
Lexington Herald 76, 78, 145, 179
Lexington Herald-Leader 209
Lexington Leader 178
Lexington's Sleepy Head House 179
Lillis 169
Lincoln Memorial University 77
Line, Jim 44, 45, 50, 51, 52, 54, 59, 64, 68, 69, 71, 74, 75, 89, 90, 91, 93, 105, 108, 109, 123, 126, 127, 142, 144, 145, 147, 149, 150, 160, 161, 162, 167, 179, 186, 187, 188, 207, 210
Linville, Shelby 68, 89, 94, 130, 168, 169, 179
Lipscomb, Pinky 146
Little Rock 160
LIU 41, 49, 96, 129, 165
Lombardi, Vince 33
London, England 60, 64
Long Island University 40, 70, 96
Look Magazine 157, 158, 166

Los Angeles Daily News 210
Los Angeles Jets 201
Louisville 17, 19, 34, 46, 48, 53, 69, 70, 71, 77, 130, 155, 160, 204
Louisville Armory 48, 54, 58, 69, 91, 129
Louisville Free Public Library 8
Louisville's Bellarmine College 195
Loyola of Chicago 16, 72, 75, 134, 135, 138, 139, 140, 148, 149, 150, 156, 157, 161, 211
Loyola of the South 195
LSU 34, 49, 58, 111
Lukswaki, Chester 179
Lumpp, Raymond 62, 65, 67, 214

M

Macauley, Ed 70, 71, 75, 82, 131
Macy, Kyle 21
Madison Square Garden 16, 35, 41, 46, 49, 54, 58, 60, 69, 70, 72, 74, 84, 85, 90, 92, 95, 96, 130, 134, 139, 140, 148, 155, 161, 173, 174
Male High School 18, 19, 20
Manhattan 165
Manhattan College 95, 96
Mansberg, Marvin 139
Marshall, Tom 158
Martin's Ferry High School 38
Martin, Slater 75
Mathias, Bob 64
Mauer, John 24, 25, 28
McGill, John 194
McGuire, Al 90, 142
McGuire, Dick 90, 141, 142
McKenna 169
McMullen, Malcolm 43, 83
Meeks, Jodie 212
Melchiorre, Gene 91, 132, 156
Memorial Coliseum 94, 120, 131, 153
Memphis Tams 194
Mexico 66
Michigan State 31, 41, 42, 57
Mikan, George 79, 82, 85, 86, 131, 201
Mikkelsen, Vern 75
Miller, Nat 129
Mills, Chris 210
Milwaukee Hawks 14, 81
Minneapolis 130, 131
Minneapolis Lakers 81, 82
Misaka, Wat 50, 115
Mississippi State 91, 92, 129
Missouri 96
Mitchum, Robert 68
Moline, IL 14
Montgomery, Ed 146, 147
Mooney, Tom 75
Moore, Bernie 171, 177, 179
Moseley, Tom 39, 40
Mosley, William "Mose" 24
Mountaineers 36
Mount, Rick 21
Mullins, Jeff 21
Mulzoff 142

N

Nagel 150
Naismith, James 23
Nashville 139, 144
National Basketball Association (NBA) 13, 81, 82, 83, 84, 195, 209
National Basketball League (NBL) 78
National Collegiate Athletic Association (NCAA) 28
National Invitational Tournament (NIT) 16, 35, 37, 49, 59, 72, 75, 92, 93, 115, 148, 155, 156, 179, 211
NCAA 68, 129, 170, 171, 176, 180, 181, 209, 210
NCAA Championship 59, 60, 67, 76
NCAA tournament 72, 74, 130, 180
New Orleans 47, 70, 90, 167, 195
Newton, Charles Martin (C.M.) 68, 89, 201, 205
New York City 16, 40
New York Knickerbockers 81, 84
New York Olympians 198
New York Times 152, 172, 190
New York University 28, 62
Nicholl 150
Nichols, W. E. 185
North Carolina State 49
North Carolina Tar Heels 91
Norton, Ken 96
Notre Dame 34, 48, 57, 62, 71, 91, 139, 155, 166

O

O'Brien, John J. 184
O'Conner, Vincent 17, 133, 134, 137, 138, 139, 140, 152, 160, 161, 162, 165, 166, 171, 185, 186, 189, 198, 199, 200, 207, 208
O'Grady 150
Ohio State 38, 40
Oklahoma 95
Oklahoma A&M 47, 59, 60, 75
Oldham, Arthur 141, 142
Ole Miss 31, 91
Olsen, Harold 40
Olympians 77, 78, 79, 80, 82
Olympic Gold 14, 67, 116
Oregon State 75
O'Shay, Kevin 57
Owensboro (Kentucky) 91, 146
Owens, Jessie 60

P

Parker, Buddy 41, 43, 46
Parkinson, Jack 32, 33, 34, 37, 39, 41, 43, 52, 105, 106, 110
Parks 145
Patterson, Patrick 212
Pelphrey, John 35
Peru 66
Phelan, Jack 143, 144
Philadelphia 40, 52, 53
Philip, Andy 131
Phillips 66ers (Oilers) 60, 61, 62, 63, 64, 65, 66, 118
Phillips Petroleum Company 60
Pitino, Rick 35
Pitts 214
Pitts, R.C. 62

Podoloff, Maurice (Poodles) 80, 81, 130, 135, 137, 183, 184, 190, 198, 200, 203, 208, 209
Pollard, Jim 131
Poppe, Henry 95
Povich, Shirley 172
Price, Mr. 200
Puerto Rico 131
Purdue 90, 94

R

Raleigh, NC 130, 159
Ramsey, Frank 94, 130, 153, 168, 169, 176, 179, 181, 182, 193, 196
Randall, Julius 176
Redding 142
Reed, Billy 205, 210
Reid, John E. 200
Renick, Jesse 61, 62, 65, 214
Reynolds Metals 196
Rhode Island 36
Rhodes, Gene 196
Rice, Grantland 32
Rice, Russell 194, 210
Richard, Maurice 54
Risen, Arnie 40, 79
Robertson, Oscar 21, 200
Robinson, Jack 62, 66, 145, 214
Rochester 95, 131, 199
Rochester Royals 13, 79
Rollins, Kenny 13, 43, 45, 46, 48, 49, 51, 52, 54, 55, 56, 57, 58, 59, 61, 62, 64, 65, 66, 68, 69, 70, 76, 80, 85, 97, 101, 109, 116, 119, 211, 214
Roman, Ed 93, 96
Rondo, Rajon 20
Rosen, Charles 8
Roth, Al 96
Ruby, Craig 24
Ruby, Earl 47, 135, 138, 139, 177, 178, 192
Rupp, Adolph 13, 14, 18, 21, 22, 23, 24, 26, 27, 28, 29, 30, 31, 33, 34, 35, 37, 38, 39, 41, 42, 43, 44, 45, 46, 47, 48, 49, 50, 52, 53, 54, 55, 57, 59, 61, 62, 63, 65, 66, 67, 68, 69, 70, 72, 74, 75, 76, 77, 80, 82, 89, 91, 92, 94, 97, 103, 106, 108, 109, 110, 114, 116, 122, 127, 130, 131, 132, 133, 135, 138, 143, 150, 152, 157, 158, 163, 164, 165, 170, 172, 174, 178, 179, 181, 182, 191, 192, 193, 194, 205, 207
Rupp, Herky 8
Rupp's Runts 193
Russell 168, 169

S

Sale, Forrest (Aggie) 25
San Diego Conquistadors 196
San Francisco 73, 148
Schaeffer, Carl 83
Schayes, Dolph 131
Schmidt, Esther 24, 26
Schu, Wilber 32, 33, 34, 37, 39, 43, 110
Scott, Bettye 204
Scott, Ed 167, 169
Seattle 75, 193
SEC Champions 50
SEC Championship 42, 72, 129
SEC Tournament 34, 48, 58, 59, 67, 71, 91, 92, 129
Sheboygan Redskins 81, 86
Shively, Bernie 31, 47, 154, 164, 194
Shropshire, Larry 178
Sigler, Ken 44
Sirignano, William 135, 136
Smith, Leroy 96
Snell, John 9
Sonnenberg, Ray 168, 169
South Bend, Indiana 57, 91
Southeastern Conference (SEC) 26, 171, 177, 178, 179, 183
Spellman, Francis Cardinal 208
Spicer, Carey 25
Spivey, Bill 8, 9, 66, 68, 89, 90, 91, 92, 93, 94, 95, 112, 121, 123, 129, 130, 138, 152, 153, 157, 159, 161, 162, 166, 167, 168, 169, 179, 184, 185, 186, 187, 190, 198, 199, 200, 201, 202, 203, 204, 208, 211, 216
Sporting News, The 183
Sport Magazine 54
Sports Illustrated 126
Stanczak, Ed 87
Steinbrenner, George 201
Steiner 169
St. John's 46, 54, 69, 70, 90, 130, 139, 140, 153, 155, 159
St. Louis Billikins 70, 95, 167
St. Louis Bombers 81
St. Louis University 70, 139, 186
Stoll Field 63, 64, 113, 118
Stough, John 68, 142, 144, 145
Streit, Saul 154, 161, 163, 164, 165, 166, 170, 171, 172, 173, 174, 175, 176, 183, 185, 186, 187, 189, 199, 207, 208, 210
Strong, Guy 68, 89, 90
Sugar Bowl 91, 139, 161, 162, 164, 167, 168, 182, 186, 187, 188, 189
Sugar Bowl Classic 47, 69, 70, 90, 95
Summer, Igor 141, 142
Switzerland 65
Syracuse 168, 169
Syracuse Nationals 81

T

Temple 34, 40, 41, 49, 52, 53, 58
Tennessee 49, 57, 58, 71, 72, 91, 92, 140, 147, 155
Terrell, T.V. 166
Texas A&M 47
Tingle, Jack 32, 33, 34, 35, 36, 37, 39, 43, 45, 46, 47, 49, 72, 110
Townes 145
Townsend, William 166, 181, 191, 192
Tri-Cities 86, 131
Tri-Cities Blackhawks 79, 81
True Magazine 50, 123, 154, 157
Tsiropoulos, Lou 182
Tulane 49, 70, 72, 139, 155
Tulsa 53, 69

U

UCLA 62
United States Olympic Basketball Team 64
University of Central Arkansas 41
University of Illinois 24
University of Kentucky Athletics Association 31
University of Kentucky Special Collections 8
University of Kentucky (UK) 13, 18, 22, 24, 25, 26, 28, 30, 31, 32, 36, 42, 43, 44, 45, 46, 48, 49, 55, 60, 63, 64, 69, 70, 71, 72, 75, 78, 89, 91, 110, 129, 130, 131, 133, 134, 135, 138, 142, 143, 144, 146, 148, 149, 152, 154, 163, 172, 178, 180, 183, 198
University of Louisville 22, 31, 60
University of Louisville Library 8
University of Tennessee 28, 138
Unseld, Wes 21
Uruguay 66
Utah 49, 50, 73, 115, 148

V

Van ArsDale, Dick 21
Van ArsDale, Tom 21
Vanderbilt 49, 91, 129, 139, 140, 155
Vanderbilt Commodores 144
Varnell, Lou 210
Villanova 46, 74, 90, 156
Volker, Floyd 84
Volunteers 43, 92
Vukovich 144

W

Wabash 47
Wall, John 20
Walther, Paul 84, 95, 146, 147
Warner, Ed 93, 96
Warner-Robbins, Georgia 66
Washington 58
Washington Capitols 80, 81
Washington Generals 198
Washington Post 172
Wassmer 142
Watson, Bobby 89, 90, 94, 130, 168, 169, 179
Wells 41
Wembley Stadium 60
Western Kentucky 21, 72, 129, 148, 158
Western Ontario 55, 90
West, Jack 176, 185, 186, 187
West Virginia 36, 50
Wetherby, Lawrence 152, 153, 154, 160, 165, 185
Wheeling, West Virginia 195
Whitaker, Lucian (Skippy) 68, 89, 94, 130, 169, 179
White, James 14
White, Sherman 96, 183, 199, 207
Wildcats 33, 34, 36, 37, 41, 42, 47, 53, 57, 59, 61, 62, 65, 69, 71, 72, 73, 74, 75, 76, 89, 90, 91, 92, 94, 129, 130, 140, 141, 142, 143, 144, 145, 146, 147, 148, 149, 150, 168, 179, 183, 208, 211
Wilkes-Barre Barons 199
Willett, Hugh 129
Williams, Owen 164
Woods, Fairce 76, 77
Wyoming 40, 75

X

Xavier 53, 58, 139

Y

Yale 74

More Sports Books
Published By Acclaim Press

Better Than Gold: Olympian Kenny Davis and the Most Controversial Basketball Game in History

An Olympics like no other... Every four years, the whole world turns its eyes upon a single gathering of the planet's best athletes for a series of sporting events. In the summer of 1972, however, there occurred such an Olympic gathering much unlike any other before it or, thankfully, since.

An unprecedented terrorist attack had invaded the tranquility of Olympic Village, leaving 11 Israeli athletes dead and the world aghast. As the USA's team took the court, there was an unnerving tension building as they prepared to play against the best and most experienced Soviet Union team ever assembled.

This is the story of Kenny Davis, captain of that very team, a sharp-shooting farm boy from Kentucky, cast onto the world's center stage in the challenge of a lifetime. Discover what Davis and all of the members of his 1972 USA Olympic Basketball Team did in amidst tragedy and injustice; something much more valuable than just winning a ball game, something much Better Than Gold.

Kentucky Colonels of the American Basketball Association

An inside look at one of the most intriguing times in the history of professional basketball; and the city of Louisville and the state of Kentucky were enjoying every bit of it.

And then as quickly as the Colonels appeared, they were gone. They had been around just long enough to win a world championship and showcase not only some of the best basketball players in the history of the game, but also some of its most colorful characters.

Kentucky High School Basketball Records & Facts

Never has there been anything like it: every team, every school, every year from the beginning of high school basketball in Kentucky through 2013!

In cooperation with the Kentucky Association of Basketball Coaches and the Kentucky High School Athletics Association, included are every high school basketball team in the state, boys and girls, from 1906-2013; all postseason scores including district, region and state games; Sweet Sixteen All-Tournament Team members' names and high school team; All-State Teammembers' names and high school team; Coach of the Year winners; Mr. & Miss Basketball; Ted Sanford & Joe Billy Mansfield Award winners; All A State Classic teams and scores; photos of every state championship team; complete roster of current coaches.

The Boys From Corbin: America's Greatest Little Sports Town

What do the Los Angeles Lakers, St. Louis Cardinals, New York Knicks, San Diego Chargers, Oakland Raiders, Kentucky Wildcats, Louisville Cardinals, Western Kentucky Hilltoppers, Furman Paladins and the Eastern Kentucky Colonels all have in common? They have had all had star athletes who began their careers as Corbin Redhounds.

For four decades, the 30's, 40's, 50's, and 60's, Corbin High School sports were the glue that held the town together. For those who worked on the railroad, cut or hauled timber, or chiseled and drug coal from the nearby mines, football and basketball were a diversion from the daily chore or providing for their families. Sports were the common denominator that transcended the economic levels of Corbin's citizenry.

The Boys from Corbin—America's Greatest Little Sports Town is not just a story…it's a phenomenon.

Factors Unknown: The Tragedy that Put a Coach and Football on Trial

As young men across America begin training and conditioning their bodies in summer practice sessions for that ever-demanding, grueling battleground of athleticism known as football, we all know it will happen. Somewhere, somehow, somebody is going to die.

On a sultry August afternoon, it proved too much for a young sophomore at Pleasure Ridge Park High School in Louisville, Ky. He gave his all and then collapsed, never to rise again. But this time was different, very different. Some unknown factors precipitated this tragic outcome. Somebody would pay for this – in prison.

This is that story, the case of Coach David Jason Stinson and, ultimately, the sport of high school football, on trial.

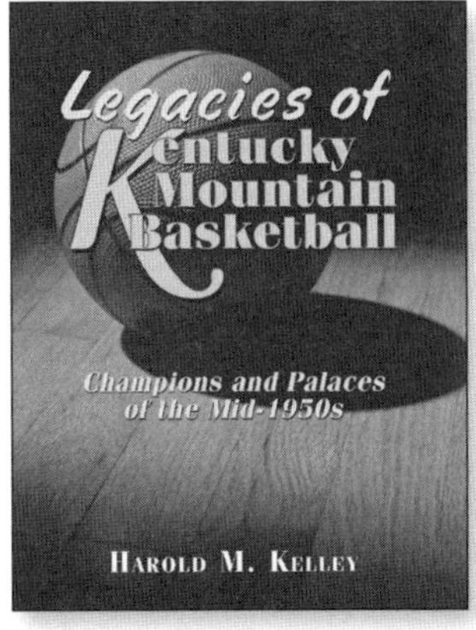

Legacies of Kentucky Mountain Basketball: Champions and Palaces of the Mid-1950s

A look back at what once was the heart and soul of sports in the beautiful, but rugged mountains of Kentucky is what Legacies of Kentucky Mountain Basketball does with photographs from today.

Legacies of Kentucky Mountain Basketball … is about the golden era of high school basketball in Kentucky, high school basketball that was as close to the original game as we will ever see again.

This book features the towns and high schools of the 13th, 14th and 15th Regions of the Commonwealth, including detailed accounts of the 1953-54, 1954-55, and 1955-56 seasons.

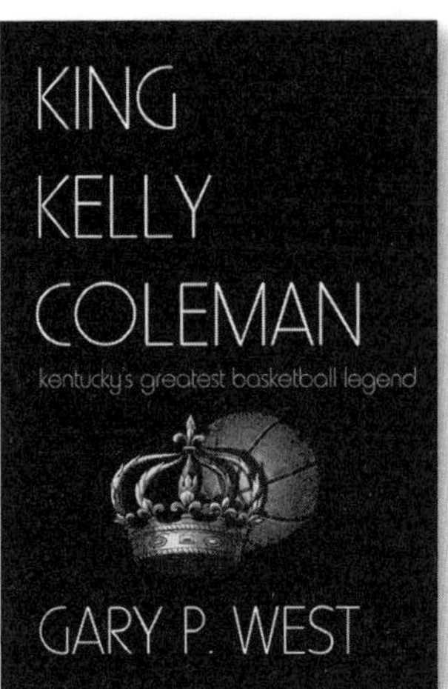

King Kelly Coleman: Kentucky's Greatest Basketball Legend

In a state where the love of basketball itself is legendary, there are its rare heroes who also, through the dispassionate lens of history, rise to legendary status. When that legend rises so far above the others as to acquire mythical or rather, folk hero, proportions – and then enigmatically vanishes- you have King Kelly Coleman.

This shy, humble mountain boy blessed with extraordinary talent and drive captured Kentucky's hearts and its all-time record books with performances that have yet to be equaled – even half a century later. Never before in print, the authorized King Kelly Coleman story, is told by award-winning author Gary P. West, from actual interviews and information from Coleman himself.

Pioneer Spirit: One High School's Rise From Tragedy to Glory

The amazing, true story that will inspire all....

The indomitable spirit of the Simon Kenton Pioneers blazes the trail from horrific devastation and seemingly insurmountable obstacles to basketball supremacy and sports legendry.

Follow the accounts of Simon Kenton High School's devastating explosion and their come-back to win the 1981 Kentucky State Basketball Championship.

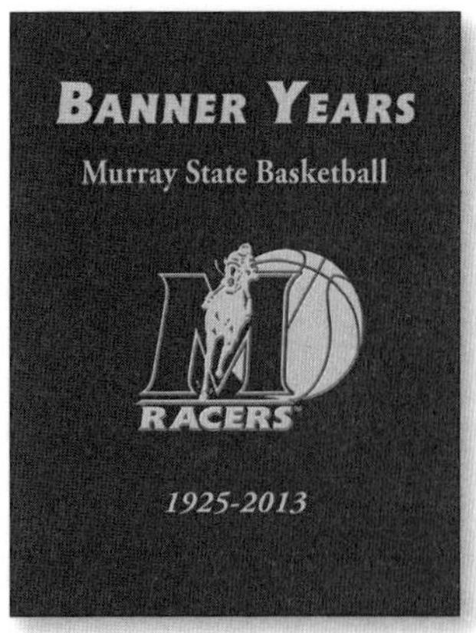

Banner Years: Murray State Basketball 1925-2013

Murray State Racer basketball has a long history of great players, great coaches and great teams. Its winning tradition is unmatched in the Ohio Valley Conference and has brought national attention to the university. Mention the Commonwealth of Kentucky and three things automatically come to mind: good bourbon, the Kentucky Derby...and basketball. Mention Jeff Martin, Popeye Jones, Isaiah Canaan...and the Murray State hoops program immediately comes to the forefront.

Buy yourself a copy of Banner Years and you will have a 368-page coffee table-style book that tells in words and pictures the story of the first 88 seasons of Murray State men's basketball (the 2013-14 season represents MSU's 89th).

Suggested first by Racer legend Bennie Purcell and published by Acclaim Press, Banner Years is truly a keepsake and something that makes it easy for you to be a PROUD RACER. (Published with Proud to Be A Racer Publications.)